THE DAYUMA STORY
Life under Auca Spears

FRONT ENDPAPER: During homeward trip to Auca settlement, Dayuma, assisted by relatives, bends to pack dugout canoe on Tapir River, in the heart of the Auca jungle in eastern Ecuador.

THE
DAYUMA
STORY

Life under Auca Spears

by ETHEL EMILY WALLIS

HARPER & BROTHERS, PUBLISHERS, NEW YORK

PHOTOGRAPHS

Rachel Saint (WBT-SIL): pages 98, 100 (center), 103 (top left), 104, 105 (bottom); 106-112, endpapers.
Cornell Capa (Magnum Photos): pages 97, 99, 102 (top).
Elisabeth Elliot: pages 103 (top right, bottom), 105 (top right).
Lincoln Beals (Wheaton, Ill.): page 100 (top left).
Robert Griffin (WBT-SIL): page 102 (bottom).
Impact Photos, Inc.: page 101 (center, bottom).
Larry Montgomery (WBT-SIL): page 101 (top left).
Richard Surman Television Kinescopes: page 100 (bottom).

To Lawrence and Katharine Saint,
parents of Rachel and Nate,
in appreciation of their helpfulness
and encouragement in this undertaking

CONTENTS

7

PREFACE

AS I flew in a tiny plane over the Auca forest of terror, deep in eastern Ecuador, on my way to meet Dayuma and Rachel Saint, the reality of a fantastic—but not fictitious—story came alive to me for the first time. Down there, somewhere in that dark greenness stretching endlessly under the tiny plane, Moipa had driven his spears into Tyaento. Tyaento's young daughter Dayuma then fled for her life to the outside, to a jungle hacienda. Eight years later a missionary-linguist found her there carrying heavy loads of bananas from sun to sun, and an almost incredible story began. I wanted to check the facts before committing them to print.

It was almost dark that September evening when the jungle-hopping plane touched down on the grassy strip chopped out of virgin forest. I was welcomed not only by my good friends Dayuma and Rachel but by Dayuma's relative Kimo and his pretty wife Dawa, Aucas who only a few days before had arrived at the Limoncocha Base of the Wycliffe Bible Translators on their first adventure away from their forest home. Kimo—the muscular young Indian who had participated in the spear-killing of Rachel's brother Nate and four fellow-missionaries almost four years earlier! At that moment I felt that I had been dropped into the thick of a thrilling drama.

For more than a month Rachel and I cross-questioned Kimo and Dawa for confirmation of Dayuma's story. My inability to speak the Auca language was fully compensated by Rachel's fluency, with satisfying results. Two earlier months in Quito I had devoted all my waking hours to ferreting out the story from documents made available to me: heaps of Rachel's personal letters, reports, and voluminous amounts of Auca text recorded by her since 1955 when she began the study of Dayuma's mother tongue. But I had many queries that were resolved during those unforgettable weeks in the jungle with the Aucas.

Rachel had been asked by Harper & Brothers in 1958 to write this story. But then came an unprecedented invitation to her and Elisabeth Elliot to live in the Aucas' midst, an irresistible opportunity. Living under extremely primitive conditions, with primary concentration on Auca language study, was not an ideal book-writing situation. In July, 1959, at the request of Wycliffe Director Cameron Townsend, I went to Ecuador to lend Rachel a hand in the project. Although I was reluctant to leave my own work with the Mezquital Otomi Indians of Mexico, I was nevertheless glad to share an assignment with Rachel—and thus enable her to continue her work with the Auca tribe with less time out than writing a book involves.

For valuable assistance I am indebted to other Wycliffe colleagues, particularly Catherine Peeke and Nadine Kernodle. Catherine, who speaks Dayuma's second language, Quichua, double-checked crucial points of the story. She also undertook research on the flora and fauna of the Ecuadorian jungle pertinent to the narrative. Her aid on the Glossary is appreciated. Nadine's willing help in the typing of the taped transcriptions for background material, as well as her careful typing of the manuscript itself, lightened the writing load considerably.

Other Wycliffe members who gave invaluable help were Kenneth Kensinger, who spent many hours on the Auca kinship material; Dorothy Jackson, who prepared Dayuma's genealogical chart; and Katherine Voigtlander, who drew the maps.

Dr. Ward Goodenough of the University of Pennsylvania graciously gave valuable suggestions for the preparation of the genealogical and kinship materials.

Eleanor Jordan of Harper & Brothers, who readied the manuscript for publication, was a valuable member of the team. For her sympathetic interest in the project, as well as for her skilled technical assistance, I am gratefully indebted.

It was a pleasure working with Cornell Capa, of Magnum Photos, who gave generously of his time and photographs for the book.

And Dayuma herself co-operated unstintingly in the telling of her story, although the implications of a book in English about her adventures were vague to her. Nevertheless, she cheerfully answered interminable questions and patiently repeated information obvious to any Auca but baffling to a foreigner unfamiliar with her culture. (And I suspect that she had her own reservations about the intelligence of an interrogator who required so much repetition!) The manuscript was completed in early February, 1960, when Dayuma left with Rachel for their Auca home where the rivers surge with succulent fish, and where the forest is alive with monkeys to be had whenever the hunters decide to appear with their blowguns. There on the banks of the sparkling Tiwaeno, foreigners who plague one with questions are few. But as I write this there is one—Dayuma's friend Rachel, who is out there now "carving" a Book intelligible to Dayuma and her people: the Holy Scriptures in their own musical Auca language.

ETHEL EMILY WALLIS

Philadelphia
February 27, 1960

NOTE TO THE READER

The pattern of Auca life has been totally unknown to the civilized world. The reader will be assisted in understanding the habitat and the unfamiliar names and relationships within the tribe if he will refer to the materials found on the final pages of this book:

1

"I DON'T REMEMBER"

IT was a still, sultry afternoon in the Ecuadorian jungle, but Dayuma's brown hands glistened with cold perspiration. Her large wide-set black eyes glanced quickly from Rachel Saint to the microphone of a tape recorder.

"Don't be afraid—just talk," coaxed Rachel in her limited Auca vocabulary as she held the microphone toward Dayuma.

But the unusual brightness of the Indian girl's eyes and the half-nervous rubbing of her hands betrayed the inward excitement, shadowed with some apprehension, of one poised on the brink of a totally new experience. She looked again at the blue-eyed foreigner whose smile reassured her. Then accepting the challenge she reached daringly for the strange metal object. Rachel felt the moist coolness of Dayuma's hands as they touched hers.

"Tell me about your home in the forest before you came here," the foreigner encouraged gently.

With much repetition and some hesitation, but in a clear strong voice Dayuma began to review her life in the Auca forest before she had fled to the outside world and to Don Carlos Sevilla's hacienda.

With scarcely two months' study of the Auca language Rachel did not understand every spoken word of the tragic tale. But she could read the terror and torment which flashed from Dayuma's eyes and shook her voice as she forgot the foreigner's machine and poured out her past. Dayuma was back in the jungle reliving the horrors of her childhood. And Rachel without warning was drawn with her into the Auca forest, bristling with cruelty.

"I was born on Fish River.
Afterwards we lived well on Palm River.
We saw the high hills far off clearly.
We saw far downriver.

"My big brother was Wawae.
My father was Tyaento, my mother Akawo.
Nampa my brother was a small child.
Oba my sister was still younger.
My big sister was Onaenga, my other sister, Gimari.
My mother's relatives were many.
My uncles were Wamoñi and Gikita.

"Moipa and Itaeka did not do well.
Fleeing and hiding we came, far, far downriver.
We went by canoe. Then we went back.

"When did they spear? They speared at night.
My father escaped into the water.
They dug a grave for him and he was caused to die.
But he didn't die right away.
I didn't see it. They spoke and I heard.
My relative said, 'I buried him.'

"Moipa and Itaeka speared.
Where did they go, did they say?
On a small stream upriver we returned.
We didn't see them.
We drank the water of maeñika fruit.
It rained, we got wet.
The jaguar growled, the monkeys called.
We climbed the trees when the jaguar came.

"Then we fled.
We came at night in the moonlight.
We speared gyaegyae fish.

"We were planting peanuts on Palm River.
The outsiders came with guns and shot.
Their dogs barked.
We went into the water, then fled on the other side . . ."

Even after eight years of peaceful living on Don Carlos' hacienda, out of reach of the spears that had killed her father, fear and hate were still hot in the Auca girl's heart. The smoldering embers of revenge needed only to be stirred into sudden flaming life—and in a few moments the docile day laborer of the banana fields was transformed into a wild girl of the jungle. Murder gleamed from her angry eyes as she was transported to the land of spearing and fleeing, of violence and vengeance.

"Moipa—I hate him!" And every utterance of the name of her father's murderer fanned her fury into higher flame as the chronicle gathered momentum. Rachel watched in awe as the girl's passion burst into a fire of frenzied hate. Dayuma had forgotten that the listener was a stranger to the world of spears into which she had been plunged.

The language curtain had begun to part, and through the narrow opening Rachel caught a glimpse of the struggle still in progress a few miles east of the hacienda. She had known that the Aucas killed on their borders, but now she learned that intratribal feuds were fast exterminating the group itself.

Soon after Rachel's arrival at Hacienda Ila in February, 1955, she had heard about Moipa, notorious killer of the forest. Dayuma in drunken despondency had asked Don Carlos to sell her a gun. "Teach me how to use it," she had begged. "I want to go back to my home and kill Moipa. One with nine shots will do." And now Rachel saw that in sober hatred Dayuma still desired to avenge the death of her father Tyaento, a duty which would normally fall to his sons.

Rachel was unprepared for the emotional upheaval caused by

the recording. In the days that followed she was to appreciate more fully the monumental achievement it had been for Dayuma. That brief narrative recounted in the Auca language was to mark the beginning of a new chapter in the history of an unsubdued Ecuadorian tribe.

When Rachel had begun writing down the first Auca words from Dayuma in February it soon became dishearteningly apparent that the girl had all but forgotten her mother tongue. Her previous life and language lay smothering under a foreign blanket grown thick by years of Quichua Indian customs and speech.

Dayuma had purposely tried to forget her native language while living with Quichuas, who ridiculed the naked and savage Aucas. She now wore the traditional Indian dress of the region, a straight dark skirt and loose-hanging long-sleeved blouse. Her black hair was parted on the side and hung down over the ears, half covering the large holes in the lobes which once held chunky round plugs of balsa wood. At home in the forest her hair had been cut in bangs which extended back well beyond the ears.

But as far as Dayuma was concerned, Auca hair styles and patterns of speech had been fast merging into oblivion when Rachel met her.

"The chonta palm I planted when I arrived here, it has given its fruit five times," Dayuma had told Rachel. To indicate past time, Dayuma had turned down three stubby fingers Indian fashion to account for the three years of growth necessary to produce the delicious bright orange palm fruit.

Rachel's keen disappointment was understandable, for she had searched several years to find someone who spoke the language of the dread killers of the jungle. The only available Aucas outside the tribe were living at Hacienda Ila. She would have to learn the language there, away from the spear-marked boundaries of the hostile race. And Don Carlos himself had invited her to come with her companion Catherine Peeke to study with the four Auca women who worked for him.

However, within a few days of their arrival at the hacienda it had been sadly evident that three of the four women, Umi, Ominia, and Wiñaemi, could recall nothing of their language even with much persistence. The struggle with them had been futile. By comparison Rachel's efforts with Dayuma had been encouraging. During a few precious hours gleaned after the girl's long days in the fields, Rachel had patiently and laboriously struggled to dredge up from the murky recesses of the Indian girl's memory words learned as a child. After pronouncing a few words recollected with obvious effort, Dayuma would exhaust her Auca verbal supply and say with simple resignation, "Wi mponimopa—I don't remember," the first phrase that Rachel learned.

Rachel says, "I could almost see her think. Her lips would move voicelessly over and over for some time. But very often after trying hard she would look up at me and repeat those discouraging words, 'I don't remember.'"

The girl's delight in a determined effort to win the battle for Auca words had given Rachel heart for the tedious siege. Though ground was gained slowly at first, by the end of a month Rachel had extracted many pages of words and phrases from her willing helper. In fact, she now had recorded phonetically more Auca words than were contained in any list available to her. In an earlier search for Auca clues Rachel had collected several brief word lists. One was recorded by the scientist Tessman (published in 1930), and three by others who through the years had tried to establish a contact with the tribe. The most recent was a brief vocabulary Dayuma had given a missionary three years before Rachel arrived at the hacienda.

These lists though very limited had served the fruitful purpose of inspiring the alert Indian girl to revive the use of her own language. "Dayuma was quite surprised when I could look at my paper and approximate a pronunciation of the words," writes Rachel. "I was amused when she began to look at my notes with great interest, just as if she, a completely illiterate primitive girl, could really read!"

Rachel also recalls that "informant time was scarce. Many a day we watched the Indian girl, from whom I had hoped to learn the language, go off to the fields at dawn, machete in hand, a huge basket hanging lightly from its bark strap across her forehead. She often turned back as she took the trail, to see if she could see us at the upper windows of our new home, and usually we did not see her again until after sunset. She cleared weeds all day, then returned heavy-laden with bananas or yuca, her strong back bent low beneath the heavy load she carried. My heart would hope that she would be given time to come to our room, but often I climbed under the mosquito net at the end of the day disappointed. I had seen Dayuma only from afar!

"Occasionally the jungle rain would bring all the servants home early from the fields. Then we would wait expectantly for Dayuma to come bouncing into the room with an air of importance, sit down cross-legged on the wooden floor, and unconsciously wiggle her big bare toes as she contemplated this new turn of events which was already beginning to affect the routine pattern of her life as she had lived it for many years at Ila.

"Having no language in common with Dayuma since I had not studied Quichua, I was forced into what we had jokingly called in our courses at the Summer Institute of Linguistics, 'ye olde monolingual approach.' By motions and gestures I elicited the names for objects. The room was gloomy, so I invited Dayuma to sit near the window where I could watch her face and decipher her motions, too, for it wasn't long before she also was using the monolingual approach with me!

"I tried sitting on the floor beside her, but I just wasn't trained for that. So I compromised and sat on a low wooden box, my notebook on my lap and pen in hand eagerly ready to write down the data that would enable me to analyze this language."

Sometimes the bright Indian girl, capturing the idea, would act out the words for Rachel by crawling like a baby, or throwing herself down in a feigned fit of anger. Such antics were always accompanied by hilarious laughter, which made informant hours great entertainment.

"How do you say 'sun'?" asked Rachel one day, supplementing her limping language with gestures.

"*Naenki*," responded Dayuma, then brightening, "*apaika*," and "*nimu*." She had also offered the words for moon and stars.

Later when Rachel asked for the Auca names of the Napo and Curaray Rivers she was overjoyed when the girl went right on and named the other rivers which she had known so well as a child. And she began to recall in detail what had happened on them. The gap between the almost forgotten past and the present was being closed by the powerful association of language.

And now those scattered words and sentences which came so hard at first had formed a coherent pattern crystallized on a historic magnetic tape. It was a short but moving story of why a daring Auca girl in her early teens risked her life to find something better than useless death in a cruel forest. The same valiant spirit prompted the untaught jungle girl to share her returning language with a mysterious machine and a curious stranger. Of that milestone Rachel writes,

"As I watched this young Auca girl my heart welled up with

thanksgiving that the Lord had sent me to her. As I looked out beyond our thatch-roofed hacienda home to the east I knew that somewhere beyond that ridge in the endless jungle lived Dayuma's people, and that some day the Lord would send me to them, too."

In the months that followed, Rachel, who had been working with Dayuma whenever opportunity afforded and analyzing the language recorded on tape and paper when she was not available, was able to fill in the details of the girl's story. And the more Rachel learned the more convinced she became that the Aucas had earned their dreadful reputation.

"Speared him dead"—the phrase recurred with striking frequency as Dayuma described the sordid end of many of her relatives. Very soon the name Moipa began to dominate the narratives. Yes, Dayuma hated him with all her heart, for this brutal killer of the forest had been responsible for many murders.

"They buried my father and he died," Dayuma had said. "Buried and died"—this phrase also began to show up in various contexts. Was it a misplaced order of words? As Rachel questioned the Auca girl she learned to her horror that the word order was true to the facts: it is Auca custom to bury alive. Because of the greatest of their fears, that of death without a burial, dying Aucas often beg to be interred before they expire. Dayuma's own father had died in his grave. Her cousin Umi, who fled the forest with her, had been a witness to the death groans which became fainter and fainter, and ended in silence.

Babies and even older children are thrown into the graves with their fathers, or left in the jungle to die alone.

In cases of extreme hate and anger, victims are dug up and speared again, the avenger shrieking his wrath and railings while plunging his spear into rotting flesh. Moipa deserved such a death,

Dayuma had said vindictively, but so far as she knew no one had been able to kill him.

Was there no limit to the cruelty of the savage tribe to which she had been called? Rachel was grievously appalled as she listened to Dayuma.

"The devil of the forest sucks our blood and we die," the girl reported matter-of-factly one day. "You can even see the black-and-blue spots on the bodies." This devil and other evil spirits existed for Dayuma, even on the civilized hacienda. The fears of the forest had pursued her relentlessly.

"Being cursed my father died"—ah! that was the real reason why Moipa's spears had finally succeeded after several earlier attempts. The curse of an enemy spells almost certain death for an Auca.

Stories of cannibals, the foreigners who ate Auca flesh, also began to find expression in Dayuma's conversation. She described in repulsive detail the fate that had befallen Aucas who ventured beyond the safety of their own guarded borders.

"I was afraid because they said the foreigners would eat me when I ran away," she reminisced, "but I knew that Moipa would spear me if I stayed."

All foreigners were to be feared—and killed if possible. Through the years they had ruthlessly shot down Dayuma's people with their guns, and had stolen their yuca and bananas. They were a threat to the Auca food supply, and to their very existence. Outsiders merited the undying hatred of her people.

As Rachel heard such verification of reported Auca hostility, her prospects of crossing the deadly borders became more remote. Even if she did learn the language from Dayuma, how could she ever set foot on Auca soil? Apart from miracles it would be folly to consider it. But the conviction was firm that some day God would make a way to the tribe, so she plowed steadily ahead on language study. Rachel had determined to use only Auca with Dayuma, for if she learned Quichua there would be no real need for the girl to recall her own language. She often thought wistfully of all the Auca conversation going on constantly not many miles away.

Rachel sighed for the day when she would be able to put enough Auca words together to tell Dayuma about the living God. How would she begin? She had noted a word for a creator-god, but what did the term mean to the Aucas? She would need to tell Dayuma of God's Word—but how, when she had no word for "book" or "writing"?

One day a little yellow airplane flew over and dropped a bag of mail at the isolated hacienda for Rachel. In it was a letter from home, a letter written by her mother. Rachel recalls,

"I showed Dayuma the letter and told her it was from my mother far away. She immediately responded with the words, 'bara ndiwaemonga—mother's carving.' It was a term used for gashing a tree to mark a trail or signal a message."

"God's carving"—perhaps that would do for the expression "God's Word." And Rachel jotted the phrase down.

Dayuma was curious about the letter. How could one so far away carve a message for her daughter on a little piece of paper? What did it say to Rachel? And who brought it to Rachel's brother Nate so that he could carry it in the yellow wood-bee to Rachel? She already knew that Nate flew the wood-bee which often buzzed overhead as it crossed the sky above the hacienda. As a pilot of the Missionary Aviation Fellowship he served isolated workers dependent upon air communication. There was no airstrip at Ila, but he often dropped a welcome package.

As the months went by Dayuma's curiosity about the rare foreigner at the hacienda grew. Travelers often came and went, but this one was here to stay until she learned all the words of the

Auca language. No one had ever shown so much interest in *her*, Dayuma thought, and no one had ever asked so many questions.

Then came the day when Dayuma began to ask Rachel questions.

"Why do you want to learn my language?" With still very limited conversational ability in Auca, Rachel was on the spot. Mustering all of her available vocabulary she managed, "So that I can go to your people, and teach them not to kill, and to live well."

A wondering look was Dayuma's eloquent reply. She had understood the words—but why would anyone want to go to the killers of the forest? She herself had no intention of returning to the place from which she fled for her life.

"But if you go," she commented significantly, "see if my mother lives, see if my sister Gimari lives. Returning, you can tell me about them."

Dayuma was beginning to wonder again about her family over the ridge. When she first came to the hacienda she had cried for them each night, but eventually her tears dried completely. Now Rachel's queries renewed her concern.

There were other questions brewing in the active Auca mind.

"Who sent you?" was the next challenge. Using the Auca word for God, Rachel replied, "Our God, the other God, sent me to learn from you." That was a big sentence and Rachel wondered if Dayuma understood. However, her reply was reassuring, for with a puzzled expression she said,

"It must have been your God." After a pause Dayuma then asked, "Why did you come?"

"So that I can put God's carving into your language, and teach your people what He says."

"Who taught you?"

That required a longer answer. Many people in Rachel's land

knew God's carving. Her mother, and her father, and her brother who flew the wood-bee knew it. Even her grandmothers and grandfathers had known, and they taught her. Now she could read God's carving for herself.

Dayuma began to ply Rachel with more questions about her family. When would she see her mother again? How many brothers and sisters did she have? Did they all live with her mother and father?

Dayuma's answers to Rachel's questions about her family were much sadder.

"Does my mother live? I don't know. Maybe she has been speared. Maybe a snake has bitten her and she has died. Maybe she died with a fever long ago.

"Does my sister Gimari live? I don't know. Do my brothers live? Maybe they have been killed by Moipa's spears."

In spite of her bitter past Dayuma's desire to know more of the new things she was learning grew with each day's conversation. There was unmistakable curiosity about God, but the language barrier was still frustratingly high.

"Is there dwelling-ground above the sky . . . ? Is there dwelling-ground beneath the earth . . . ?"

Questions, questions, and more questions. Dayuma worked hard to remember her language to teach Rachel. Then she, in turn, could give the answers which Dayuma was sure she knew.

"Why didn't you come when I first ran away?" Dayuma asked one day, after a linguistic skirmish. "I would have remembered my language fast then."

And Rachel thought how much easier it would have been to learn Auca from an informant who was more fluent.

Eight precious years, apparently lost.

"Why, indeed, didn't I come sooner?"

2

SHAKEN FROM THE NEST

WHEN Rachel had announced to friends in New Jersey one day in 1948 that she would be leaving for South America, they were thunderstruck. They had worked happily with her for years, and assumed she had settled in permanently. But Rachel had, in fact, been listening for the message that was to change the course of her life that year. It meant leaving a comfortable, happy place of Christian service and heading toward a primitive home somewhere in the tangles of Amazonian jungle.

Rachel had quickly recognized the hand that shook her cozy nest. The time had come to try her wings of faith in a distant land where countless Indian tribes were dying without God's Word.

Rachel had known that her task would involve learning an unwritten language, the key to communication with primitive people, and therefore applied for study at the Summer Institute of Linguistics. It was the first step in joining the Wycliffe Bible Translators, a mission team devoted to sharing God's Book with neglected tribespeople the world over.

In the summer of 1948 Oklahoma heat pressed down on several hundred trainees for Bible translation as they struggled with sounds and syntax for eleven weeks of intensive linguistic analysis on the state university campus at Norman. At times Rachel would slip away from the books to a quiet shade by the football stadium where under towering white clouds she could talk with the Lord who had thrust her out on this new venture. As she read His Word and waited on Him for the next step, the assurance deepened that God would lead her to an unreached tribe. She knew that there would be many opportunities to help in pioneer work already under way, but God's will for her was a tribe untouched by the Gospel. A verse from the Berkeley version of Romans reinforced the conviction: "Those who have never been told of Him shall see and those who never heard shall understand."

After the course at the University of Oklahoma the next step was Jungle Training Camp in southern Mexico where Rachel learned how to live in rustic surroundings. She observed Wycliffe translators Phil and Mary Baer with the Lacandon Indians, one of the most backward tribes of North America. It was a small tribe, and cultural barriers slowed spiritual advance into the group. Perhaps a similar challenge awaited her in the Amazon area.

In 1949 Rachel packed her duffel bags and footlockers with equipment for living far from the benefits of civilization, and was soon on her way to Wycliffe's advance in Peru. En route she stopped in Ecuador to visit her brother Nate and his wife Marj. Nate was flying missionaries stationed in the eastern jungle of Ecuador. He told Rachel of the tribal work in progress in the sparsely populated jungle forest east of the Andes, the undeveloped Oriente. But there was one tribe where missionaries were not welcome—the hostile Auca.

"I don't fly over them," said Nate. "I fly around them." Foreigners down through the years had tried unsuccessfully to live peaceably with the Auca tribe. A forced landing in Auca territory meant certain death, and Nate believed that his work for isolated missionaries was too vital to take the chance.

Rachel comments, "Nate was always fearless when duty demanded facing any kind of danger, so I knew there was good reason for his cautiousness. This was the first time I had heard of the Aucas, and my heart was strangely drawn to them. If there was ever an unreached tribe, I thought, this was surely it."

In Peru Rachel worked with the Piro Indians. Esther Matteson was already well into the language and had begun the initial stages of Bible translation. But this was not an *unreached* tribe, so Rachel could not settle in comfortably when there were others— like the Aucas—who had heard nothing of Christ.

In another tribe of Peru—the head-hunting Shapras—two Wycliffe translators were due for furlough after several years of living in extremely rugged circumstances. Doris Cox and Loretta Anderson had learned to speak Shapra and began to give the Word of God to Tariri, the head-hunting chief, and others of his tribe. There had been little response to their message, however, and they were reluctant to leave their work for a much-needed rest. Finally they decided to take their furloughs separately, if a temporary partner were available for continuing work in the tribe. Rachel willingly offered to serve as a partner first to Loretta, then to Doris.

While living with the Shapra Indians, Rachel came to love Chief Tariri and his wild people. But the chief was not yet in-clined to leave the brutal practice that was his claim to tribal leadership. Decked out in his bright-colored feather headdress Tariri was an imposing figure as he set out with his spears for a roundup in the forests of the Amazon headwaters, where northern Peru merges undramatically into Ecuador.

After two and a half years of jungle work in Peru Rachel spent a month's vacation in Ecuador, visiting again her brother Nate and his wife Marj. She heard more about the untamed Aucas. People on the streets and in buses were discussing the recent Auca attacks on Quichua Indians and Ecuadorians living near their borders in the jungle. Several attacks on the personnel of the Shell Oil Company base at Arajuno had hastened that company's withdrawal from the area. In Quito Nate took his sister to visit an engineer of the company who gave more details of the ferocity of the Auca attacks. He said that he even had a feather headdress, souvenir of a raid.

"May I see the headdress?" Rachel asked.

"Certainly"—and the engineer promptly sent his son to fetch the trophy.

"It is exactly like Tariri's!" Rachel exclaimed in amazement. "Why, these people must be like the Shapras of Peru!"

During her days in Ecuador a quiet, deep assurance settled on Rachel. These unapproachable Aucas were "those who have never been told of Him." This was the unreached tribe to which she was called. And as she left Ecuador and returned to Peru she knew that one day she would be going to the Auca tribe. Rachel recollects,

"I hardly knew what to do with this new assurance, for Wycliffe was not working in Ecuador and I had no leading to leave Wycliffe. I loved this group which was as dear to me as my own family, and I couldn't think of leaving. I didn't mention the matter to anyone except a Peruvian pastor, a godly man who promised to pray for me and the tribe to which I had been called."

Rachel began to pray and plan for her future work among the Aucas. She thought of possible reasons for the Lord's having placed her for a time with the primitive Shapras. The feather headdress had been an exciting clue. Perhaps there was a cultural connection between the two tribes. If so, they might belong to the same linguistic family.

While at the Yarinacocha Jungle Base in Peru Rachel visited with other Wycliffe workers who had been stationed for months in tribes throughout the Peruvian jungle. Among them were Catherine Peeke and Mary Sargent who had returned from the

Záparo Indians on the Pastaza River near the Ecuadorian border. Although several days by canoe from the Shapra tribe, the two young women had been Rachel's closest "neighbors." As they chatted they compared tribal notes and discussed future plans.

"Will you be returning to the Shapra tribe?" was a very natural question for Catherine and Mary to ask Rachel.

Rachel hesitated. She knew that she wouldn't return to the Shapra tribe, but how could she tell about her future plans?

"No . . ." she said. "My tribe is across the border."

"Across what border?"

"Across the border in Ecuador. The Aucas—"

"In Ecuador! How? Wycliffe isn't working there."

"I don't know, but I am sure that I will be working there. God will make a way . . ."

The conversation which continued during the meal was interrupted for an important announcement which Director Cameron Townsend wanted to make.

"I would like to read a letter which has just come from the Ecuadorian ambassador to the United States, inviting us to work among the Indian tribes of Ecuador . . ."

Busy days of planning and packing followed as the first members of the Ecuadorian advance, volunteers from among the workers in Peru, began to move northward. Though eager to begin her search for the Auca tribe, Rachel was not among the first recruits to reach Ecuador. When after a number of delays she finally arrived, however, she was delighted that there was fresh news concerning the tribe. She heard of an Auca girl who was living in Quito in the city home of Señor Sevilla, an Ecuadorian hacienda owner from the Oriente. Since there was no safe way to enter the tribe at this time, Rachel investigated the possibility of working with an Auca speaker to gain a knowledge of the language before the door into the tribe opened.

One afternoon when Rachel and Catherine Peeke called on Señor Sevilla he graciously offered the services of one of his maids who spoke Auca. As Rachel wrote down the words pronounced by the girl Catherine whispered, "This is not pure Auca—she is mixing Quichua with it." Catherine had learned Quichua while working with the Andoas Indians, and she recognized the linguistic hybridization.

In her disappointment Rachel frankly told Sevilla that this informant would not do because she evidently did not speak the Auca language.

"That is understandable," said Sevilla, "for she is a Quichua girl who was captured by the Aucas and lived with them for many years. It is very possible that she doesn't speak pure Auca. But if you want to work with Aucas we have four of them working on my hacienda in the Oriente."

"You do?" asked Rachel, trying to conceal her excitement.

He then told of Dayuma and Umi who had fled from their Auca home and arrived at Hacienda Ila several years before. The other two women, Wiñaemi and Ominia, had come out later. These Aucas would be available for informant work at the hacienda.

From Señor Sevilla's home Rachel and Catherine went immediately to join other Wycliffe workers for an audience with President Velazco Ibarra of Ecuador, to whom Cameron Townsend was to present the members of the first group of translators. Rachel, who lacked a proper hat for the occasion, had been encouraged by Townsend to wear the bright feather headdress which Chief Tariri had affectionately presented her upon leaving his tribe. She had converted it into a fashionable headpiece by the addition of a veil. As President Ibarra cordially received the band of missionary-linguists, he displayed great curiosity when the young woman with the Indian headdress was introduced as a future Auca worker.

"What?" he said. "You mean that you expect to work with the Aucas? When I flew over them they threw spears at the plane. No white person has ever been able to live in the Aucas' territory. . . . Do you really intend to go to the Auca tribe, Señorita?"

"Yes," answered Rachel confidently. "I believe that God will make a way."

She was frightened later when she reflected on her boldness. "It sounded like presumption—but I was so sure that it just tumbled out!"

Finally in February of 1955 Rachel, accompanied by Catherine Peeke, arrived downstream on the Anzu River in a Wycliffe float plane, almost at the front door of Hacienda Ila. The Anzu is one of hundreds of feeders that tumble down the waning slopes of the Andes and finally succumb, many jungle miles later, to the huge and hungry Amazon. An hour by canoe downriver from Hacienda Ila the Anzu joins the Jatunyacu to form the wide and winding Napo that cuts a muddy channel through giant jungle and wanders on erratically across the Peruvian border. But the Napo's main reason for being, as far as the Ecuadorian settlers are concerned, is that it safely separates them from Auca territory.

Hacienda Ila, on the western side of Auca territory and protected from spears by several rows of intervening mountain ridges, had been hand carved out of virgin jungle by the industrious Sevilla family. Over a period of thirty years they had subdued the fertile area once covered by huge trees thickly draped with gigantic vines and ferns, a formidable green barrier to civilized progress. Nature always threatened to reclaim what man had taken by force, but Don Carlos Sevilla was a match for the constant challenge.

Aided by an entourage of faithful Indians, he made the hacienda an extensive model of efficient jungle production.

The huge two-story thatched home of the Sevilla family was surrounded by various smaller buildings for the workers, guest houses for travelers in the jungle, a kitchen house, and even a small school for the children of the Indian laborers. Beyond the buildings lay the cultivated fields of sugar cane, bananas, yuca, and pasture for the cattle and horses. Fruit and palm trees dotted the landscape.

Hacienda Ila bore the stamp of Don Carlos' remarkable ingenuity and industry on every hand. To dry the harvested cotton, rice, and corn he had rigged a novel all-weather platform where produce could be quickly shielded from sudden shower. The oblong drying platform was covered by a corresponding thatched roof which revolved on a central pivot. By pulling a rope a small Indian worker could turn the entire roof which would cover the platform, or, if turned crosswise, would leave the ends of the platform exposed to the sun. Nate Saint had observed the interesting contraption from the air.

In a room on the ground floor of the thatched "castle" where Rachel and Catherine lived Don Carlos had stored machinery obtained from the Shell Oil Company when it had ceased operations in the jungle in 1949. For several years the enterprise had sought to drive a wedge of men and machines into Auca territory but were repeatedly repulsed by Auca spears. Their large base at Shell Mera, as in Arajuno, was finally abandoned and equipment disposed of locally.

Living quarters at Ila reflected much of the history of the place, according to Rachel:

"The guest room the Sevilla family graciously offered us was a large one on the second floor. Like the rest of the house it was constructed of hand-hewn timbers from the forest that had been cleared to make way for the jungle mansion. From the walls several portraits looked down upon us out of their massive wood frames. There was one of Don Carlos' mother wearing a necklace of huge gold nuggets. Her whole gracious manner spelled old Spain. Another was of a robed and bearded priest, a mark of the Old World visible to the present day along the route of Orellana.

"The place reminded me in many ways of a medieval castle, with the turrets replaced by palm thatch, and the moat by the racing river. We were served our meals in the spacious dining room where one or more members of the Sevilla family presided. We were offered the best fare the jungle affords adorned by Latin culinary arts and served by well-trained Quichua Indians. The conversation of our hosts and their many guests who always made Ila a stop-over gave us a liberal education in the ways of the jungle."

One familiar topic was certain to be mentioned—that of Auca spearings. Don Carlos was well qualified to lead such discussions for he himself had been the victim of those spears. While hunting rubber on the Curaray he had had several encounters with them. His prize story was of a hand-to-hand combat when the Aucas surprised him on the river. He dived into the water, swam to the other side, and climbed a fallen tree up the steep bank. One Auca who pursued him threw a spear which wounded him. The others rained spears at him, but he managed to use the same spears for counterattacking, and finally drove the Aucas off. Then burning with fever and his spear wound squirming with maggots, he walked eight days out of the forest. His faithful dog was his only companion.

The wild stories that she heard from Don Carlos and his venturesome visitors would have discouraged one with less conviction than Rachel. But she seized every opportunity to study the language with Dayuma.

After a discussion about the fierce tribe one day at the table

Sevilla's son suggested that Rachel would probably write a book about the Aucas.

"Yes, perhaps after I have lived with them for twenty years," she replied.

"You don't expect to live among the Aucas for twenty years, do you?" he asked incredulously.

After that dialogue Rachel wrote in her diary: "No outsider has ever lived long in their territory. It would be sheer presumption apart from God's call."

During the few precious hours when Dayuma was free from her work in the fields she faithfully taught Rachel as much of her language as she could remember. She gained confidence in the friendly foreigner who listened so sympathetically. As Rachel learned Auca, Dayuma was encouraged to recall more of it herself as a medium of detailing her early life revived through the powerful association with her mother tongue.

In the first days of study on Auca when Rachel was extracting words by gestures and signs, it occurred to her to show Dayuma the photo album compiled during her stay with the Shapra Indians. The response was immediate. When Dayuma and the other Auca girls saw the picture of Chief Tariri with his feather headdress, they gasped and announced with assurance, "Auca!" The album was the key that unlocked the door. They pointed to the long hair, the blowguns, the monkeys, and the spears, and reacted as if they were seeing pictures of their own people back home beyond the ridge. There was one difference: their people didn't wear clothes, while Tariri's did.

Dayuma was intrigued by Tariri and his family, and the fact that Rachel had actually lived with them. She asked Rachel to teach her the names of Tariri's wife and children and relatives. Rachel says, "I was amazed from the very first at Dayuma's keen memory. She never forgot one of those names."

As growing fluency in the language permitted, Rachel told Dayuma about the tribes in which she had lived and described some of their customs. Whenever the practices of other Indians struck a familiar note the girl would brighten or display a startled expression. How could this newcomer know so much about the way Aucas lived? One day when Rachel casually mentioned that Tariri's tribe strangled babies, Dayuma became curious and wanted to know more about the Shapra custom. Very soon the Auca girl was explaining to Rachel the methods of infanticide in her tribe.

During the months of patiently pulling Dayuma back into her language Rachel saw that God had wasted no time. Every step had been perfect preparation for understanding and winning the heart of a wild girl of the forest only superficially tamed by the accouterments of civilized society.

As Rachel recalled with gratitude the way God had led her she knew that He would some day complete the journey right into the heart of the forbidden land. From her home at the hacienda she wrote early in 1955:

"About a year and a half ago I flew over the eastern jungle with Nate on one of his routine runs. Perhaps twenty minutes out of his back yard at Shell Mera he turned to me and said, 'See that ridge?' I did. It looked just like the rest of the jungle except that it dropped out of sight on the horizon.

" 'Just beyond that ridge is where your Aucas live,' he volunteered.

"And a way of reaching the Aucas then seemed just as vague as the green nothingness that was lost on the horizon. But the Lord's call and the Lord's promises seemed just as solid as the jungle ridge, the visible boundary between the Aucas' territory and the rest of the jungle. The real boundary was marked, however, by years of killings which had repulsed all foreigners.

"Now I am closer to Aucaland. As I dream out of the window

of the hacienda to which the Lord has brought me, I am close to the land of the Aucas, although I cannot see it. What I see is a ridge, rising from the swift Anzu River to the east, in an ever-changing tapestry of jungle verdure, varied with tropical sun or dark rainstorms. The ridge is ever there, just as solid as faith's promises, the first thing I see in the morning, and the last as the lingering sun sets.

"As I look off across the ridge to Aucaland, with perhaps not one but several groups of people living there without God and without hope, I wonder myself just how the Lord will make the way. Somehow, I feel that when He does, it will be a safe one, for He doeth all things well."

3

"WITH MY FATHER
IN THE FOREST"

SOMETIMES on dark jungle evenings after Rachel had given up
hope of seeing Dayuma, she would hear the muffled thumping of
bare feet on the stairs. Overtones of giggles and whispers announced the arrival of Dayuma and her companions for a late visit.
The women would chatter and chuckle around the smoky
kerosene lamp. Occasionally they would oblige with a rhythmic
nasal chant from the forest. In Auca falsetto they would sing the
same syllables over and over, refrains from ancestral tunes too
ingrained to be forgotten.

In such a mood Dayuma would be inspired to recount the happy
hours of her childhood when her relatives would gather for whole
nights of singing and dancing. Dayuma would lead her partners in
a spritely demonstration of how they used to sing and sway in long
rows, hands clasped together, in a heel-toe dance.

For days before a big party the jungle would ring with shouts of
glee as the children joined in the excitement of the coming event.
On tall poles outside the thatched huts were fastened the back-
bones of jungle fish which attracted clouds of pretty butter-
flies. They danced gaily in the bright sunshine as if anticipating
the celebration.

Under the fluttering butterfly clouds the men laughed heartily as they wove brilliant headdresses of red and yellow toucan feathers to be worn at the dance. Some crowns were completed with several tall soft white feathers of the heron or scissorshawk placed majestically at the back. Bright-colored feathers hung loosely down from the stand of white plumes. Upper arm bands of colored and white feathers, and chest ornaments made of animal teeth and bones completed the costume. Red achiote paint from jungle seed smeared on bare brown bodies was the finishing touch which announced it was dance time.

Above the swinging, swaying rows of dancers, palm flares placed at intervals under the thatched roof cast eerie, flickering light. The only other light was furnished by the cocuyo, giant lightning bugs caught for the occasion and tied together with fine palm fiber to be hung from the upper arm bands. Their green phosphorescent body lights and their big red tail lights glowed brightly as the men moved to the rhythmic rattle of bone ornaments and the nasal, repetitious chants. Gradually the women would join them, first the young girls, then the young mothers as their babies were put to sleep. On and on through the night the slow swinging dance continued, forward and backward in time with the music, broken only by occasional fast solo dances by the men.

The children wished they could have a party every night, and climb trees and play all day. But unfortunately there was hard work for every little Auca. Fast-growing jungle weeds had to be cleared for planting yuca and bananas, and there was always firewood to be chopped. Dayuma's cousin Umi was her faithful accomplice in jungle escapades. They would often get spanked with nettles by Uncle Gikita or big brother Wawae for not doing their chores. How those nettles did sting!—but the punishment was soon forgotten and off they were for another gay fling in the forest.

Sometimes Uncle Gikita grabbed Dayuma by her shoulder-length hair and administered a sound whipping. Finally, in angry determination to prevent a recurrence of this dreadful punishment, Dayuma took a pair of sharp shells and cut her hair so short as to restrain Uncle Gikita. The younger girls, impressed by her example, promptly hacked their hair in an inconveniently short style. It was a happy day for Dayuma when Uncle Gikita married Maengamo, for after that he seemed to be occupied with activities other than beating little miscreants.

There were so many exciting places to play, especially the big forbidden landslide. "You'll die!" warned the parents. But Auca children were seldom afraid of anything. They loved to climb high up the slope, clinging to jungle vines, then come whooping and yelling down the steep landslide. After a big rain it was especially treacherous—but that was when it was the most fun for Dayuma. One day just after they had slithered down the hillside there was an avalanche of earth large enough to have buried them. That time Dayuma's father Tyaento brushed the stinging nettles over every part of their bare bodies, raising huge welts.

In a while Dayuma's mother Akawo missed the young culprits.

"Where are the children?" she asked. "They've gone again to the landslide!"

"I'll beat them this time," Uncle Kiwa said. He found them high on the dangerous sliding earth, screeching in ecstasy. And oh! how the nettles stung that time.

Angry with Kiwa they plotted revenge. "Now what shall we do to Kiwa? He's mean. Let's put thorns for him to step on—*that* will hurt!" They selected the sharpest palm thorns and made a bed of them right in the path where he would return from hunting. Carefully, they covered the trap with dirt.

"Ay! ow—ow!" yelled Kiwa as he stepped on the sharp thorns. "My feet hurt! I'll really nettle those children this time!" And again Uncle Kiwa punished them. Dayuma told Rachel,

"Kiwa nettled us a lot. One day being very angry with him we went to his peanut patch and pulled a lot of peanuts and ate them. When Kiwa came he said, 'Who's been eating my peanuts?' Father asked me, 'Did you eat those peanuts?' When I said no he said, 'Don't you lie!' And *he* spanked us with nettles!

"Later Kiwa married Natani and they had a little baby. Moipa came and killed Kiwa. 'Now who will nettle us?' I said, because Kiwa spanked us with nettles more than anybody else."

One of the greatest joys of the forest was to splash and play with the alligators on Fish River when the sun was hot. It was great fun to tease the sluggish animals sleeping lazily on mahogany logs by the water. The children punched and poked them with sticks to make them move. Finally the creatures would tire of the torment and plop down into the water.

Tyaento would often take the children to a deep place in the river where they could dive and stay under the water a long time. One of their sports was to put huge stones on their shoulders or weigh themselves down with stones on their chests so they would sink. The one who could stay on bottom the longest was the champion.

Back home after play in the river there were many things for children to learn. Young boys had to be taught how to spear. The men would take their sons with their spears to a field of banana trees. "Do it like this, then when you grow up you will understand," they would instruct as they plunged their spears into the pithy trunks. "Spear it like this! There! That's the way! Harder!" For days the spear training would continue until the young boys could hit the target accurately and bring the "enemy" down.

Boys had to learn to spear fish and blowgun monkeys and birds. Tyaento would take his sons into the forest to teach them, and Dayuma, as her father's favorite, would often accompany them.

Those trips were the happiest days of her life. Sometimes monkeys and baby toucan birds were caught alive and kept for pets.

On one of the trips Tyaento left Dayuma with her little brother Nampa while he went deeper into the forest to blowgun monkeys. While he was gone Nampa heard the call of the baby toucan birds, high up in a big tree. He tied a vine around his ankles for support and started to shinny up the tree when Dayuma spotted a big nest of wasps. "Don't go up there!" she called. "The wasps will sting you and you will fall and die!" But the boy climbed right on up. And the wasps stung him! Howling, he quickly slid down the trunk of the tree. But when their father returned he climbed up the tree, tapped on the hollow limb where the baby toucans lived, and out came the long black and yellow beaks of the babies expecting food from their mother. Tyaento grabbed them by their beaks one by one and took them home for dinner.

Dayuma's memories of her mother were not so pleasant. She had never forgotten Akawo's threat when she was still very small, too young to sense the anxiety when Tyaento was several days overdue in returning from the forest. Akawo had seen the spears strike many times in her own family, and she dreaded the day when she would be left alone to provide yuca and meat for hungry children. In her fear she said to Dayuma,

"If your father doesn't come back tomorrow I will kill you. Choked with a vine around your neck you will die. Then I will bury you in a rotten tree trunk."

"Why does my mother talk like that?" wondered little Dayuma. "Why will she kill me if my father doesn't return?"

Akawo's apprehension had been mounting for seven days. Tyaento had gone upriver to hunt, and it was upriver that Moipa had gone to live, promising that some day he would spear his relative Tyaento with whom he had quarreled.

Surely by this time Tyaento's body, pierced by chonta spears, lay unburied in the forest. Now who would bring home meat for so many hungry mouths? A partial solution lay in reducing the number to be fed. Dayuma was the youngest, a skinny little Auca who probably wouldn't live anyway. She often suffered from high fevers, and chances for survival seemed very slim.

In her hammock that night Dayuma looked up at the steady, luminous stars keeping vigil over the jungle forest. She kept wondering about her mother's firm words as she had threatened, "I will kill you tomorrow . . ."

"Will my father come tomorrow? Will he come . . . ?" Tormented by the prospect of being choked by a strong jungle vine tied firmly around her thin neck, the child sobbed softly in her hammock. Finally, weary with fear and wondering, the tired Indian girl fell asleep.

Nearby the swift Fish River, tumbling down from the melting snows of the Andes, raced eagerly on toward the Curaray. Only the ceaseless singing of the water, or the occasional howl of a monkey, broke the silence of the dark forest.

Akawo could not sleep. From her hammock she stirred the embers of the dying fire, and planned for the future. After choking Dayuma, should she take the other children and flee? Moipa was sure to come and kill her and them. He often killed women and children, and he would not be satisfied with Tyaento's death. But where should she flee to be safe from Moipa's spears?

When Dayuma awoke, the first rays of light were filtering through small scattered peepholes in the dense green wall of palm and giant fern. Sleep had revitalized the thin body. Her keen mind was instantly wide awake.

"If my father doesn't come *today* she will kill me!" Then quick as a flash of jungle lightning she said to herself, "She won't choke me. I'll run away. I will hurry up and run fast. I will flee to the bramble patch—she won't get me there. If my father dies I will live as an orphan, I will live all alone. I will take a small pot and cook yuca and eat alone. *Then I will live to grow up!*"

The little Auca's will to survive was strong, and plans for escape were being firmly plotted in her young mind. She sprang out of the hammock and looked around with the alertness of a canny animal of the forest. Akawo was muttering as she poked the fire and plunked a big clay pot on to boil. Dayuma glanced around the thatched hut and made a quick inventory of its scant equipment. She saw a small clay pot in the corner beside her mother's hammock. That one would do, she thought. And she looked again to see if the long fire stick was in its place above the fire. Yes, there it was wrapped in a leaf—she would take that to make her fire. She had twirled the stick before when she went with her father into the forest, and she could do it again.

Though very young Dayuma had heard of many Auca children thrown out in the forest for the animals to eat, or choked with vines, or buried alive. She had heard so much that she knew her mother was not "just talking wild." Many were the times she had fallen asleep in her hammock as her mother and father and grandfather reviewed tribal spearings and fleeings and infant killings.

There was the tale of the woman who had two children, one big enough to play and the other a small baby. When the foreigners came—one of the many groups of outsiders who periodically invaded Auca territory—the woman fled. In the jungle the baby cried a lot. "Why should I keep this baby? He cries so much," said the mother. And she threw it away. "In the jungle the baby died alone" was the matter-of-fact conclusion of the tale.

There was also Natani, Kiwa's wife, who was carrying her baby up a hill by the Tiwaeno River. She left her baby there in the jungle and the baby died. Some time later Natani's father said to her, "Where is your child? I haven't seen her lately." But Natani didn't answer, and her father wondered about it. Then one day another child was born, a very tiny baby. "Watch out, don't you throw this one away," cautioned her father. And that one grew up.

Then there was Aka, one of Moipa's wives, who said that if the foreigners attacked she would take her boy and girl, tie their hands and feet together, and leave them behind.

"Let the foreigners have them," she commented.

"Where will you live if they kill all the Aucas? Then where will you live?" someone asked her.

"I will live with the deer. They eat *tipa* palm nuts and underbrush. They drink water. I shall do the same when I live in the deer's house."

"But the deer have no house. They just live in the jungle."

"Then I will live in the jungle, too," pursued Aka. And all the Aucas laughed and laughed.

But one day Aka did throw a child away. When Moipa came home from spearing, he said,

"Where is my child?"

Aka didn't answer. Then her old mother spoke up,

"The baby cried and cried when we went to the jungle. We dug in the ground and buried her."

"Why did you do that?" asked Moipa. "That wasn't good."

"Later she will bear another child," said the old mother. "She threw this one away for no good reason. Later she will have another one."

"Well, then, don't act like that again," said Moipa.

In her childish bewilderment Dayuma didn't know which would be worse—to be choked to death or to be buried alive. What would it feel like to be thrown into a hole and have the dirt heaped on you until you died? She remembered the child who was born without a foot. "How will he get about without his foot?" asked the mother. Then she dug a hole, buried the baby, and it died. Another deformed child was born and the mother did the same thing. "Having dug the ground she buried it. Later it died" —the story could be repeated for many Auca infants.

All morning Dayuma watched her mother as the jungle sun rose higher in the sky. She did not turn her back on her mother, but observed her every move. How happy she was when her mother sent her to the stream for a small pot of water! There at the water's edge she looked again at the path leading off into the jungle, and decided that she would flee downriver.

"Perhaps I could run away. I could live with the deer in the jungle and eat palm nuts," she thought, remembering Aka's plan.

"If your father doesn't come by this afternoon, yes, I will kill you," Dayuma's mother reminded her when she returned with the water.

Dayuma watched the sun anxiously. Soon it would be noon.

Then that day, sometime before noon, her father came home. Dayuma was very happy. "Now my father has not died after all. My father is *alive!*" she said joyfully.

In the afternoon when Tyaento had put his spear away and had his banana drink he went down to the water's edge. A happy daughter followed him. When they were alone Dayuma said, "Father, Mother said she was going to kill me. 'If your father doesn't come by this afternoon, yes, I will kill you,' she said. And I cried and cried."

"But I am alive," said Tyaento comfortingly. "Now you will grow up with me. Then when you are grown up I will say, 'No, don't do things for your mother. You work for me.'"

But for a long time Dayuma didn't grow. Monkey meat and the banana drink which ordinarily made children plump had no effect on the ailing little Auca. This made her mother angry. Then later she grew and became fat. Her father was very happy. "Now my child has become big," he said. Then her mother said, "Now you make things. You are no longer sick with a fever. Who is going to clear the weeds in my banana patch? and in my yuca patch?"

Dayuma was very angry. "When I was a little child I did lots for you," she said, "but you were angry with me. You were going to kill me. Now I will not work for you. I will work for my father, yes, but I won't work for you."

However, several years later when her sister Gimari was born Dayuma did help her mother who was sick and could not care for the baby. Dayuma would sling the infant in a bark cloth on her back and bound off into the forest to play in her favorite spots. Baby Gimari loved riding on her big sister's back where she jiggled and jogged up and down as the lively little mother, nothing daunted by her constant charge, pursued her fun.

Dayuma's childhood throbbed with thrilling adventures in the forest, and fun with brothers and sisters and other playmates. It was only when the horrible spears struck, or when overpowering storms threatened to destroy the forest and all those living in it, that the brightness of life was overshadowed by sorrow.

One hot, humid day when Akawo was crying with the pain of a ray fish sting, Dayuma's younger sister Onaenga went to the river to fish. Dayuma stayed home with the younger children, Nampa and Gimari. Her father and older brother Wawae had gone farther downriver to spear fish.

The family had recently moved to a new settlement still surrounded by tall trees. An epidemic had weakened the men soon afterward and they were unable to clear the heavy forest dangerously close for jungle storms.

Dayuma watched as the clouds darkened and began to drop heavy rain. The wind moaned and swayed in the big trees. Just as Onaenga returned from fishing the wind burst through the clearing, howling angrily and whipping the tops of the trees. It whirled down and snatched vines and pieces of the thatched roofs, tossing them crazily into the torrents of rain now flooding the ground. Lightning gashed the black sky followed closely by blasts of thunder which rocked the forest.

Suddenly large trees were ripped up by the roots, and others crashed as if they had been chopped. The huts upon which they fell were demolished.

Onaenga grabbed little sister Gimari as Dayuma took baby brother Nampa in her arms and started running. She watched the giant trees to see which way they would fall, then threw Nampa ahead of her, out of their path.

"If I die, I die," Dayuma said, "but Nampa will be saved. Get out of the way quick!" she called to the others, but they couldn't hear in the roar of the storm. Onaenga was killed, but somehow Gimari survived.

Akawo couldn't run fast because of the pain in her foot. She was struggling up one of the paths leading away from the hut when a big tree thundered down in front of her. Had she been running the tree would have caught her. Dayuma, who thought her mother had been killed, was near enough to call,

"Mother, Mother, were you killed?"

"Oo, oo—" came a faint answer. And there was her mother, right in the bramble patch!

As Rachel listened Dayuma exclaimed,

"How happy I was to hear my mother's voice!"

Happy to hear the voice which had threatened to choke her a few years before . . .

4

"MY GRANDFATHER
TOLD ME"

"LET's ask Grandfather to tell us a story!" said Dayuma one day to
the other children playing in the forest. They ran back to the clearing and saw Grandfather Karae squatting by the pot of monkey
as he tore the meat apart with his fingernails. With no teeth it
took much longer for him to eat. He was working away on the
monkey leg laid carefully on the top of his foot.

"What story would you like to hear?" asked Grandfather, licking
and sucking the dinner from his fingers.

"Tell us about how our ancestors got their spears," said little
Nampa.

As Grandfather climbed into his hammock with the palm fiber
from which he was weaving a fishing net he began to tell the old
tale, often repeated, to his young listeners.

Long ago the Aucas didn't have spears, they had only chonta
palm clubs which they decorated with human teeth. It was the
son of the moon who taught them how to make spears, and to
sharpen them with "living stones with bright things inside."
When the son of the moon grew older he took an old man of the
tribe out to the forest and taught him how to kill another man.
Since that first time the Aucas have never stopped killing. Later,
people from under the earth taught them how to sharpen the
spears at both ends.

Dayuma's favorite was a monkey story. Long ago when God was still on the earth, there were people who lived like Aucas. They climbed high up in the trees and picked dyuwi fruit and drank the juice. One would climb up high and throw the fruit down to the others. As one of these people was picking fruit one day, both thumbs were split off and he lost the use of his hands.

"Now what will I do?" he said.

"You will become a monkey," God said. Then hair grew all over his body and he became a spider monkey.

Another favorite was the jaguar story. Once a girl was born on the trail where her mother was walking. When the mother went to get some water in which to wash the newborn baby, a jaguar came and took the child. When he arrived at his lair, another big jaguar asked,

"What animal's child have you brought?"

"It's an Auca baby. I have brought it to eat."

"You eat the placenta and I will keep the child," said the big jaguar.

Thus it was that the little Auca girl was saved and raised on raw meat. Her teeth grew big like a jaguar. When she was grown she asked about her mother.

"You were an Auca child," the jaguar told her. "I took you when you were born. Then I said, 'When she is grown she will become my wife and I will be her husband.'" Then the Auca-jaguar wanted to visit her mother. So the jaguar husband "became like an Auca," and together they went to visit the mother.

They surprised her mother who thought that her child had been eaten by a jaguar. Later the mother accompanied her to the jaguar's lair. The daughter deceived the mother into eating some raw deer meat which caused her death.

The Auca-jaguar had seven sons who grew up to be Aucas. Their jaguar father died. The sons were making their yuca fields and their mother would come to visit them where they were cutting down trees. Whenever she would see someone good to eat she said, "He is fat," bit his head off, and cooked him for her sons. She did that several times, then finally she was speared. Those who speared her cut her head off, and hid it in the bottom of the pot where they cooked her. The sons came home for dinner and ate the stew in the pot. Finally they discovered that they had eaten their own mother. They knew her by the big jaguar teeth!

"Now we are going to be speared, too!" they said. So they ran to the lake to escape to the other side. But in the lake the alligators bit them. On the other side they managed to drag themselves around on one knee. They made spears and speared right up into the sky—which in those days was very near the earth. They pulled themselves right up into the sky on their spears, and God turned them into stars—the constellation of the Pleiades. And there you can see them now, the Ones-Who-Were-Bitten-by-the-Alligators.

"Tell me about the people who live under the earth, Grand-father," Dayuma asked one night. And old Karae told her about the *babitari*, the closed-mouth ones who live far down under the earth. He said that their mouths would not open but that they have teeth and tongues with which they talk, and you could under-stand them. At least Grandfather knew what they said. They cook yuca and wild boar, but live from merely sniffing the fumes. Day-uma never saw the *babitari*, but Grandfather knew all about them.

He told many stories of the devil of the forest who came at night and ate Aucas. He could name many Aucas who had died in this way. And sometimes you could plainly see the black-and-blue spots where the devil had sucked the blood until the Auca died. The hawk and the owl are friends of the Aucas, and they often warn when the devil approaches to kill them. When they see the devil coming they squawk, "Wake up! The devil is coming! All of you wake up fast! He is going to eat you!" Then the devil is very angry with the hawk and the owl and says, "Why do you talk? Why are you selfish with the Aucas?"

There are good ocelots who are friends of the Aucas, too. They guard the huts at night so that the devil of the forest will not come and eat people. He whistles to signal that all is well.

"Having heard his whistle we all sleep very well," said Grandfather. "If the ocelot doesn't whistle we say, 'The devil will come,' and we are very much afraid." And if the ocelot doesn't watch the big thatched hut the devil comes and eats Aucas.

Grandfather told of one man who always slept with one eye open because the devil came so often. Finally he moved away to another hut after the devil had eaten his father.

Although Dayuma never saw the devil of the forest, nor the jaguars and ocelots who guarded their dwellings, they were surely there, for Grandfather heard them and knew what they said.

There were other jaguars who lived inside people. Two of them lived inside Grandfather and would speak to him. They spoke to him of many things that were going to happen. One night they said to him,

"There are quite a few of you Aucas living now. But you will spear each other and there won't be many of you left. You will spear others, and they will spear you in return. Thus there will not be many Aucas left. Then the very few children who are left will grow up, and they will spear. Then only ten will be left. Again there will be spearings and only four will be left.

"Then the foreigners will come and take all of your land. Both of us saw the foreigners. How many foreigners are there? Lots and lots and lots of them. There are others who live where the trees don't grow. Far away across the big water we went, and we saw them there. The ones who live right here near are short, like the Aucas, but the others are tall. When the foreigners come there won't be any Aucas left. They will take all the land. We don't just say this. All of you will die," warned Grandfather's jaguars, "if you don't spear them first."

Dayuma had heard about such jaguars from her mother Akawo whose grandfather was inhabited by them.

"My grandfather was speared and he died," Akawo had said. "My grandmother buried him in the hut. As she was coming along the trail one day with my mother she saw two jaguars. My mother said, 'Those aren't just plain jaguars, those are the ones who lived in your grandfather's body!'

"After my grandfather had died my mother and others were sitting in the hut where he was buried. My grandfather's jaguars became like baby ones. They went right out of a hole in the hut. All of them sitting there with my mother saw it happen. Two big jaguars took the little jaguars in their teeth, and carried them off. Then my grandmother closed over the hole, and my mother cried and cried. After that lots of wild hogs came. The jaguars had brought them. The Aucas speared the wild hogs and ate them."

As a child Dayuma had wanted to know about God. Akawo would tell her all she knew, which wasn't much. She told her that long ago God created all the animals, and all the rivers, and all the Aucas.

Turning to Tyaento, Dayuma asked, "Father, where does God live now?"

"I don't know where He lives," Tyaento answered. "But He won't become old and die. A long, long, long time He will live."

Then he sent Dayuma to old Grandfather Karae who knew much more. The old man informed her that not only did God create all the animals, but that when He created the ugly big black tapir the Aucas were very much afraid of it. But God just laughed at them.

Along with his stories of creation old Karae would sing a song,

"God created, God created everything,"

over and over again. There were several verses telling how He created first man, then animals.

In the beginning God created three Auca men and three women. When the women became pregnant the men sharpened bamboo to make knives so that they could perform Caesarian deliveries. Although the babies survived birth, the women all died soon afterward.

Later when one of the girls grew up and was going to give birth, her husband sadly went out into the forest to sharpen the bamboo. Meanwhile, a rat appeared in the form of an Auca and told the woman how to massage to help her child to be born. He told her how to pull a cord out of the hammock to make a hole through which the child could drop. He further instructed her to put a piece of bark across the hammock to which she could cling when her pains were severe. The rat had stationed his children to watch for the return of the Auca man. As the warning was given, the rat and his children ran away. When the man arrived the child was already born, and the mother hadn't died. He was amazed and delighted. And because of the rat's instruction the women lived, and their children were brought up on mothers' milk.

After God had finished creating man and animals He went up to the skies, never to return.

"How sad," thought Dayuma as a child, "that God would never come to earth again."

She often wondered what would happen to her after she died. She asked her father,

"Having died, what will become of me?"

"Your body, having died, will rot," he answered.

"Then what?"

"Then your skeleton will decay."

"Then what?"

"I don't know. Ask your grandfather. He will know."

Then Dayuma asked Grandfather Karae the same question, and he, as usual, knew more than anyone else. He knew much about life after death.

"When your body rots," he said, "your soul will live."

"Where will I live?"

"You will go high up in the sky."

"Where is the trail?"

"It is just a very small trail. It goes up there on the plateau. Then it goes down and down. There is just one trail, there is no other. There is only one trail by which you may go. Having arrived over there you will see a huge worm, as large as a full-grown tree. All who die go along that trail. If one doesn't return he will go fast over the top of the worm and up into the sky. But if he is afraid he will return here, and then become a termite. Here, where they buried you, up in the crossbeam of your house, you will become a termite."

"Then what will happen to me, Grandfather, if I become a termite?"

"I don't know. That is the end. You become a termite."

"But I don't want to become a termite, Grandfather!" Turn into an insect after she died? The thought troubled the child as she continued to ply him with questions.

"Then what happens to the ones that go high up in the sky?"

"There high up in the sky it is like the top of a hill. There they will eat fruit. All of those who die and go there, in the same way they will eat fruit, high up in the sky. Then they will live."

"Then will they die again, Grandfather?"

"Yes, they will die again. In the same way others will kill them."

"Will they kill the soul?"

"Yes, they will kill the soul."

"What will they eat, high up in the sky?"

"Well, if they have just been speared they will eat chonta palm nuts. If they have been killed by a poisonous snakebite, they will eat yuca. If they die from fever, they will also eat yuca and peanuts."

Grandfather knew a great deal about what would happen to her after she died, but there was much more that Dayuma wanted to know. At night around the fire she would ask Grandfather to tell her more about God and the things one couldn't see. But not even Grandfather could answer all her questions.

5

OUTSIDERS

As a very small child Dayuma had noticed a long scar on Grandfather Karae's bare body. It stretched all the way across his abdomen.

"How did you get hurt, Grandfather?" asked Dayuma one day, looking at the scar. Then he told her of the attack of outsiders when he barely escaped with his life.

It happened one day as he and some of the other relatives were out in the forest hunting monkeys. All of a sudden "the foreigners came secretly and shot their guns." Karae's daughter was killed. As her mother, for whom Dayuma was named, picked up the body, she was killed. Dayuma's father Tyaento was slightly wounded, but a bullet tore across Grandfather Karae's abdomen, making a big hole. The wound was so deep that the liver was exposed, and he bled a great deal. It looked for a time as if he wouldn't live, but he recovered slowly.

The long scar was a perpetual reminder of the danger from the outside world. Aucas had to learn to watch and be wary of strangers, and to defend themselves from attack.

Her father's grandmother Wagingamo was down at the stream one day with several relatives beating out *barbasco* roots to extract poison for fishing. Strangers suddenly appeared over the hill and began shooting at the Aucas. Wagingamo's son-in-law was killed, but she and two small children were captured. As they were being hustled along the trail they came to a steep hill. Wagingamo said to her oldest grandchild, "This is where we will flee from the outsiders. They don't understand our language."

Then Wagingamo turned on the trail and said in Auca to one of the foreigners behind her, "What is that I see over there? Look!" And she pointed to a distant ridge. When he turned, she quickly pushed him over the side of the hill, gun and all. By the time he had scrambled up the hill Wagingamo and the two children were out of sight. Back home she reported her escape to her relatives, who "just laughed and laughed."

Among the Aucas themselves there were differing opinions regarding those who lived outside their borders and who were never welcome within their territory. Some said there were no good outsiders, that all non-Aucas were very bad. Others believed because of firsthand experiences that outsiders living downriver on the Curaray were exceedingly bad, but that those living downriver on the Napo were fairly good. Around the fires at night the discussions continued loud and long, and incidents were cited to strengthen each, either pro or con.

To the Aucas all outsiders were foreigners, whether they were of the extensive Quichua tribe surrounding Auca territory, or whether they spoke the language of the Spanish conquerors or of other white men. The Aucas made no distinction between the groups that composed the outside world.

From time to time outsiders made successful raids and captured Aucas. Some never returned, but a number escaped and were reunited with their families. Karae told the story of one captive who had lived for years with strangers on the other side of the Napo. But one night she escaped. "Downriver where the Napo was very big, swimming she crossed the river," Karae said.

When she arrived at her former home, however, her own relatives didn't understand her, for she spoke with a strange accent. "Why don't you speak well?" they remonstrated. After a while she sounded again like an Auca.

Still another group of outsiders were known to kill Aucas and cook them with salt. Since salt is not native to Auca diet this was proof to them that the cannibals were not of their tribe. Miipu, who had been captured by the cannibals, witnessed the killing and cooking of one of his own relatives, Awaenga, also captured with his wife and their small child. The wife escaped but Awaenga was tied to a tree and shot. Then when he was "a little bit rotten" his captors hacked up the body and threw it into a pot with salt. Miipu was forced to eat his relative's flesh, much to the delight of the cannibals. He escaped, went back to his people and reported, "There you will not live well. They are not good foreigners."

Little wonder that through the years the tribe feared they would fall into the hands of those who ate Auca flesh. In making contacts with any outsiders this hazard had to be considered.

Because the Aucas spoke no language in common with outside dwellers they constantly misunderstood and clashed with all who approached them regardless of their motives.

Grandfather had a great store of tales about the Wiñatarae, a group of Aucas living in a different area of the jungle. They were very large and made long spears. They also made huge pots, two or three feet high, and when turned upside down were a good hiding place. Once during an attack some of them hid under their pots and were not killed.

As a child Dayuma heard the odd speech of the Wiñatarae. Her father could understand them, but she could not follow their conversation.

Earlier, in her grandfather's day, a group of the Wiñatarae had silently settled themselves in an empty Auca hut near the banana and yuca fields of their neighbors and were helping themselves to a rich supply of food. Two Auca heroes, Tipayae and Ima, on discovering their big thatched hut and land appropriated by the thieves, planned to wipe them out.

They built themselves a palm-thatched shelter, high up in one of the largest trees of the forest above the enemy and hidden from their sight in the crotch of the tree. They even cooked in a small clay pot over a fire made by friction sticks. There they lived for more than a month. Every time they went down for water or food they would spear one or two Wiñatarae. After killing a few they would circle way around, "just like jaguars," and hide once again in the tree. Thus they killed many of the Wiñatarae, the siege continuing until their spear supply was exhausted.

One of Grandfather's favorite stories was of a very short Auca man who had a narrow escape from an outsider. He was so anxious to get his peanuts down from the rafters of his hut when the outsiders came that he didn't have time to run away into the forest. So he ducked under a canoe which was turned upside down. The outsiders came and one of them sat near the canoe. The short man quickly reached out from under the canoe, grabbed a club, and gave the intruder a fatal blow on the head.

"For one year, and for two years, the outsiders didn't come back to the Aucas' huts," laughed Grandfather as he finished the tale.

The approach of outsiders was usually heralded by the barking of their dogs, a warning for the Aucas to be on guard. An Auca man who had never before seen the foreign animal, killed one when it wandered into his clearing. Some of the children listening to Grandfather had never seen dogs either, but they laughed anyway as he told the story.

Moipa and his brother Itaeka, who had become part of Karae's family after their parents were speared, would discuss the problem of outsiders with Tyaento. "Why don't we make friends with

foreigners?" Tyaento often asked Moipa. But Moipa had no desire
for peaceful contacts with any of them. He hated them all. As a
young man he began to make raids on those living on Auca borders. Tyaento was of another persuasion. He reasoned that if the
hostility continued the outsiders would eventually gather their
forces, come in and take all the Auca territory.

The years only increased Moipa's hatred of outsiders—and of
several living in his own land.

6

MOIPA

"LONG, long before you were born," old Grandfather Karae once told Dayuma, "there were many of us. Then our people began spearing among themselves. They killed and killed until there were only a few left. Finally someone said, 'Now we have killed enough. Why do we kill so much?'" Others agreed, and for a long time the tribe lived without many spearings.

However, within Dayuma's own family group occasional murders left an imprint of terror on the young child's mind. While still living in Tyaento's home Moipa and Itaeka killed the father of little Gomoki, Dayuma's relative and playmate who with her parents also lived in the same group. It was the first spearing that Dayuma witnessed. She could remember with horror:

"Very early in the morning Moipa and Itaeka spear-killed. 'Why do they have Gomoki's father in the middle of the hammock with one of them on either side of him? Why are they doing that?' I was there in the hut watching. Being a child, I was playing. Then I saw one of them blink his eyes. 'Why is he doing that? Why is he blinking his eyes?' Then quick as a flash they grabbed Gomoki's father. 'Hurry! Spear him!'

"Moipa grabbed a spear. Then I ran away. To the vines and the underbrush we children fled—there were several of us—and I was terribly frightened. After they speared Gomoki's father my father came looking for us and called, 'Where did you go? They have killed our relatives, now you can come back.' Moipa had killed

Gomoki's father, and her mother, and her little sister. I saw her father lying there looking alive. He didn't die fast, he died after a long while. When they spear in the throat one dies fast, but he didn't die fast. I was very much afraid. My mother was there, but she didn't speak.

"Gomoki was very little then, when they speared her father. Then my father took her and she grew up with us. She was an orphan. Three little children my father took at that time."

Not satisfied with this cruelty, Moipa returned later and speared the three-year-old daughter of the same family. Then he took Gomoki and Aepi, a young captured Quichua girl who was living with Dayuma's family, and attempted to torture them to death. He tied their wrists together and, according to Dayuma, "threw them in the deep water. What could they do in the water like that? They were tied up tight. They went down, then they bobbed up again. Then they breathed, and went down in the water again. Then Moipa threw them out of the water, then he threw them in again. My father found them there and helped get them out of the water. I went there but Moipa had gone. He was nowhere to be found. I went and the two of them were about to die. Then I pushed their stomachs which were huge. Then they threw up all the water.

"I was just small then. But they got better. Then my father said to Gomoki and Aepi, 'Don't you two stay in the hut or they will kill you. Both of you follow me.' So they went everywhere with my father and they both lived to grow up. If my father hadn't found them in the deep water they would have died."

Through the years, Tyaento rescued other children orphaned by spearings, and raised them as his own.

At that time the Aucas lived in large oval thatched huts. Dayuma's family group occupied ten such huts, each containing many people. In one, for example, there were eleven men with all their wives and children. Altogether there were several hundred in the related group living on or near the Tiwaeno River.

Dayuma's two lower front teeth were just growing back in when her relatives started to kill one another. There was a nightmare of chain-reaction spearing. Within a few days the Aucas living in the ten large huts were reduced to a handful of survivors who occupied only four small huts.

Moipa and his brother Itaeka were comparatively inexperienced spearers when the big feud began. The lull in intratribal killing was brutally broken. Aentyaeri, Dayuma's relative who initiated the mass spearing, had observed Moipa's budding ability as a killer, and knew that his chance of wiping out his enemy Mingi would be multiplied with Moipa's help.

Aentyaeri was still a very small boy when his hatred for Mingi began. Mingi and his followers had declared that through a vision it was revealed that Aentyaeri's father was a witch doctor. With his forces rallying around him, Mingi speared not only Aentyaeri's father, but also his mother. Then Mingi threw their bodies out in the forest for the buzzards to eat. He was smug in the confidence that there would be no one left to avenge their death.

Cold and hungry, Aentyaeri and his younger brother would walk out to the forest and watch the vultures consume the decaying bodies of their parents. Then the forlorn orphans would return to their fireless hut and weep pitifully. But finally some relatives discovered their plight, took them in and raised them to manhood.

All through his childhood Aentyaeri brooded on the death of his parents. His hatred for Mingi increased with his years. Later Aentyaeri married and went to live on another river.

As the years went by Aentyaeri grew to be a very large fellow. When word of his strength began to spread in the forest it dawned on Mingi that the orphan who had seemed so weak and insignificant might some day soon be plotting to avenge the death of his parents. Uneasy, Mingi conspired with his accomplices to spear Aentyaeri before any possible plans for reprisal would have had time to hatch.

Meanwhile, Aentyaeri went to visit his foster mother whom he had not seen in some time. Upon arriving at her hut, however, he discovered that she long since had been speared and her body stuffed into the trunk of an old tree.

His foster mother's cruel death was the final blow. With the gnawing memory of buzzards eating the rotting flesh of his mother and father, he went to old Karae for advice.

"Now what shall I do?" asked Aentyaeri. "Shall I kill them or not?"

"If you want to kill them, kill them," counseled Karae, "if you don't, don't."

Aentyaeri invited his own brother and Moipa and Itaeka to go on the raid with him. For four days they made spears furiously, coloring them with red seed paint and decorating them with feathers. Then they practiced out in the banana patch, jabbing the spears angrily into the soft trunks and shouting, "In this way we will spear our enemies!"

On the fifth day they went to Mingi's hut on the Tiwaeno River. Mingi was immediately ill at ease, for he had been planning to kill Aentyaeri the next time he went hunting. Mingi asked him why he and his companions had come.

"We have decided to go and spear the foreigners who live down on the Napo River," Aentyaeri began, "and we need your help."

"I am just a young man," continued Aentyaeri. "I have never speared anybody before. You are an old experienced warrior. Come with us and help us kill the Napo foreigners."

"But I don't have any spears," objected Mingi.

Aentyaeri looked around the dark interior.

"There is one overhead, and there are three, and we'll each give you one of ours. That will be enough. Come with us. We are going to leave tomorrow morning."

When Mingi still hesitated they showed him the masticated yuca dough wrapped in leaves in preparation for the journey. Mingi, convinced by this apparently sincere sign of readiness for the warpath, consented to go. Little did he realize that the lumps of yuca dough were only wads of mud.

As Mingi prepared for the journey he was still uneasy. He'd been hunting that day but had had no luck in killing birds—an omen that he was cursed and would be killed.

Before settling down for the night, Aentyaeri and his friends took a firebrand from the fire and went outside. When Aentyaeri returned alone, without the ember, Mingi was suspicious.

"I heard a jaguar call so I dropped the fire and ran," Aentyaeri explained.

But he had given the fire to his companions hidden in the trees nearby. They were to watch the big hut and spear anyone who tried to flee, while Aentyaeri would spear inside.

Sleep did not come easily to Mingi that night. And it seemed to Aentyaeri and those waiting outside that Mingi would never fall asleep. Finally when he did Aentyaeri quickly struck him with a stone ax. Moipa and Itaeka rushed in with their spears to finish the killing. In the fracas several of Mingi's companions were also speared.

As Mingi was dying he cried out, "Why are you killing me?" and Aentyaeri answered, "Long ago you speared my father and mother and left me to starve and die. Now let your children starve."

He was conforming to Auca tradition, "an eye for an eye, and a tooth for a tooth," retaliation in every detail.

After killing his enemies on the Tiwaeno River, Aentyaeri went the same night to Fish River in search of others who had participated in the spearing of his parents.

Meanwhile, an Auca in one of the huts there was dreaming that Mingi was speared, when sounds were heard in the thatched roof. The fear of attack was dismissed, however, when someone said it was "just a rat."

The "rat," of course, was Aentyaeri and his party who were making holes in the big thatch which went down almost to the ground. Carefully, they pushed the thatch apart until there was an opening large enough to enter. Then plunging suddenly through the thatch, they fell upon two brothers sleeping inside, and speared them to death.

At dawn they surprised another enemy who was spearing fish. In a short time they killed him and his wife, as well as several of their children and some of their relatives.

When Aentyaeri finally returned to his hut he found that a part of his thatched roof had been burned. His mother-in-law who had quenched the fire with water said that "the lizzard had burned it," a common Auca superstition. Aentyaeri was not so sure. Upon inspecting the ground around his place he found feathers which had dropped from the spears of the retaliating party. He also discovered footprints, which led him to Tyaento's hut where the avengers had gone to kill Moipa.

In the bloody clash that followed with the sympathizers of each of the opposing parties, many Aucas were killed. The total of dead men rose to twenty-two. Tyaento's clearing in the forest was strewn with speared bodies. When the battle was over he dug a big grave and buried them all.

Instead of waiting to be speared by his enemies Aentyaeri fled to the foreigners, far from the scene of the mass spearing. However, he was soon killed at the hand of strangers.

Moipa had escaped. He was now an experienced killer, and vigorously perpetuated the tradition of spearing within the tribe and on its borders. His hatred of outsiders increased.

Eventually Moipa and Itaeka withdrew from Tyaento's home. But two other relatives, Kimo and Dabu, brothers whose parents had been speared in Aentyaeri's war, stayed on in Dayuma's family.

When Dayuma was still a small girl her people found that large numbers of outsiders were pressing close to their borders, and some had even crossed the line. Moipa had investigated this encroachment and discovered "a big house where many foreigners slept." He had noticed the foreign wood-bee buzzing overhead and dropping things on the edge of his land. Moipa was highly displeased with these activities.

Unknown to the Aucas, the Shell Oil Company had, by 1940, established a base on the Arajuno River, serviced from the larger base of Shell Mera at the foot of the Andes. Moipa resisted the approach of these foreigners who were nosing into his territory, and speared six of them before disappearing into the forest.

One day he saw a number of men walking on a small trail. He watched them take a larger trail to the river.

"I am going to kill those people," he said. "Why do they come here?"

With the help of his brother Itaeka, he followed the foreigners' trail to the big house. There they speared several of them before being bombarded by bullets. Moipa narrowly escaped death when the bullets grazed him.

"They just couldn't kill Moipa!" exclaimed the other Aucas.

When Moipa returned home he began to gather full forces for an attack which would wipe the foreigners out. He threatened Dayuma's father and her brother Wawae if they refused to go. They went along, although Tyaento was reluctant. When the party arrived at the foreigners' camp, however, there were no people in sight. But they plundered the settlement, overturning, destroying, and throwing away most of the equipment. Barrels and bags of rice and flour were dumped. "What could this possibly be?" they asked one another as they tasted something very sweet. It was sugar, a food of which the Aucas had no knowledge or appreciation. "This is no good," they decided, and threw it away.

Then they took "the foreigners' bed clothes." "Now we will sleep covered," said those who had observed how the invaders slept. But after covering themselves with the strange bed clothes, they said, "They stink!" and threw them away also. They took home some of the "foreigners' yuca" for their wives to see. Secretly at night the wives added it to their own prepared yuca. Then in the morning when the men had their yuca drink they said, "What might this be? It stinks!" So they threw it all out and "laughed and laughed."

Later Moipa observed the foreigners' wood-bee buzzing over the Curaray where it would drop bundles in a certain spot. He followed the air trail and discovered a lone foreigner chopping down the trees and making a camp.

The distant outpost was manned by a Negro of the Shell Company who was preparing the way for an exploration team to follow. The plane dropped food, clothes, and other supplies at the isolated spot.

Moipa went to Tyaento's place and tried to enlist a raiding party to halt the advance of the foreigners in the area. Dayuma's brother Wawae listened with interest. He was a lazy fellow who tried to avoid work as much as possible. He begged chambira palm fiber from other relatives instead of cutting and preparing his own material for weaving hammocks and fishing nets. Wawae did enjoy hunting, however, and it was he who often brought Dayuma her favorite monkey meat.

The idea of a raid with Moipa appealed to Wawae, and he went with him to the Curaray. There they found the solitary foreigner strumming a guitar. They speared him and stole his clothes, which Moipa and Wawae wore home. They never removed them, until finally the clothes rotted away and dropped off. Never having had clothes, it didn't occur to the men to wash them.

Each time Moipa returned from attacking the foreigners it was evident that Tyaento disapproved his action.

"Moipa does not do well," he would say morosely.

Tyaento and Moipa differed on other scores, too. Moipa was taking one wife after another, and had already speared one who was thin and who did not please him. Tyaento argued that if this continued there would be no women left for the younger men to marry. The friction between the two men grew steadily.

Others of the tribe had counts against Moipa, too, and he knew that some day his luck would run out and he would be speared. In preparation for that day the chief killer had selected a successor, young Naenkiwi, whom he trained to spear his enemies and resist further attempts of foreigners to take Auca territory.

Dayuma's concern for her father's safety increased with the years. As her apprehension grew she talked with her father of the possibility of his being killed by Moipa. What should she do then? Should she stay and be killed by his spears that were certain to fall on other members of the family, or should she flee outside to the foreigners and take her chances? Tyaento considered the foreigners a safer risk.

Dayuma saw the glumness clinging to Tyaento one evening when he returned from hunting. He had had little success. The monkeys he hit had refused to die.

"I am cursed," he said darkly. "Moipa will kill me soon."

Not long afterward Tyaento, in need of yuca for the large family, set off through the forest for the yuca patch. Old Karae went along, and Gimari and cousin Umi. Dabu joined the party as they started on the overnight trip.

They slept under a big felled *giminiwae* tree, the base of which had several compartments formed by wall-like roots fanning out in all directions and providing convenient sheltered nooks.

Stealthily, Moipa had followed the little group. He waited until they had fallen asleep before attacking. He fatally wounded Karae while the others escaped. Tyaento was speared in the knee.

Someone ran back through the forest to warn the others who had stayed home. Dayuma fled at the first shout of danger. Her brother Nampa said to Akawo, "Quick, Mother, let's flee." She snatched baby Oba and ran out into the night.

Shortly Moipa arrived at the big hut and started spearing. An old uncle who had not been able to flee was his first victim. Moipa drove his spears into the old man who cried out, "I fed you, I brought you meat—when you were young I killed animals in the forest and brought them for you. Why do you kill us now?"

"Oh, just because—" yelled Moipa. "And I'll kill all the foreigners, and kill all of you off, and I alone will live!"

In the shuffle several small children had been left behind. Moipa hacked Dayuma's little sister Nimu to pieces with his machete. He wished that more of Tyaento's children had been within reach.

But by dawn Dayuma, along with several companions and Aepi —who had taught Dayuma some Quichua words against this day— were deep in the forest, heading for the Curaray.

7

BEYOND REACH
OF SPEARS

FROM the day that Dayuma disappeared downriver flanked by dark forest, her mother Akawo had watched for her return.

"She is very young," thought Akawo. "She will hide in the forest. When she is sure Moipa has gone to his hut she will return."

But Akawo was wrong. Dayuma was already several days down the Curaray. Although in her early teens, she was an intrepid pioneer, the valiant leader of the venture. Her companions wanted to turn back as they began their hasty departure down the Curaray, but Dayuma spurred them on. She poled the canoe downriver in spite of hunger and driving jungle rains. Dayuma was determined that nothing would turn her from her purpose.

But suddenly, at a bend in the river, she saw a relative with her baby on her back. She had cut through the forest and overtaken them. She poured out details of the raid which Dayuma had anticipated. Moipa had attacked the family, killing men, women, and children. Dayuma's little sister had been hacked to death with a machete. Her mother? She did not know whether Akawo was dead or alive. That was too much for Dayuma. She must know about her mother.

Turning the party back, she poled upriver for five days, looking all the way for signs of the escaping relatives. Eventually her search was rewarded. There on a beach was the familiar print of her mother's foot.

"My mother is alive! She lives!"

Dayuma's voice trembled with joy as she followed the footprints from the beach to the forest, then through the trail until she found her mother.

"Mother, come with us," she begged immediately. "Come with us to the foreigners' houses. If you stay here you will surely be speared."

But Akawo preferred death in the forest to fear of the unknown beyond, and refused to go. So once again Dayuma set out for the Curaray, accompanied now by her cousin Umi and Aepi.

Umi had been with Tyaento when he was speared. As they traveled downriver she gave Dayuma the details of her father's death. After Moipa's barbed spear had pierced his knee, Tyaento knew that he would die. He hid in the forest along with other survivors, and was without food and burning with fever. He then begged his relatives to bury him alive.

They dug his grave and put Tyaento in it. Then after covering him over with bamboo slats, they began to fill the hole with earth as Tyaento groaned in pain. The moans became fainter and fainter.

"In the morning we heard nothing," concluded Umi. "I saw it. Your father is dead."

Dayuma, weeping bitterly, continued her way down the Curaray, poling the canoe with strong, determined strokes. As the three girls traveled they discussed their destination. Dayuma's mother had lived downriver before she married Tyaento.

"She lived in Ima's big hut before she went upriver," said Dayuma, "but I don't know the trail to Ima's place. My father would know. He always remembered very well. He would say, 'Here is the trail,' or 'There is the trail,' and we would go."

They came to a huge settlement of foreigners who gathered around them and stared. The three girls quickly retreated and hid in the bushes beside the river. But the foreigners treated them kindly, giving them food and clothing. It was the first time Dayuma and Umi experienced the feel of covering for their bare bodies, although Aepi had worn clothes and explained the foreign custom to them.

The site was an obsolete rubber-hunting camp manned by Quichua Indians stationed on the Curaray for their patrón, Señor Sevilla, who lived on a hacienda far to the west on the Anzu River.

Señor Sevilla had ordered that any Aucas who came out on the Curaray should be treated kindly and brought to him at Hacienda Ila. Word was therefore sent ahead to Sevilla, and after a stay of two months on the Curaray the three girls found themselves being taken to Camp Arajuno, en route to the hacienda. When they had crossed the Oglán River, Señor Sevilla himself met the girls, bringing with him new clothes to replace the ones given them earlier. Then they continued their way to Camp Arajuno.

There at the Shell base Dayuma suddenly found herself in a new world. Someone offered her a cigarette. Tobacco was unknown in the Auca forest and she hated the smell of it.

Her greatest shock came without warning as she found herself suddenly face to face with a big black animal displaying huge teeth. It was a beast of terrifying proportions which could surely eat one alive with such monstrous teeth! She had learned to cope with jaguars and boas, but never had she seen or heard of a horse.

A little further on at a river crossing a guard asked for one of the Aucas as his fee for permitting the party to pass. Dayuma understood his bargain and, grabbing a heavy stick, threatened to kill him. One look into Auca eyes, flashing fire, convinced the guard that Dayuma meant business, and he quickly retreated.

Finally Dayuma, with Aepi and Umi, arrived at the hacienda.

Now there were advantages in this outside world which Dayuma was quick to see. They were given food and clothing; the threat of Moipa's spears seemed far, far away. But also there was a price to pay. The wild, unbound life of the forest was replaced by a long, daily round of chores—planting yuca, gathering bananas, pounding the hulls from rice, or harvesting sugar cane. There were heavy loads of firewood to carry for the hacienda kitchen which furnished dozens of meals a day to the family of the patrón, his guests, and the large corps of field laborers.

Dayuma did not mind the hard work, for she was young and strong, but she did miss the trips into the forest and carefree larks down jungle rapids. When the girls were hungry for monkey meat Señor Sevilla would send someone to hunt for them. And when time allowed there were occasional swims in the Anzu.

Occasionally, the price of freedom seemed too great to Dayuma. Three times she and her companions, overcome with homesickness, tried to leave. But each time they were brought back and set to work at their treadmill of hacienda chores.

Back in the forest Akawo watched for Dayuma's return. The days and weeks passed with no word from the runaways. Three times the moon grew large, three times it shone down in shimmering brightness on the swift Curaray, but still there were no signs of Dayuma. Often Akawo would walk far into the forest, looking for footprints along the trails and on the beaches. She knew Dayuma's well, but she saw nothing resembling the familiar track. At night she would steal away from the fire and the hammocks and go as far as she could without danger of being attacked by a jaguar, and listen. Perhaps Dayuma would come quietly through the trees after dark. But days and nights came and went, and her daughter did not return.

Had she been killed by a wild animal? Or had she starved to death out in the forest? Had she reached the world of the foreigners, and had they killed her—and perhaps eaten her? Tyaento had loved his daughter and Akawo knew of his advice that Dayuma flee when Moipa speared him. Now she alone lived to be concerned for her daughter.

After three long months of watching the black beyond which had swallowed Dayuma, Akawo could no longer bear the strain. She must know about her daughter. She commissioned Ominia, Dayuma's step-grandmother, and young Wiñaemi and her mother to search for Dayuma.

"Look well for her," Akawo said. "Go far downriver and along the beaches. If an animal has eaten her flesh, look for her skeleton along the trails. If you don't find her in our land go to the outside to the foreigners and look for her. Go until you find some sign of her, and bring me word again."

The little party of three set off through the trees and down the river, following the trail which Dayuma, Umi, and Aepi had taken three months before. Their keen eyes scanned the beaches for familiar footprints. They looked and listened, poling far downriver. One day they heard noises in the forest, the hacking and cracking of trees being cut. There was the shot of a gun. Frightened as a deer Wiñaemi's mother jumped quickly from the canoe, swam through the water, and disappeared into the forest on the other side. But old Ominia and Wiñaemi poled the canoe to the side of the river and waited. Perhaps the foreigners were not shooting at them.

Then the foreigners spotted them and came over and talked. But Ominia and Wiñaemi could not understand these strangers— they chattered like monkeys! The men were kind and offered them food. Tired and hungry, Ominia and Wiñaemi accepted their hospitality. Afterward the foreigners gave them a place for the night.

Later the men took Ominia and Wiñaemi away downriver, then up another river. After several months they came to an open place, beyond the forest, where there were many more foreigners—and there was Dayuma, living well in a big house! She persuaded them to stay at the hacienda.

Meanwhile, Wiñaemi's mother had returned alone to Akawo with no word from Dayuma. Neither could she tell what had happened to Ominia and Wiñaemi after she herself fled in fright into the forest.

Akawo, struggling to feed her brood of fatherless children, had no way of knowing of the vicissitudes that followed Dayuma even beyond reach of the sharp spears. The pangs of homesickness that had driven Dayuma to attempt a return to her widowed mother in the first months at the hacienda were deadened by exhausting labor that brought welcome sleep each night.

After several years had elapsed another way of escape attracted Dayuma. A young Quichua worker at the hacienda, Miguel, asked her to marry him and live down on the Curaray. This broke the pattern of daily drudgery from which there seemed no release. For a time Dayuma was very happy.

But six months after Dayuma's second son was born tragedy suddenly struck again. The family was infected with measles, a disease for which jungle Indians have little resistance. Miguel, burning with fever, soon died, followed by the baby boy, and Dayuma wavered between life and death for many days. During her illness she lost all her hair when the high temperature threatened to claim her life.

Dayuma's dead baby lay on the mat beside her with no one to

bury him. The Quichua settlement was also struggling to survive the epidemic. Finally a neighbor came and buried the baby beside his father. Stunned by grief, Dayuma lost all desire to live. She was too low to care—even for her older son—and longed only to be buried with her husband and baby. In her despair she attempted to take her own life.

"If I could get down to the river, I would drown myself," she thought. But she was too weak even to crawl to the water.

"Then I will starve myself," she decided. For two days she ate nothing, but life still refused to loosen its hold.

"Why can't I die?" she wondered in anger.

When Dayuma realized that she wasn't going to die she began to think of living again. Jacinta, a Quichua woman in the next village and a relative of Miguel's, had offered to care for her if she could get to her home. Dayuma crawled slowly over the long trail to the woman's house. There she was faithfully cared for by Jacinta and her little daughter Maruja, who looked after Dayuma when her mother went to the fields. The child brought her gourds of yuca or banana drink as she lay on her bamboo bed.

It was many months before she was strong enough to return to work at Hacienda Ila, where she carried loads of bananas and yuca in exchange for food and clothing. Across from the hacienda lived Olimpia, Miguel's aunt, who offered Dayuma and her son a home.

Just as she began to regain a foothold, death struck again. Olimpia was suddenly snatched from Dayuma. This was a staggering blow, almost too heavy for the strong Auca spirit. Despondent, and still under the influence of liquor customarily consumed at Indian funerals, Dayuma went to Señor Sevilla and asked for a gun to kill Moipa. She had for the moment almost forgotten that Señor Sevilla selected her to teach Rachel her language. The first days of instruction had been interrupted by Olimpia's death and funeral.

As Auca study was resumed Dayuma's sadness began to pass. She found an unexpected motive for living in the friendship with the señoritas which had opened a peephole into a new kind of fascinating life. Through conversation first with Catherine in Quichua and later in Auca with Rachel, Dayuma began to learn things which she had never heard in the forest, nor at Hacienda Ila. She began eagerly to anticipate the few hours when she was free to teach her language to this queer foreigner who wanted to learn Auca but didn't speak Quichua. It became a game and Dayuma joined the fun with zest.

Then came the days when Dayuma had remembered enough of her childhood language to teach Rachel to speak Auca. Communication was on a simple level to be sure, but coherent enough to give Dayuma important clues to unanswered questions. Maybe at last she had found someone who could tell her things which she had wanted to know for years. Her curiosity about God and His carving grew, but Rachel's efforts to tell her what the carving meant were only tantalizing. And Dayuma struggled to remember more Auca so that Rachel could tell her more about God.

Suddenly in June, 1955, when they seemed to be gaining momentum in Auca conversation, Rachel had to leave. This turn of events was hard for Rachel to understand, much less explain to Dayuma. But Rachel and Catherine knew that circumstances were the Lord's signal for departure.

"Will you come back?" asked Dayuma wistfully as Rachel turned to go.

With faith in the God who sent her to Dayuma, Rachel replied,

"*Otyae imaenti pongimo*—Returning I will come back."

8

POST-PALM BEACH

MONTHS of serious illness and other delays hindered Rachel's return to the hacienda. Finally in March, 1956, she and her new partner, Mary Sargent, found themselves on a jungle trail trudging toward Ila. River conditions had made the landing of the float plane impossible, and the overland route was the only way in. Catherine Peeke had gone to the States for furlough, but Mary was happy to replace her as Rachel's partner.

The long, hot trail to Ila provided many hours for reflection and anticipation. Much had happened since Rachel left the hacienda the year before. In the multitude of thoughts that crowded into her mind two questions kept cropping up.

Would Dayuma actually be at the hacienda? Although Señor Sevilla had cordially invited Rachel to return, she heard that Dayuma was away from the hacienda. She hoped that she would see her when she arrived.

How would she talk to Dayuma about Palm Beach? How much would the Auca girl know about the massacre of the five missionaries, including Rachel's brother Nate, three months before? From all that Rachel had learned about the Auca pattern of killing foreigners there was no doubt in her mind that Dayuma's people had killed her brother. If Dayuma knew this, would it cause strained feelings? Would Dayuma expect Rachel to avenge the death of her brother?

The death of the five men at Palm Beach, the code name for the spot on the Curaray River where they were killed on January 8, 1956, had been a shock to Rachel, as it was to the whole world.* Now on the trail back to Ila the memory of the little yellow plane that used to fly over and drop mail from home brought alternate waves of pain and joy as Rachel thought of Nate. From the moment that she heard of the death of her brother she wondered about a connection with Dayuma's family. Would Nate's pictures of Palm Beach provide clues for eventually finding those relatives from whom there had been no sign or sound for nearly nine years now?

Immediately after Palm Beach Rachel had written her parents,

"Among the things brought back by the ground expedition is a picture found in Nate's camera of the two Auca women who first came with one Auca man. I keep wondering if they could be Dayuma's mother and younger sister. . . .

"For you two, so far away, we pray the Holy Spirit's comforting. I told the Lord I was willing to make any sacrifice to reach these Indians—and this is the first thing He has asked of me. As you know Nate was precious to me. We rejoice that he is in the Lord's presence now. . . .

"May God yet give me the privilege of going to these same Indians and translating His precious Word for them and seeing the harvest from the five grains of wheat planted way down on the Curaray River in Auca soil."

By the time Rachel could return to the Oriente many pictures taken by the five men had been published. Which of these had Dayuma seen, and what had been her reaction? Rachel had pic-

* The story of the martyrdom of Nate Saint, Jim Elliot, Pete Fleming, Roger Youderian and Ed McCully is told in detail in *Through Gates of Splendor* by Elisabeth Elliot (Harper, 1957). See also *Shadow of the Almighty* by Elisabeth Elliot (Harper, 1958), and *Jungle Pilot* by Russell T. Hitt (Harper, 1959).

tures of the gift articles from the bucket which Nate had dropped from the plane. Upon seeing those Rachel had written,

"I felt so near the Aucas handling the gifts they put back in the little basket attached to the bucket—ear plugs, seed ornaments, a beautiful feather headdress, peanuts, cotton, a parrot—all things for which I have words in the language!"

Should she discuss those Auca articles with Dayuma—if she were at the hacienda?

As Rachel and Mary rounded the last bend of the trail and came in view of the hacienda, Rachel's first big question was suddenly answered. Dayuma had spotted Rachel and came running out to meet her, giggling with delight and chattering away in Auca.

"You came back!" she exclaimed. "You didn't die!"

Then she told Rachel that she had been wishing and watching for her return for many moons.

"Sometimes I would go out by myself and call to the air, 'Rachel! Come back!'"

In those first few hours of joyous reunion all of Rachel's wonderings were swept away.

It was easy to talk about Palm Beach, since the widespread publicity had thoroughly penetrated back into the Oriente where the story began. Dayuma had seen the pictures and knew that they were her very own people. As a matter of fact, she had immediately recognized the older woman who had come to Palm Beach as Aunt Mintaka, her mother's sister. She thought that the man known as "George" was a relative who had grown up in her home. She wanted to believe that the young girl "Delilah" was her younger sister Gimari, but try as she would, she could not. No, it couldn't be Gimari. Gimari was a very little girl when Dayuma left the forest—but she couldn't have changed that much! And if Aunt Mintaka lived, perhaps her mother Akawo and Gimari lived, too, somewhere in the forest!

The pictures and the conversation about them transported Dayuma back to the land of her childhood. This was the first glimpse of home in nine years—almost tangible hope that some of her family still lived.

Rachel wrote her parents,

"I wish you could have seen Dayuma's face when she saw the color picture I took of all the things Nate brought back in the basket. She named them all—each type of basket-weaving, etc. I kept wondering about the tiny houses around the big house in Nate's photos. Now I know—a monkey house, a parrot house, a guacamayo house! Dayuma's face brightened at the recollection."

Within a few days of their arrival at Ila, Rachel and Mary moved with the Sevilla family and Dayuma to Hacienda San Carlos, their new location on the Anzu River. With the move Rachel observed a significant change in Dayuma's position: she had graduated from the status of "hewer of wood and drawer of water" to the rank of house girl. Her duties in the main house of the hacienda enabled Rachel to see her more frequently than when she had spent long hours in the yuca fields, or gathering firewood. But informant hours were irregular because of her obligations.

Of her new acquaintance Mary Sargent wrote,

"We call Dayuma 'the Patchwork Girl' from the Wizard of Oz because she wears a dress now and it has several patches both front and back. When Rachel and Cathy were here before she worked in the fields and wore the traditional Indian blouse and skirt. Then one day the family took her to the city and she came back wearing a dress. She waits on the table now as only a 'Patchwork Girl' can —running back and forth in her bare feet like a padded doll! Her ears are pierced and the holes in the lobes enlarged by the type of ear adornment she used to wear, but her straight black hair cut off at the shoulders hides that mark of identification. Her eyes are smiling and friendly—they can be serious, too. She's an extrovert, impish, alert, a good teacher, and we love her.

"The other three girls are with her here. Looking at them a strange realization wells up, almost as though it couldn't be: they belong to those others out there in that forbidden part of the jungle over the ridge.

"Two nights ago they came to our room to sing their songs for us. I hadn't heard them before, and they were in a mood to sing. Umi and Omiñia, the singers and still in Indian dress, sat on the floor between our beds. Dayuma sat next to Rachel on her bed, and Wiñaemi next to me on mine. The light from our kerosene lamp just barely pushed back the darkness and made great black shadows on the walls about us—shadows that moved when we moved and that made the room seem small and very full. Still other shadows pushed in, a dark-skinned audience of little people come to hear the Auca girls sing.

"The girls' dark skin and black hair made little contrast. Their song was as unusual as the stories of their people: a repetition of the same words over and over again in a rhythmical pattern more like a chant yet at the same time musical, fascinating. Suddenly coming to the end of one song they would laugh a little, look up, and then start trying to remember another song out of the past. . . .

"Father, out there in the jungle over the ridge and two days away on the trails, kinfolk may be singing the same songs tonight as these girls are—but out there they are not dressed even in Indian clothes. And while the women sing, their men may still be talking of the five white men whom they attacked. Thou alone, O my Father, art able to penetrate their thoughts and direct the intents of their hearts. Guide them, please, to do Thy will, to receive those who are trying to reach them. Bring Thy Word to them and grant that soon they may be singing Thy praises."

Rachel wrote to her parents of the renewed opportunity to work with Dayuma and of her hopes for the Auca tribe.

"The picture has changed considerably," she stated. "A year ago we were the only ones taking an active step toward learning the Auca language, and now the whole world is interested. This has made it exceedingly difficult for me. I will appreciate your *special* prayer that the Lord will enable me to do my part quietly. I have no desire for publicity—but I do feel I should continue with Dayuma. I have a love for her and she for me, and the Lord knows my heart. Nate himself always hoped the way would be made for me to reach the tribe. . . ."

But the days of "quietly" doing her part were gone forever as the eyes of the world focused upon the forest-hidden tribe of killers. The pressures resulting from Palm Beach publicity complicated the program of Auca study which Rachel had hoped to follow. Many travelers found their way to the eastern jungle of Ecuador. A steady trickle of curiosity seekers, adventurers, and some desiring commercial gain from firsthand information began to seep into the hacienda. Great pressures were exerted on Señor Sevilla to share Dayuma's scant informant time. Her value as an Auca speaker was evident.

"All the forces of good and evil have converged upon the Aucas," wrote Rachel to close friends who were praying about the situation. "God has shown us in a very personal way the value He has put on this tribe. Now more than ever we need those who will stand with us and pray."

She wrote to another friend, "I told Mary I'd like to write a novel of things just as they are happening day by day. She said, 'No one would believe you!' Every once in a while I say, 'The plot sickens'—but we expect a wonderful climax some day!'"

The golden opportunity for language study that seemed to be theirs upon arrival soon began to fade into almost no study time with Dayuma. There were days when she did not appear, and was seen only as she trotted in and out of the breezeway, serving the table. She was near—but unavailable for teaching her language. Rachel's diary entry for April 2 suggests the struggle:

"Easter Day has come and gone. I meditated on the resurrection—verses that say a spirit has not flesh and blood. Contemplated my kid brother in Gloryland; prayed for the folks at home, and Marj and the children especially. Looked away across the ridge and then at the four Auca women and Dayuma's half-Auca boy who all seem so precious to me. Prayed for faith to continue without discouragement. Only the Lord can prosper the work while we're hearing the language only about three hours a week—but He can, or He can change the circumstances. . . . Perhaps before next Easter we will be able to tell Dayuma. . . ."

There were frequent references in the diary to the ridge, and the desire to go "beyond the ridge, where our hearts are." But Rachel knew that she could not go beyond until she could speak Auca.

Furthermore, there was the imminent threat of losing Dayuma completely, for her services as a guide into Auca territory were being sought. However, Dayuma's own hesitation at re-entering her tribe where brutal customs had not changed gave her pause. Rachel was surprised at the answer the girl gave Señor Sevilla one day when he proposed an Auca trip:

"When God tells me to go, I will go."

Meanwhile, there were others interested in reaching the tribe with the Gospel who felt that more contacts should be attempted. Some felt that Dayuma could fly over and by use of a loudspeaker invite her people to come out. The idea appealed to Dayuma for she was very eager to go up in a plane. But in one letter answering a request for Dayuma's co-operation Rachel presented reasons for delaying such a project:

"In spite of all the pressures that would seem to indicate that this is the time to make another attempt, from our standpoint here, it seems to me to be premature. There are several circumstances that would point to that. First, Dayuma is still unsaved, and no one could be quite sure just what she would say if she got that near to the people who have killed so many of her family. When we were here before she expressed a deep hatred for them.

"If she did give a message now, our language work has not progressed sufficiently to be sure exactly what she did say. There are still many words in the language to which we cannot yet assign a definite meaning. We wish we had more time with Dayuma so that the work would progress faster, but so far the Lord has not opened up the way.

"Another big question in my mind is whether it would be right to take the only language informant available to our cause, and put her in what as your letter expresses might become a dangerous spot. I say that for her sake, since she says plainly that she does not know God, and for our sakes—those of us who are so anxious that her people be reached. . . ."

And to her parents Rachel wrote,

"Some feel that it is time to take my informant temporarily, but somehow I feel that for me the cloud has not moved. Much as I long for a better opportunity to learn the language, it seems to me that we should continue here (unless the Lord miraculously opens the way for us to do so somewhere else) until we have facility in the language. . . ."

On a day crowded with many problems Rachel received heartening news. Dr. Kenneth L. Pike, the linguistic expert under whom she had studied at the Summer Institute of Linguistics in Oklahoma, was in South America to consult with Bible translators about language problems, and offered to visit Rachel and Mary at the hacienda. As an added blessing Señor Sevilla consented to the extra informant time which Pike's visit would entail for Dayuma. For several days before his arrival Rachel and Mary worked diligently to assemble all of their Auca data for Pike to consider.

Rachel recounted the benediction of Pike's visit in a letter written on May 21 to family and friends:

"Last week Dr. Pike took precious time out of his busy schedule to travel by plane, canoe, and trail to the hacienda. We desperately wanted and needed the help Dr. Pike was able to give us. We talked to Dayuma about his coming. We showed her his picture, recently published in the April 30 issue of *Time* magazine. We told her that he was like our brother. . . .

"When he asked her to repeat and repeat certain words of the language she patiently did it. In the midst of the phonetic work-out Dayuma asked me, 'Does the Doctor understand my language?' 'No, he understands *my* language,' I replied. Her only comment was, 'You understand *both* languages.'"

Pike's skill in repeating and quickly grasping the meanings of Auca words impressed Dayuma, and gave Rachel a boost in the analysis of the language. His spiritual counsel and advice lifted the morale of both Mary and Rachel who had been patiently struggling at times against great odds. Pike encouraged them not to be weary in well-doing but to continue the good fight of faith. Surely God would reward them in His time.

After Pike's visit Rachel wrote to her friends,

"There is still so much we don't know how to express in Auca. But I decided that I can talk freely to God about Dayuma, and all the other Aucas fifteen minutes away by air, out in the forest. And some day, because you, too, can talk freely to God about them, may it be that we will be enabled to talk freely to them about Him. Dr. Pike's visit, the added advantage of Mary's help in the tedious analysis of Auca as she works with me here, and the new prayer backing of many Christians now interested in these Indians will surely be used of God to hasten that day.

"After Dr. Pike's visit, I was rechecking my data with Dayuma and came to the word for a bone-instrument which Chief Tariri of the Shapra tribe had given me. Dayuma's Quichua friends, seated on the floor, listened to the discussion in Auca, and asked Dayuma what it was all about. Then she told me in Auca what she had explained to them in Quichua: 'I told them that Tariri made it out of a monkey-bone. That long ago you lived in his house, and learned his language, as you are learning mine, and that now Tariri and his people don't spear any more. Now they live well with God. . . .' These are the encouraging things for which we praise God. . . ."

Another cause for thanksgiving was the new airstrip at the hacienda that greatly facilitated transportation. Señor Sevilla, who desired the services of the planes of the Instituto Lingüístico de Verano, had had it made.

As Dayuma thought of the swiftness of travel now possible for Rachel, she asked her one day,

"Are you going home to your mother soon?"

"No," Rachel told her, "I would like to visit your mother first, down on the Curaray. But perhaps your people will spear me if I go?"

"If you speak well to them in their language they won't kill you," Dayuma answered matter-of-factly.

"But I still do not know how to speak their language well. You must teach me every day."

And Dayuma said she would.

9

LAZARUS

"who are they?" asked Dayuma one day, holding up a picture of Mary and the baby Jesus.

"This is God's Son Jesus, and His mother Mary," answered Rachel.

Rachel told her as best she could about how He came to earth, lived and did good, but was killed, and how He rose from the dead and now lives in heaven with His Father.

"Will He come to earth again?" asked Dayuma, studying the picture again.

"Yes," Rachel replied, "He will come in the clouds, and when He comes again my brother, who is buried on the Curaray, and Don Jaime [Jim Elliott, whom Dayuma had met], and the other three who died with them will come to life again and go up to meet Him in the air."

She showed such keen interest that Rachel was encouraged to try more. She was most curious about the resurrection of Rachel's brother Nate.

As Dayuma plied her with questions Rachel sensed that her interest sprang from her old Auca beliefs concerning death and burial of the body. Other foreigners had gone in at the risk of their lives to find and bury the men who had fallen on the Curaray. This followed a good tribal pattern of burying those who had died by the spear. But what of this new angle to death that she was hearing for the first time? Was it possible that a dead body could come to life again?

Eager to follow up Dayuma's interest in the resurrection of the body, Rachel began to work out a simple explanation in Auca of this basic Scriptural truth. It occurred to her to start with the story of Lazarus. She later related,

"I worked out the story of Lazarus verse by verse. It seemed cumbersome, but late one evening when Dayuma lingered I felt it was the Lord's time to read it to her. She followed each word, apparently with understanding, but at this stage in language study one can never be quite sure. At Mary's suggestion I asked Dayuma to tell it back to me. This is her résumé:

" 'Lazarus was very sick with fever. Later he died. Martha and Mary cried very much. There was a big stone over the hole, Lazarus being inside. Jesus having come said, "Lazarus, come out fast." He came alive again. Later, cloth untying, he was all well. Very much like God Jesus did.' "

Mary Sargent, who watched Dayuma's face as she told back the story, recalls,

"Her eyes fairly shone! I knew that she was understanding, and I felt that she was believing what Rachel told her. Later I said to Rachel, 'I am sure that Dayuma is born again—she is so responsive!' "

Dayuma's hunger to know more inspired Rachel to translate simple Bible stories into Auca and to begin teaching her the life of Christ. "Line upon line" she learned of the miraculous birth and life of Christ, and His power to raise the dead, heal the sick, and still storms. It was all utterly new to Dayuma. Grandfather never told her stories like these.

Christmas, 1956, was crowned with an unexpected joy for Rachel. Dayuma was given permission to accompany her to Quito where the holidays were spent with Wycliffe and other Christian friends, a novel experience for the jungle girl. The association with people who all believed what Rachel had been telling her left an indelible impression.

Back at the hacienda Dayuma shared the story of creation and other narratives with Wiñaemi.

"If you teach her about God she will come to love Him," Dayuma said to Rachel. "Now she loves Him just a little bit. I will tell her lots and then she will come to love Him lots. . . . Why was I not caused to love Him long ago?"

Such signs of spiritual comprehension encouraged Rachel "to believe that Dayuma may now have a grasp of salvation."

But there was the ever-present barrier to progress in the study of the Auca language: lack of time with Dayuma who was continually busy with necessary hacienda chores. In the early months of 1957 Rachel prayed for more opportunity with her.

One day Rachel was surprised by a radio message from Señor Sevilla who had gone to Quito. Cameron Townsend was passing through Ecuador and had called upon Sevilla to discuss the Auca work with him. It appeared that Sevilla, known as the "Daniel Boone of Ecuador" because of his amazing experiences with wild Indians, was to participate in a television program featuring the Indians of South America. Dayuma would also appear on the telecast, and Rachel's services as an interpreter would be required. She would have to sharpen up on Auca conversation, so Sevilla was releasing Dayuma for two hours of language work a day.

It seemed a roundabout way of Auca analysis, but Rachel was grateful for any means of learning more. With the unexpected impetus Rachel's fluency in conversation with Dayuma improved a great deal within a few weeks.

Suddenly the new schedule was interrupted by a message that left Rachel aghast and reluctant to comply with a request that had been made of her. Would she leave immediately by plane for

California with Dayuma to accompany Sevilla on the *Daniel Boone* television program?

Her first reaction was no—she would not snatch the jungle girl out of her environment and drop her suddenly into Hollywood. The shock would be too much for Dayuma—and what if she should get sick? Rachel objected, anticipating the negative reaction on Dayuma under extremely contrasting conditions. It would be like taking her to Mars.

Peace of mind finally came to Rachel when the Lord assured her that the program would provide a means of sharing her own burden for Bibleless tribes with the American public. The fear that Dayuma would die away from her native land was also removed from Rachel's heart.

10

"THIS IS YOUR LIFE"

"THE big water I saw, I came well," Dayuma was telling Ralph Edwards in her own Auca language.

"The stars like light I saw clearly in the big water."

The Auca girl used to swift-flowing jungle streams had been impressed by the calm Caribbean over which she had flown en route to California from Ecuador. Air-lifted from the backwoods of South America she now faced the dazzling lights of a Hollywood television studio.

The shock was almost as great for Rachel as it was for the Indian girl. In one sense the strain was greater, for in a running Auca commentary she was trying to keep the Indian girl oriented on the drama of which they were unconsciously the center. The situation was complicated by the fact that Rachel believed this was only "a rehearsal for a TV interview." Nor did she realize that *her* life, rather than Sevilla's, was being featured on Ralph Edwards' *This Is Your Life* program that unforgettable evening of June 5, 1957.

Ralph Edwards had taken Dayuma and Rachel to a platform decorated with palms and a jungle thatched hut. Rachel recollects that he was talking with them casually when—

"Suddenly, from somewhere offstage, I heard my father's voice. I thought that these Hollywood people certainly had gone to a lot of trouble to get him to make a tape recording for me. And then before I knew what was happening my own Dad appeared before me!"

Rachel, suppressing her emotion, took her father over to meet Dayuma. She continues,

"Scarcely had I recovered from the shock of my Dad's appearance when I heard the voice of my oldest brother Sam! Then *he* appeared!"

Sam Saint, an airline captain, had been flown with his father from the east coast of the United States for the event honoring his missionary sister. As he left the center of the stage he passed Rachel again, kissed her, and whispered,

"Don't make it hard for Ralph, Sis, he's working against time."

"And it was at that point," Rachel says, "that I woke up to the fact that this was the real thing! We were appearing on TV before thousands of viewers!"

Later in the program she heard Ralph Edwards say that *thirty million* people were watching.

Almost simultaneous with Rachel's realization of Ralph Edwards' dilemma, he, in turn, realized Rachel's problem of trying to explain a fast-moving mystery to a bewildered Indian girl who knew no English.

Rachel heard the voice of her lifetime friend Beryl Walsh Adcock, and she too appeared, to Rachel's increased amazement. Then her old friend Dr. Addison Raws of the Keswick Colony of Mercy in New Jersey, with whom Rachel had worked before she went to Peru, emerged from nowhere. Next Lorrie Anderson, her former partner from the Shapra tribe of Peru, walked in. She was followed by Rachel's co-worker from Ecuador, Don Burns, who was escorting Señor Sevilla to the lights.

"Señor Sevilla was the only one I wasn't surprised to see," Rachel said after the program, "because I thought the 'interview' was to feature him!"

While yet gasping "at the rapidity with which things happen in Hollywood" she heard yet another voice. "That was the most fantastic of all—when *Tariri* came in to greet me!"

Her good friend, the Shapra chief, now a vigorous and radiant Christian, had been flown from the north Peruvian jungle and dropped in the middle of Hollywood to greet his "sister" Rachel.

In a half hour members of her family and her closest friends from different parts of the world had greeted her—"a group I hadn't ever dreamed of seeing together this side of heaven!"

Masterful poise and presence of mind enabled Ralph Edwards to pilot the program to a successful conclusion, co-ordinating a motley array of Indians and missionaries who had been living by the sun, not by split-second studio clocks. He had politely but anxiously watched the measured minutes tick away as he sensed the problems involved for Rachel and her informant, and had graciously solved them on the spot.

After the program Ralph Edwards' guests were escorted to the Hollywood Roosevelt Hotel where the happy reunion continued with less tension. Understandably curious patrons of the hotel were fascinated by the befeathered Indian chief and the Auca television star as they were ushered into the lobby. Although the jungle Indians exhibited remarkable poise and aplomb under the exotic circumstances, the fashion and fare of the luxurious hotel were indeed life on another planet for them. When the strain of the public pressure began to take its toll, how grateful they were for private rooms with doors. Meals served in their rooms proved to be more successful than gay dining-room conviviality, complicated for folk of the forest by confusing arrays of silverware they did not know how to use, and oddments of foreign food. A Wycliffe translator from Los Angeles who had lived in the jungles of Peru sensed the predicament and smuggled a big pot of plain boiled rice and chicken into the hotel for the disorientated Indians. They hungrily devoured it to the last grain.

Dayuma had been delighted to meet Tariri at last, and he was equally happy to meet her. His first question upon seeing her had been, "Does Dayuma know the Lord?" This was his chief concern, far outweighing other features of the exciting evening. He had prayed for her conversion.

Weary but happy, Tariri left Rachel and Dayuma as he turned to go to his elegant room in the hotel.

"Good night, my big sister," he said to Rachel.

Then turning to Dayuma, "Good night, little sister."

The next evening Rachel watched at the bedside of a very sick Indian girl. The shadowy fear which had threatened her in Ecuador lay before her in tangible form: Dayuma was burning with a high fever.

Rachel remembered having met a doctor earlier that evening in the lobby of the hotel. He was in company with friends who had shared the telecast. Perhaps he was still in the lobby.

Without realizing that Dr. Ralph Byron, Jr. was an eminent cancer specialist, the director of The Tumor Hospital of The City of Hope Medical Center, Rachel was grateful for his prompt arrival in the room where Dayuma lay ill. Neither did Rachel know that Dr. Byron was an earnest Christian who had been praying for Dayuma long before her trip to the United States.

Dr. Byron, with Rachel interpreting, gave Dayuma a simple, direct testimony of his faith in Christ.

"Are you trusting the Lord Jesus, too?" he asked Dayuma in conclusion.

"Yes!" was the spontaneous answer. "I think of Him day and night!"

It was the first testimony of personal faith in the Lord that

RIGHT: Dayuma's pet parrot seems to reflect her happy mood at Hacienda San Carlos on the Anzu River in the eastern jungle of Ecuador.

ABOVE: Quichua Indian dress and hairstyle disguise Dayuma's Auca origin.

TOP RIGHT: Hacienda San Carlos.

RIGHT CENTER: Auca language study: Missionary-linguist Rachel Saint (*right*) with Mary Sargent and Dayuma.

RIGHT: Children of hacienda laborers pose outside school building with mothers and teacher.

BELOW: Wycliffe pilot Capt. Larry Montgomery chats with Dayuma and Rachel hacienda airstrip, as Mary Sargent and Carolyn Orr look on.

RIGHT: Reminiscences of joys and horrors in the Auca forest are recorded for Rachel.

BOTTOM RIGHT: Dayuma recalls an incident when she was "just so big."

BELOW: Hacienda owner Don Carlos Sevilla points to spear scar—souvenir of Auca attack.

Wheaton, Illinois: Baptism of the first Auca Christian by Dr. V. Raymond Edman, President of Wheaton College.

RIGHT: In Sulphur Springs, Arkansas—thousands of miles from Ecuadorian jungles — Dayuma and her son Sammy enjoy the snow.

BELOW: Kinescopes of the television program "This Is Your Life" honoring Rachel, who appears (left) with host Ralph Edwards and Dayuma. A picture of Nate Saint (center), Rachel's brother, is flashed on the screen. Nate, with four fellow missionaries, was killed by Aucas . . . relatives of Dayuma (right).

15965

LEFT: Atop Hotel New Yorker, Rachel shows the Indian girl a new kind of "jungle forest with endless trails."

RIGHT: Rachel and Dayuma on speaker's platform at Billy Graham New York Crusade, Madison Square Garden, July 7, 1957.

BELOW: Thousands at Crusade meeting are inspired by Auca adaptation of Bible story.

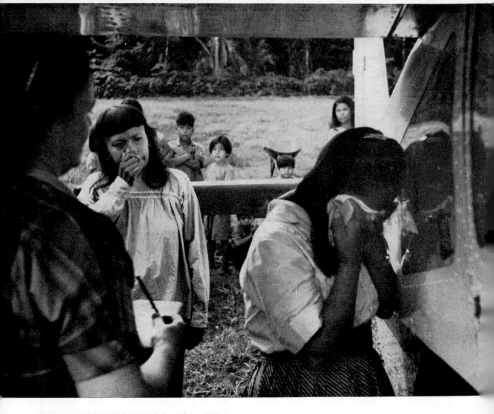

Heartbreaking news of brother Wawae's murder, confirmed at Limoncocha Base, causes Dayuma to
sob as her Aunt Maengamo and
Rachel offer comfort.

After Dayuma's first trip back into
the forest to see her family, she
returns with friends who invite
Rachel and Betty Elliot to come
and live with them.

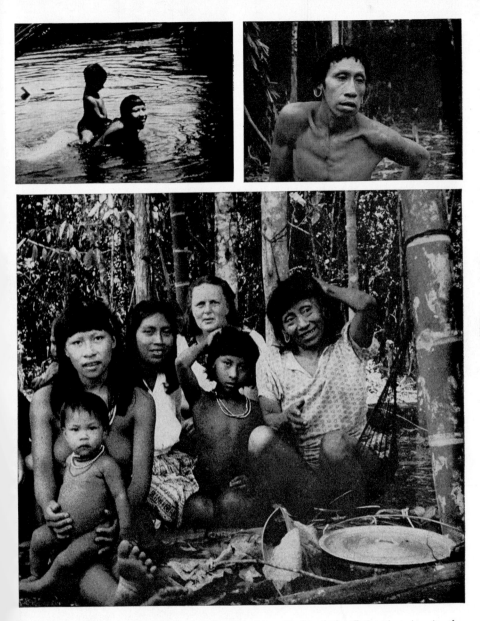

TOP LEFT: Gimari ("Delilah" of Palm Beach) with her baby Bai swimming in the Curaray.

TOP RIGHT: Storyteller Uncle Gikita, one of the Auca band that killed the five missionaries in 1956.

BOTTOM: Family portrait: Mother Akawo (*right*) with (*left to right*) daughter Oba and her baby girl Adyibae, daughter Dayuma, Rachel, and daughter Ana.

Modern Auca housekeeping in open palm-thatched hut: Dayuma and her mother enjoy a family chat while preparing succulent wild hog. Sammy, born outside the forest, is being taught Auca handcraft by his cousin Gingata. Horizontal pole holds palm-fiber carrying basket and fishing nets woven of finer palm.

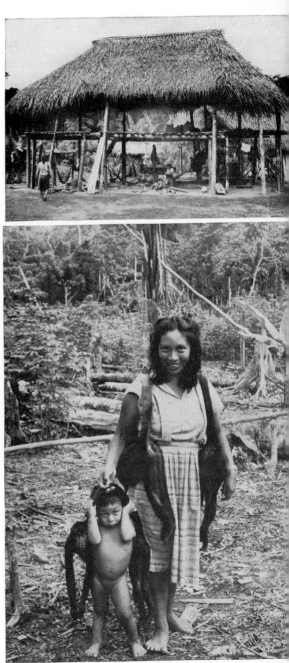

op right: Shelter in the Auca forest was built for Rachel by Dayuma's relative Kimo.

ight: Auca forest teems with many varieties of monkey. Dayuma and nephew Bai return from hunt with four of the creatures to be roasted and eaten later.

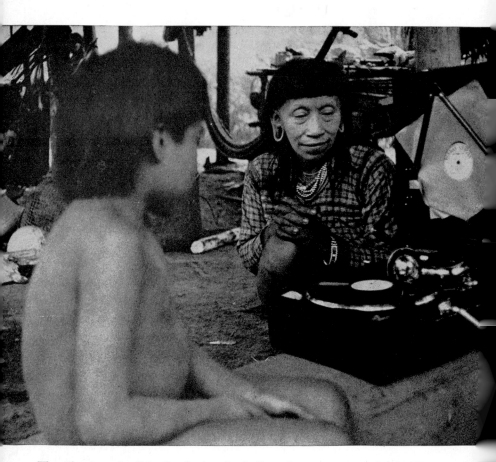

The "foreigners' talking-box" plays back Gospel messages recorded by Dayuma for her people. Mother Akawo and children often listen for hours at a time.

RIGHT: Dayuma's half-brother Minkayi is ready for a hunting trip. Machete in hand and blowgun resting on his shoulder, he will use poison darts held by his small son (left) whose brother poses with small blade in imitation of his father.

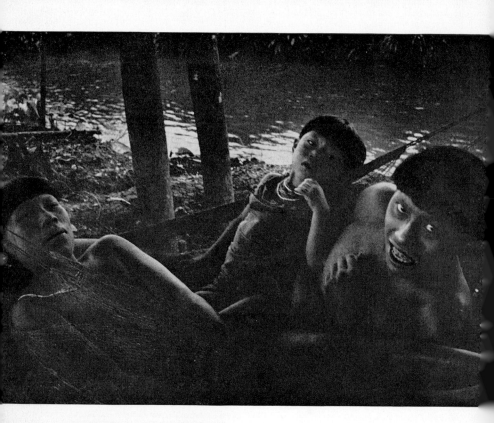

ABOVE: Relaxing is a favorite pastime. Monga (*right*) with his wife and child in a typical scene.

LEFT: Uncle Gikita's daughter Biba poses gracefully on abandoned dugout canoe.

RIGHT: Dayuma's sister Oba makes fi in the primitive way. Fire-stick of ha chonta wood twirled into softer wo produces sparks to ignite tuft of kapo

Childbirth in the jungle: Wiba, a member of Dayuma's family group, will bear her child unaided. She clutches woven strip overhead as labor increases.

RIGHT: Wiba cuts and ties umbilical cord of her newborn child, whom she has lifted from the ground after he dropped through a specially-made hole in the hammock

Heads bow in prayer as Dayuma concludes a Bible lesson.

Kimo interrupts his poison-dart-making to join the group in prayer.

Rachel had heard from Dayuma's lips. And Rachel caught again the look of aliveness which had shone from Dayuma's eyes on first hearing the story of Lazarus.

Dr. Byron prayed quietly, giving thanks to God and requesting healing for the Auca girl.

By morning the fever had disappeared and Dayuma was back to normal.

11

NEW FRIENDS

"IT *stings*—" spluttered Dayuma as she tasted ocean water for the first time. A trip to the beach was her introduction to the wonders of California after the television program. The aggressive waves frightened her. What if the big water should go on a rampage and cover the land? Rachel explained that God had set its bounds and that she needn't worry. However, Dayuma rather nervously watched the water seething under her as she stood on the pier, and did not relax completely until she was again on solid soil.

From Los Angeles, Rachel and Dayuma traveled to central California where they visited the family of Wallace Lindskoog, brother of John Lindskoog, one of Rachel's Wycliffe colleagues in Ecuador. Wallace flew them in his private plane to the famous Redwood Forest near Santa Cruz. As they walked among the giant trees the Auca girl brightened. Now *this* was like home! Did they have trees as big as these in her land? Wallace wanted to know. Oh yes—big just like these. And how long would it take her people to cut one of them down? he asked. It would take two days, Dayuma said, with foreigners' axes. But it would take ten men, changing off, to do it in two days. With stone axes, of the kind their ancestors used, it would take much longer.

"Why don't they blowgun those squirrels and eat them?" asked Dayuma when she saw many of the animals jumping from limb to limb high up in the redwoods. The touch of home thrilled the

Indian girl who had begun to think that trees and animals belonged to a land very far away.

As they flew in the plane Lindskoog talked of radio beams, "trails marked in the sky," which told pilots where to go. Although Dayuma couldn't see them she took his word for it, and made a firm mental note.

On the Lindskoogs' farm Dayuma was quite at home, although she had never seen animal life on such a scale. A Lindskoog relative owned one of the largest turkey farms in the area at the time, and Dayuma marveled at acres and acres of the big birds. She also exclaimed at the unbelievable amount of milk—extracted mechanically—from the huge cows. At Hacienda Ila she had seen small quantities of milk squirted by hand into gourd shells. She was overwhelmed by the size and strength of the cattle. One prize bull had just brought Lindskoog twenty thousand dollars.

During their conversation Lindskoog asked Rachel what she needed most for her Auca work. Rachel knew that as a successful businessman he was thinking concretely in terms of dollars and cents, but her answer took little time.

"What we need most is an entrance into the tribe. And only God can give us that."

The Lindskoogs, who had been praying for the Auca tribe, assured Rachel they would ask God for that opening.

While in California a wave of homesickness inundated Dayuma and one day she wept forlornly. Rachel had dreaded this reaction. She recounts,

"As I lifted my heart to God in prayer for the homesick girl, a little bird began to sing in a tree outside the window. Dayuma bounded out of the room, climbed the tree, and became engrossed in watching a nest of newly-hatched birds. Her homesickness left, and never recurred with the same intensity."

In the traveling and excitement of those days Dayuma was most concerned with when she would see Rachel's mother. That was supposed to be one of the purposes of the trip to the States, but it was very slow in being realized. Rachel had difficulty in explaining satisfactorily that there would be several stops between California and Pennsylvania.

The first leg of the journey was to Oklahoma, where Rachel would see many of her good friends on the staff at the Summer Institute of Linguistics then in session. In a stopover at the Dallas airport en route to Norman a tall elderly gentleman spoke to Rachel.

"I saw you on the television program and I would like to meet you. I'm Charles Fuller."

"Not Dr. Charles Fuller of the Old-Fashioned Revival Hour!" exclaimed Rachel. "Take off your dark glasses so that I can get a good look at you!"

Rachel told him that for many years in far-off jungle spots she had listened to his Gospel broadcasts and had prayed for him.

In the terminal another person walked up to her and said, "You won't remember me—" She was a young airline hostess from Rachel's home town who had seen the television program. Then a well-dressed woman, a stranger to Rachel, walked up to her and said quietly, "We liked your program." She was the wife of an oil executive from Venezuela.

Rachel became increasingly aware that her private life was gone forever. Her trip to Oklahoma was only the beginning of a chain of contacts from the west coast to the east indicative of the widespread impact of the television program on people from every walk of life. A sampling of reactions assured Rachel that a large audience had been alerted to the existence and need of Bibleless Indian tribes and the part Wycliffe translators were having in meeting that need.

Later Rachel was encouraged by a comment from Ruth Graham, wife of evangelist Billy Graham. She was being consulted about a possible *This Is Your Life* surprise for her husband, and said she would consent to the arrangement if the program would present a clear-cut testimony for Christ "as Rachel Saint's had done."

A letter to Cameron Townsend from Pete Kyle McCarter, vice-president of the University of Oklahoma, expressed gratitude for the program:

"Last week I happened to be watching the right television channel at the right time to see *This Is Your Life* when Miss Rachel Saint was the subject.

"My feeling, as the program went along, was one of very deep gratification that the Linguistics Institute is a part of the University of Oklahoma. Just as Miss Saint's association with the Institute does honor to the Institute, so the Institute's affiliation with the University brings honor to the University. All of us here at Norman are very proud of being associated with an enterprise which merits the kind of favorable attention which Miss Saint's television appearance must have brought to the Institute."

When Rachel arrived at Norman with Dayuma it was indeed a glorious home-coming. Dayuma was especially overjoyed to see Dr. Kenneth Pike, her good friend whom she had met at the Ecuadorian hacienda where he had made a trip to study her language.

Again Rachel was grateful for Pike's help on the Auca language during her brief stay at Norman. The circumstances for study had changed a great deal. The television program had been the technical means of releasing Dayuma for informant work. In an advanced linguistics laboratory course Pike used Dayuma as an informant while he worked with Rachel on further Auca analysis. The hours, though profitable for linguists, were hot and long for the Auca girl. Fortunately, Dayuma quickly learned the secret of the magic cold-drink dispensers in the halls of the university buildings. During the long linguistic sessions when Dayuma became bored and restless she would suddenly disappear, only to return a few minutes later with an ice-cold "coke."

Dayuma enjoyed the freedom and informality of the school where all of Rachel's friends were interested in Indians from various tribes of the world. She was delighted to meet informants speaking Indian dialects of Oklahoma. And they were interested in the Indian girl from the distant land of Ecuador.

From Norman, Rachel and Dayuma went to New York where the Billy Graham evangelistic crusade was in progress. When Graham had heard that Rachel and her Auca friend were in the United States he invited them to give a testimony and report in Madison Square Garden. Again Rachel was challenged with a brusque change for the uprooted Auca girl. How would she explain to Dayuma that she would be appearing before thousands of people? How would the girl react? Suddenly Rachel remembered the thousands of turkeys on the California farm. So she told Dayuma there would be as many people in the meeting as she had seen turkeys a few weeks before.

When Rachel suggested that Dayuma tell the huge audience a Bible story in Auca, all reticence left her. She happily selected one of her favorites—the raising of Jairus' daughter. With a great deal of enthusiasm and Auca animation she recounted the story with gestures, while Rachel translated it into English. The story was joyfully concluded as the young girl was raised to life by Jesus who told her mother to "cook that she might eat. And her parents were very, very, very happy!"

The experience brought much blessing to the New York listeners and to Billy Graham, who was deeply moved by the testimony of the first Auca Christian.

When the invitation to accept Christ was given at the close of the meeting and hundreds found their way to the platform,

Dayuma was amazed that so many people in the United States hadn't already accepted Christ. She had thought all the people in Rachel's land would know the Lord because they had God's carving in their own language. A few weeks earlier, after having landed in Miami, Florida, and upon seeing great crowds of Americans, her first question had been, "Do all these people love God?"

Before they left New York for the Saint home in Pennsylvania, Rachel showed Dayuma some of the sights of the city. As they stood atop the Hotel New Yorker surveying the skyscrapers, Rachel noticed Dayuma's attention riveted on an object on a window of one of the neighboring buildings. It was a window cleaner. How did the man stay on? What if he fell? She was much more impressed by his precarious situation than by any of the skyscrapers.

From another angle they viewed the Hudson River, where large ships were gliding along. Later at close range Dayuma saw a huge airplane carrier in the dock. What were those wood-bees doing out there on that "big canoe"? Dayuma had seen airplanes at the hacienda in Ecuador, and she was used to dugout canoes, but this was a novel combination of the two. Rachel explained that the top of the big canoe was an airstrip, and that planes could fly right off of it in mid-ocean into the air.

At last they reached Philadelphia, where Dayuma finally met Rachel's mother "who had sent the carving across the big water." As Dayuma met others of the Saint family she became more convinced that these relatives of the pilot who had been killed by her people had no intention of retaliating, of "killing in exchange." This conviction was later to lead toward opening the door to the Auca tribe. Dayuma had seen the dead foreigner's relatives and talked with them—and they still loved the Aucas.

In a quiet cabin in the pine woods of Pennsylvania Rachel and her parents spent several happy weeks with Dayuma. Again the similarity to her own forest home in Ecuador revived many memories, both pleasant and unpleasant. As darkness began to fall each evening Rachel noticed a return of fear in the girl's eyes. The devil of the forest was lurking near in the big trees, Dayuma warned, and perhaps tonight he would suck their blood! Rachel observed that when swarms of mosquitoes would gather, Dayuma started swatting them frantically. Soon Rachel learned that these insects were considered to be evil spirits, whose bites would bring dire results. The Auca girl, though far from her jungle home, was still haunted by dreads and fears. Hour after hour she would unburden her soul to Rachel, who could now understand and help. But for the casting out of these lifetime fears, Rachel knew that only the power of God Himself was sufficient.

Often at twilight Dayuma would tell the jaguar tales she had heard from her grandfather. One of them was about the man suddenly caught face-to-face with a jaguar on a trail in the forest. He had no spear, only a blowgun and poison darts. With great presence of mind he blinded first one eye and then the other with his weapons. He called for help, and soon other Aucas came with spears and killed the infuriated animal.

She also mentioned the jaguars living inside her grandfather, although he himself was not a witch doctor. These jaguars would talk inside his body as he lay in his hammock, but only the witch doctor had power to command them. The jaguars would ask her grandfather about his enemies, saying, "Tell me whom you are angry with, and we will go and kill them." And Grandfather had very bad headaches when the jaguars came.

The behavior of these other "jaguars" convinced Rachel that Dayuma was referring to demons, or evil spirits, capable of possessing and at times dominating Auca personalities. She prayed for wisdom and guidance, and searched the Scriptures for an antidote to the girl's fears.

The miracles of Jesus in casting out demons in the days of His earthly ministry would be a solution to Auca fears! She told Dayuma the story of the demon-possessed Gadarene whom Jesus pitied and restored to normal life by ordering the demons to leave and enter a herd of swine. The girl listened with great interest, especially to the climax when the swine went tumbling headlong into the sea where they drowned dramatically. That final destruction of the demons, at Jesus' command, indicated that the Savior who lived in her heart was more powerful than witch doctors or demons.

The sequel to the Gadarene story challenged the Auca girl. The Gadarene in his joy and gratitude wanted to stay with Jesus, but was told by the One who had restored him, "Go home to thy friends, and tell them how great things the Lord hath done for thee." He obeyed, and later through his testimony a great crowd came together to hear Jesus when He arrived. Rachel recognized an opportunity to plant the seed of desire for returning to her own home in Dayuma's mind. Perhaps Jesus might some day ask her to go home to Dayuma's family and friends and tell them of His power. Rachel said she would willingly go to the Aucas—would Dayuma go, too? It was quite evident the girl was pondering the question. And the old fear of Satan's power was beginning to weaken through the constant teaching from God's carving.

In September, Dayuma accompanied Rachel to Wycliffe's biennial meeting in Sulphur Springs, Arkansas, a quiet country village of scarcely five hundred people where the first Summer Institute of Linguistics had been held in 1934. This gathering of translators from all over the world was indeed a family reunion for Rachel. Many of her companions in Bible translation whom she had not seen for years were in the States on furlough and attending the conference. They were overjoyed to see Rachel, but just as thrilled and moved to see her Auca friend for whom they had prayed. The name Dayuma was already familiar to many who had been asking the Lord for her salvation since 1955.

The thoughts of Rachel's co-workers flashed back to the previous biennial conference held in September, 1955, when Catherine Peeke had challenged them with an impossible situation, except for the power of God. Catherine, who had recently arrived from Ecuador and the hacienda where she had been living with Rachel, detailed the Auca problem for the Wycliffe family. She had asked them to pray that God would give Rachel an entrance to the tribe through the language, and that He would bring Dayuma to a saving knowledge of Himself.

Now in 1957 Rachel was in their midst to thank them for their prayers, to share with them the joy of Dayuma's faith, and to plead with them to continue in prayer until the Auca door opened.

Rachel says,

"This was a group that knew how to pray. I had great confidence that their prayers would move the arm of God on our behalf, for many of them had faced impossible situations in their tribes, and had seen God work in answer to prayer."

Dayuma's eyes were opened to the world-wide ministry of Wycliffe as she became acquainted with Rachel's friends who told of transformed lives and indigenous churches in many tribes where they had translated God's carving. As Rachel interpreted the reports in Auca, Dayuma heard of how the work began in each tribe with one or two Indians whose hearts God had touched. From small beginnings there were now thousands of believers in some of the tribes.

After the conference Rachel expected to leave immediately with Dayuma for Ecuador. God had other plans for them, however. She wondered at the delay, but regarded it as divine provision of a time and place for further language study.

Rachel was in correspondence with Dr. Ben Elson, Director of the Mexican Branch of the Wycliffe Bible Translators and editor of a series of volumes of American Indian language texts sponsored by the University of Oklahoma. A book of Auca texts was under consideration. In answer to one of Rachel's letters Dr. Elson wrote,

". . . As regards your question as to whether or not the texts are of sufficient importance to spend time on when there are so many other important things to be doing—this is hard for me to say. I think the most important thing is to get the Scriptures into the hands of the Aucas. I think it is very important for you to learn to speak well so that when you go into the tribe you will be able to speak with the people well, and about all kinds of things. If you are really able to go ahead on the Scriptures, I would say let the texts go. I trust the Lord will guide you into the proper priorities. . . ."

Later Rachel wrote to Dr. Elson, "After considering the matter and praying about it, I have felt that I should go ahead writing up the Auca texts as I can wedge them into the daily schedule. Somewhere in the list of priorities is a lot of work on the grammar. Pray that some of this waiting and urgent desk work will be done. There is a law of diminishing returns as it continues to stack up, although our general knowledge and fluency in the language is considerably increased with the opportunity of the last six months."

She settled down to more serious Auca analysis, grateful for an alert informant at her side.

12

A SEARCH ACROSS TWO CONTINENTS

"CALL a local doctor? Send her to a hospital? But she's never even seen a hospital. Besides, no one would understand her language."

In the Ozark village, as she watched at the bedside of a very sick Auca girl, Rachel prayed and pondered. The Asian-flu epidemic of 1957 had affected Dayuma, who was unaccustomed to foreign diseases, more gravely than most Americans. The girl had grown steadily worse for several days and was burning with fever. Rachel knew she needed help. What should she do?

As she looked to God for guidance, she suddenly remembered that Dr. Kenneth Altig, a Wycliffe doctor from the Jungle Base in Peru, was on furlough in California. While working with the Shapras she had often conferred with him by radio over five hundred miles of jungle about sick Indians. He would know better than anyone else what to do for an Auca girl temporarily transplanted to Arkansas. She telephoned him, and in a three-minute conversation he prescribed for Dayuma. Within a few days she passed the crisis and was on the road to recovery.

Dayuma was slow, however, in regaining strength. Rachel kept vigil around the clock, feeding her liquids with a spoon until she was able to sit up and feed herself. One day after Rachel served her a cup of coffee, there was a persistent vibration between the cup and saucer as it rested on the tray.

She saw that the noise was bothering the sick girl, but try as she would, she could not stop it.

"It is the devil of the forest!" Dayuma said apprehensively.

In her weakened condition the fears of her childhood assailed her with great force.

"The devil is saying in the cup, 'Don't drink me. You'll get worse.'" Dayuma, certain she had been cursed, took the vibration as a warning.

Rachel reminded her of the power of the Lord, who was stronger than the devil. But the noise continued and Dayuma was not convinced.

"I'm not afraid of the devil because the Lord Jesus lives in me, and I will drink the coffee!" said Rachel finally.

With that Dayuma rose to the challenge.

"No," she said with resolution, "you talk to the Lord Jesus and *I'll* drink the coffee."

So Rachel prayed, and Dayuma drank the coffee!

More deep-seated fears of Dayuma's childhood were gradually unfolding as Rachel continued to study the Auca legends remembered by the girl, and chance remarks. One day Dayuma mentioned that devils attacked at night and sucked her people's blood. When Rachel challenged the old Auca belief, the girl objected,

"But you said that Satan was 'chief of the devils.'"

Rachel found that Dayuma was combining the Biblical doctrine concerning Satan with what she had learned in her childhood. Again, through patient teaching Dayuma began to see that Satan's desire was to destroy the *souls* of men. The climactic assurance from God's carving that "greater is he that is in you, than he that is in the world" inspired Dayuma with new confidence in her battle with the old fears.

During her slow recuperation the teaching of the Word, translated orally into Auca, began to penetrate her thinking deeply.

Gradually her faith in God grew, and the fears subsided. One night she dreamed she was back at Hacienda Ila, and her old companions were tempting her to sin. In her dream she answered them, "No, now I belong to the Lord—I don't live like that any more." In another dream the powers of evil were pressing down and threatened to overcome her. She told Rachel that in the name of the Lord Jesus she ordered the devils to leave—and they did. She was applying the teaching of the book of Acts. This spiritual gain compensated for the precious time Rachel had expected to invest in concentrated linguistic study.

In those critical days the assurance given Rachel before leaving Ecuador that the Auca girl would not die in the States was a comfort when she would have despaired of her life. As in Hollywood when Dayuma had been very ill, the Lord revived her body.

It was not until early November that she was able to walk again and enjoy fairly normal activity. Her progress, though slow, was steady. With no unforeseen complications Rachel knew that soon she would be able to resume study of Auca grammar. She would wait, however, until the girl was stronger.

On Monday, November 18, very early in the morning, the tranquillity of the Ozark "Sleepy Hollow" was abruptly broken by a long-distance telephone call from Rachel's brother Sam in New York. He relayed the breath-taking news from Ecuador that two Auca women had run out of the forest and were on the edge of Auca territory with missionaries. He had few details, but assured Rachel that Marj Saint, who was in California, would be calling her. She doubtless would know more of the story.

Dayuma wondered who the early caller was. When she heard the news she was puzzled—and pensive. It was a long way from home for such a message. Were these actually her people who had come out of the forest?

Rachel, forgetting the time difference between Arkansas and

California, and having waited for what seemed a long while to hear from her sister-in-law, placed a call to Marj Saint. She learned that Betty Elliot, widow of Jim Elliot who had died on Palm Beach, was with the women at the Quichua village on the Curaray where they had emerged from the Auca forest. One was thought to be the older woman who had visited with the five men on Palm Beach. If true, she was Dayuma's Aunt Mintaka. A further detail excited speculation. A third woman, much younger than the other two, had come out with them but had fled back into the forest. Who was she?

"Two women fresh from the tribe who *perhaps* spoke the same language we were studying!" The thrilling anticipation sent Rachel's hopes soaring, and her hands to packing. With the first news flash she began to prepare for the return trip to Ecuador. As she shared the details of the momentous events with Dayuma, assuming that she, too, would be overjoyed with plans for return, she sensed the girl's hesitancy. Disappointed, Rachel listened: even if she did return to Ecuador she was too weak to walk the steep trail to the Curaray. She knew what the trip entailed.

It had not occurred to Rachel that they would not leave immediately, "but I saw that the girl was not ready to go," she relates.

Dayuma asked many questions, for she had been burdened from the first call. She knew the pattern of her people well. What had prompted them to come out? Was it a decoy?

She appealed to Rachel that the missionaries be urged to take the two women and get out. "My people will surely come and kill," she warned. Her advice was telephoned to Ecuador the same day.

Although Dayuma was hesitant and apprehensive about returning immediately, she experienced an uncontrollable desire for answers to several other questions. Could the woman who had come out with her Aunt Mintaka be her very own mother? And could the younger woman who had fled back into the forest be her younger sister Gimari? The pull was almost irresistible. A possible clue to the whereabouts of her family, after more than a decade of silence! With her people moving from river to river, she had no idea where they might be living now. A delay in returning to Ecuador might mean loss of contact for another ten years.

Rachel knew that hours counted. Her concern was that the women, like the younger girl, might soon flee into the forest. If they did, the questions about Dayuma's mother and her family might never be answered. The missionaries in whose custody they were could not speak their language. It was urgent that Dayuma help.

Rachel suggested that Dayuma make a tape recording to persuade the two women not to run away. Dayuma rose to the occasion. Bundled in a warm robe and seated before the recorder, she trembled with weakness and excitement. In a voice charged with emotion she delivered a message for her people. She identified herself, pleaded with them not to run away, and asked that they send back an answer giving their names and those of their relatives.

"Long ago when Moipa speared my father," she began, "Umi, Aepi, and I fled to the outside. My father was Tyaento. I am Tyaento's daughter Dayuma. My mother was Akawo. . . .

"Long ago we did not live well, not loving God. The Aucas spoke saying that God created. Our old grandfather said that God created. All men and all women He created. Yes, I now love that God. Now I live very well. Before I did not live well.

"The foreigners who do not love God do not live well. Now those who speak to you, yes, they all speak of God. Very well they speak. You two do not return to the Auca houses. Live in the foreigners' house. . . .

"Now, you, who are you two? I do not know. You two in return speak to me, I will understand. Do not you two be afraid. Live in the foreigners' house. You two will not be afraid. I live without fear. Very well I live. . . . You are just afraid that the foreigners will shoot and you will die. . . ."

Through the years Dayuma had longed for an end to the constant friction between her people and outsiders. She had hoped for peaceful relations, and for a friendly contact to be made. She now urged the two women to encourage such a communication between the two groups.

"Go visiting to the foreigners' houses with your relatives. They will not spear, they will visit well with you. Then the foreigners in return will visit your houses. If the ones that love God visit, they will visit well."

Dayuma knew that she could not endorse the visits of all foreigners, remembering full well that exploiters had ruthlessly killed Aucas. But she urged the women to welcome foreigners like the ones with whom they were living.

"Don't you two return to the forest. A little bit later I will come to your house. There I will speak to you both. Umi and Wiñaemi do not remember our language. It has been a long time since they came, and Wiñaemi was very small when she came to the outside. Now she is grown up. She does not remember the Auca language and understands only the foreigners' speech.

"I remembered a little bit long ago. Then another foreigner came and spoke with me. She, a woman, spoke with me, and I understood. Then in return I spoke with her in my language. Very well I spoke. Now I live with her. Later, returning, I will come.

"Who are you two? I in exchange will understand. You two speak with me. When the ones you live with say, 'Speak,' do not be afraid to speak."

In a detailed account of her family, relatives, and others of her group, Dayuma told what she knew of each of them. She named those who had gone to the outside and died, and those who she believed were still living. The names of her relatives would unmistakably identify Dayuma to the two Auca women.

"My uncle is Wamoñi, my other uncle is Gikita. My mother's little sister is Gami, Umi's mother. My mother's sisters born later were Wiika, Wiwa, and Mintaka.

"What rivers do you live on? Do you live now on Fish River or on Palm River? I have not returned for a long time to your huts. Does my mother live? I don't know. It has been so long that I don't remember all the other Aucas. Tell me who still lives and I will understand. I was not able to return. I lived in another foreigner's house. I told him I would return to my people. He was angry. Now in another house I live well. That is all."

During the anxious days after the tape was sent, news coming from the Curaray was not good. There were constant signs of Aucas lurking nearby, which the Quichua Indians and the missionaries interpreted as threats.

Dayuma reacted fearfully to every report. Well she knew the spot on the Curaray where the Auca women had taken refuge first with Quichua Indians and later with missionaries. It had been the home of Dayuma's husband Miguel. Not far away he and her baby son were buried. It was there that Dayuma in deep sorrow had tried to take her own life.

The news recalled other happenings of days gone by: of death; of unhappy encounters with foreigners on the edge of Auca territory; of thwarted efforts to locate the trail that would lead to her home in the forest.

Then came the word that Dayuma had dreaded. Her people had appeared and killed the Quichua Indian who first received the two Auca women. His body had been riddled with twenty-two spears. His young wife had been taken captive.

After hearing the tragic report Dayuma began to relax.

"Now my people will not come again. They will hide in the forest."

Further word was received that Betty Elliot had taken the two women and gone to Shandia, a safe distance from the scene of the spearing. In a letter to Catherine Peeke in Ecuador, Rachel wrote,

"Dayuma is sleeping now—in the sleep of sorrow, I guess. Dear girl! She dreamed of spearings and attacks every night and never really relaxed until she heard that her aunts were in Shandia."

The tension had been high for two weeks. With her relief, however, there was an added concern for Dayuma. From the heart of the jungle far across the big water had come the news of how her people had speared, almost as soon as it happened. How could news about her people travel so far so fast? Rachel explained that Christian friends, people who were praying and who were interested in the Aucas, had sent the word by radio.

But further details of the killing worried the girl. She had been suffering with those involved, but at a helpless distance. The young wife who had been captured was Maruja, the daughter of Jacinta the Quichua woman who had nursed Dayuma back to life after her husband and son had died. Maruja was the little girl who had brought her gourdfuls of banana or yuca drink when her mother went to the fields. Now that girl, a young widow, was a captive of Dayuma's people.

"The man who lost a woman, took a woman" was Dayuma's natural explanation. She was certain that the husband of one of the women had taken Maruja.

Dr. Wilfred Tidmarsh, a missionary living nearest to Auca territory, had recorded the speech of the Auca women when they first arrived at the Curaray settlement. Word had been sent that a copy of the tape was on its way to Sulphur Springs, but to Rachel and Dayuma it seemed that the package from Ecuador would never come. Finally it was received, and Dayuma could hardly wait for Rachel to set up the recorder.

Rachel states that "Dayuma crouched over the machine, and almost crawled into it!" She was about to hear the voices of members of her family—perhaps of her mother.

To Rachel's dismay her copy of the Auca conversations was made over a vigorous piano concerto previously recorded and not erased. She recalls,

"Every time there was something particularly vital to hear, the fortissimo bass parts of the concerto boomed out."

Over the obscuring strains of the piano solo, and through pitiful sobs and sighs, the Auca voices poured out a lamentation of spearings and killings, of sufferings and fears. Dr. Tidmarsh, using the phrases and words of Auca previously recorded by Dayuma, had questioned the women and their answers were a tangle of classical chords and rapid nasalized Auca, charged with high emotion.

Rachel had wondered if the language of the two women would be in the same dialect studied with Dayuma. The first phrases of the tape were muddled, then suddenly through an acoustic clearing she understood the phrase, "Being an orphan I came . . ."

Rachel rejoiced! Meanwhile Dayuma was glued to the recorder, and would permit no interruptions for clarification or questions. Rachel longed to stop the machine to listen again to an obscure phrase, but Dayuma was too eager for word from home.

"Who is speaking?" Dayuma kept asking as she listened intently. "Is it my mother?" The possibility, overshadowed with uncertainty, seemed almost more than she could bear.

Interspersing the strains of the concerto and the sobs were vital bits of information that Dayuma began to piece together. Although the near-hysterical speaker did not give her name, she told enough family history for Dayuma to identify her as Maengamo,

Uncle Gikita's wife. And Uncle Gikita was Dayuma's mother's brother! Maengamo also divulged that her younger brother had come with her out of the forest, but for fear of the foreigners, had fled immediately. Which of Maengamo's brothers was it—Kimo or Dabu? They were both like brothers to Dayuma since they had been brought up in her home. And if Maengamo's companion was Mintaka—why, that was Dayuma's mother's sister!

When Dr. Tidmarsh mentioned Dayuma's name to the two women, there was no answer "except that piano concerto," says Rachel, "and then Maengamo broke out in the nasalized rhythmic song that the four Auca girls had sung for us at Ila." This was a severe disappointment, since Rachel and Dayuma had hoped for a favorable response at the mention of the name Dayuma.

Maengamo's monologue was concerned with past spearings in the tribe, details of Tyaento's spearing, the horrible atrocities of Moipa, and an impassioned tirade against the hated killer. Moipa had been speared, but Maengamo did not say that he had been speared dead. Was the murderer of her father still alive, after all the intervening years since Dayuma left the forest?

To Rachel's dismay, the Auca girl who had been progressing in victory over the old hates and fears was being sucked back into the old tribal maelstrom of anger and revenge.

Maengamo referred repeatedly to her fear of foreigners, and said that she and her companion were "throwing themselves" on Dr. Tidmarsh's mercy. "You would be afraid of foreigners, too . . ." but her reasons succumbed to the strong strains of the piano. Knowing the fears of cannibalism which had always dominated her people, Dayuma guessed the rest.

Aunt Maengamo told of how an airplane—"a foreigners' wood-bee"—had circled their huts and of how the Aucas called out to it, as if it could understand what they were saying. She mentioned that her people had heard a chopping sound in the forest and had said, "Let's go see." She spoke of a vine dropped down from the wood-bee.

The incoherent tragedy sobbed out on the tape threw Dayuma into a state of nervous high tension. As she listened again and again to the garbled message the girl's spirits plunged to the depths of sadness. She began to relive the grim horrors of her childhood. By day and by night she was under the shadow of the old spears. At times when the emotional tempest threatened to swallow Dayuma, Rachel would suggest a long, quiet walk in the Ozark woods where Shetland ponies and fattened pigs served as salutary tranquillizers. After a relaxing break they would tackle the tape again.

The transcription of the tape was a major accomplishment. The Auca speech was much faster than Dayuma's, and was much more nasalized. There were new Auca words and phrases. Rachel analyzed and translated the tape phrase by phrase, asking Dayuma to repeat some of the rapid ones in slower Auca. The girl also explained the new vocabulary in words familiar to Rachel. It was an exhausting assignment for one who had never heard Auca spoken in a natural context, as well as for Dayuma, who had not heard her mother tongue for many, many years.

Rachel says,

"When I finished writing out the translation of that tape into English, I felt as if I had just completed my final exams!"

In those days Rachel discovered other chambers in the great hall of horrors of the tribe to which she was called. She prayed earnestly for spiritual and mental equilibrium for Dayuma as the turbulence of her past dashed upon her mercilessly. At times the Indian girl was almost distracted by the haunting questions "Does my mother live? Does my sister live?"

Rachel dreaded the news that the next tape from Ecuador might bring—if indeed the two women had not run back into the forest.

By praying with Dayuma and teaching her line upon line God's will as revealed in the Bible, she endeavored to fortify the storm-tossed soul against any stronger onslaught.

On Thanksgiving Day Rachel was cheered by a spontaneous prayer revealing Dayuma's desire for her own people, in spite of mental torment:

"Let those who know about You speak to others. Then they will understand. If the Aucas aren't angry we will return and tell them about God. You gave us that we might eat. Your Son in exchange died."

13

A BRUISED REED

IN those days of stress and suspense Rachel was frequently reminded that faithful friends were praying for Dayuma and her tribe. One who had remembered them for many years was Dr. Raymond Edman, president of Wheaton College and former missionary to the Oriente of Ecuador. As a personal friend of the Saint family, he had known the circumstances which led Rachel to the Auca tribe, and had followed her work with keen interest and constant prayer. He and a fellow missionary, Reuben Larson (later co-founder of the Pioneer Missionary Broadcasting Station HCJB), had pioneered in the jungles of Ecuador. Through the years they had not ceased to beseech God for an opening of the Auca tribe to the Gospel.

On December 24, 1957, Dr. Edman wrote Rachel,

". . . Often we have been looking upward for Dayuma and you. Last evening Reuben and Grace Larson were with us for dinner; and a large part of our conversation was about the latest developments on the Oglán. Interesting indeed that the two Aucas who have come are related to Dayuma. The light begins to penetrate the darkness!"

The Larsons had gone to the Oriente in 1924 in the hope of reaching the Aucas with the Gospel. They had heard of the merciless killers, "without God and without hope." Of her call to the jungle Grace Larson wrote,

"In my ignorance, all Indians of the Amazon jungle were Aucas, so in answering the Lord's call to me I yielded up as far as I knew the last full measure of devotion. In March, 1924, we left the United States for Ecuador but with a fuller knowledge of the Indians, although it was still meager. Ever in the back of our minds was the drive of the ultimate—getting to the Aucas."

Later she wrote to Rachel Saint,

"Our part has been taking one step toward them into the jungle. To you has been given the priceless privilege of accomplishment, the blood, the sweat, and the tears."

The Larsons had kept three of thirty-nine chonta spears that had been used to pin a Quichua Indian to the ground near their mission station in the jungle. These spears were to them "vivid reminders of men without God." As an encouragement to prayer for the tribe they had reproduced the large, broad footprint of an Auca in an early issue of *Jungle Indian Bulletin*.

"A young engineer of a petroleum company whom we knew as an appreciated friend came in from his camp on a little river," Grace Larson wrote, "and brought the tracing of the footprint in the sand. The prints led up to his tent, and away again. He said that they were Auca footprints, and no one in that area to whom we showed it ever questioned it. We asked if we might use it to awaken prayer on behalf of the Aucas, and he gave us his full permission."

An appeal for prayer for the unreachable tribe was printed on the replica of the footprint: "A great price was paid for their redemption. Will it ever be made known to them?"

Although ill health forced the Larsons to leave the jungle, they had never ceased to pray for the tribe whose needy condition drew them to Ecuador. And through the years their prayer fellowship with the Edmans for the Aucas had continued. Now years later, in 1957, they were rejoicing in the slight shaft of light penetrating the very deep Auca darkness.

After Christmas a second taped installment of the tragedy arrived in Sulphur Springs from Ecuador. It was a continuation of the fears and sorrows of the first—without the piano concerto. Maengamo, always the main speaker, said she had left the fears of the tribe behind mindful of other fears before her in the outside world. Her second daughter had been killed by witchcraft, a fate certain to be hers also if she remained in the forest. She was quite sure that the foreigners would shoot with their "made things," or that they would eat her alive—but she had come anyway. "They will cut you up alive and eat you cooked" had been the warning when she decided to leave.

"I buried my daughter and came," she wailed incoherently over the tape.

With hysterical blubberings she jumped from the present to the past in her endless recounting of killings and curses.

Then came the word for which Dayuma had long waited. Moipa had been speared dead years ago! With agonizing detail Maengamo depicted the treachery which had ended in Moipa's awful death. "They were as mad as iwa monkeys when they speared Moipa," she said.

Dayuma gave a shout of joy, and it hurt Rachel that she was so happy over any spear-killing. Jubilation turned to sorrow a few minutes later as she heard tragic word about her family. Her big brother Wawae, who was her favorite, had been murdered a long time ago. Dayuma had begun talking about returning to the Auca forest, and was counting on living with him. "He always brought me meat from the forest. I loved him very much," she had said.

Dayuma's tears began to fall as Maengamo gave all the cruel details of the big brother's death. As she wept she listened for more news of her family. But there was not a word about her mother, nor her sisters. Again, the tape poured out more accounts of Moipa's heartless spearings.

The sobs of sorrow gave way to tears of anger as Dayuma thought of those who had killed Wawae. Old fires of hatred and resentment leaped into flame.

"I will never go back!" wailed Dayuma. Her last hope had been dashed. There was no one to go to, not even Wawae. Surely her mother had been speared, and there was no word of her sisters.

In a firm voice Rachel began to check the rising anger which threatened to undo the spiritual progress of recent weeks. Spasms of violent weeping had exhausted the heartsick girl as Rachel reasoned with her. She reminded her that the Lord Jesus had left heaven to come to earth where people hated Him, and finally murdered Him. But what did He do when He was being killed? He loved his enemies and forgave them!

Love your enemies . . . forgive them . . . Those concepts were not in Auca thinking. It was a hard lesson for Dayuma to learn in the heat of the battle.

Rachel told her,

"If the Lord Jesus had not left heaven, we would never have heard of Him. You are the only one of your people who knows God. How will they hear if you don't go to tell them? You may be the only one who can tell them of Jesus." Dayuma was thinking it over, but she was still angry, very angry with Moipa and the others who had killed Wawae.

Rachel also reminded her that the Bible taught, "Let not the sun go down upon your wrath"—and the sun was about to go down in Sulphur Springs. That was a difficult command at the end of a very sad day. But as the darkness began to settle down upon the little village Dayuma reached a momentous decision.

"Not being angry I will sleep," she said quietly.

In that time of spiritual crisis when the passion for revenge was being replaced in Dayuma by a desire to forgive, she listened carefully to the Bible lessons chosen for the occasion, and made personal applications. Rachel told her the complete story of David, including Saul's designs upon his life. David did not retaliate, but trusted God to deal with his enemy in His way.

Rachel recalls,

"Dayuma became so interested in the story that she kept wanting to know more. She pushed me beyond what I felt I was capable of teaching. When I would come to a stopping-place she would say, 'And then?' "

So it was that she heard the whole long, sad story of the kings of Israel, reinforced by Rachel with related admonitions from other parts of the Bible. "Rejoice not when thine enemy falleth" was a timely word. "Vengeance is mine, I will repay, saith the Lord" underscored the lesson. David's life gave Dayuma food for thought for many days.

On the tape from Ecuador Dayuma had heard the name of one of Moipa's relatives who escaped the spearings that wiped out his family.

"I could find him when I return and tell him about God," Dayuma said thoughtfully one day.

It was Rachel's turn to shout for joy! This, indeed, was genuine victory, a token of God-taught forgiveness. Love was beginning to replace the old Auca pattern of hate.

Later, after a discussion concerning the kings of Israel and their shortcomings, Dayuma prayed,

"God, You alone become the Aucas' Chief."

In January, 1958, the English translation of the second involved message from Maengamo and Mintaka was finished and sent back to those in Ecuador who were eagerly awaiting the next chapter.

As Rachel dropped the package in the mail she noticed the date —January 8. She thought back two years. On January 8, 1956, her brother Nate with four of his friends had laid down his life for Dayuma's people. And already the first message about God in

Auca had been sent back to two other members of the tribe. In those two years Rachel had learned to communicate with Dayuma in Auca, and had led her gently to a love and knowledge of the Living God. There was good evidence that as a child of God she was maturing in her Christian life. The travail and the trials had not been in vain.

Rachel remembered the Watch Night Service in the Wycliffe Home in Quito on the eve of 1957. As various members of the group voiced their petitions to God, Mary Sargent had asked Him for something which startled Rachel. She confidently requested that during 1957 there might be a fruitful contact with the tribe. Now Rachel recalled Mary's prayer of faith which God had honored. It was in November of that year that Dayuma's aunts had run out of the forest.

Rachel remembered another prayer, one she uttered on January 1, 1956. She had asked the Lord to reach the Auca tribe, "with me or without me," adding that she was willing to make any sacrifice to that end. A week later her beloved brother Nate died on Auca soil. She traced God's hand in the events of the last two years. His ways had proved to be higher than hers, and His sovereign purposes were being realized.

A convincing proof of divine planning was the continued presence of Dayuma's relatives with Betty Elliot. Although separated by thousands of miles from Dayuma and Rachel, communication by tape and written message kept the aunts waiting hopefully for Dayuma's appearance. One day when a letter from Betty enclosed a picture of Mintaka and Maengamo, the homeward pull was very strong. Once again the tug brought tears to her eyes, but now of joy at the sight of her very own kin.

"Let me talk to them!" she said eagerly. "I want to speak to my relatives!" Rachel quickly obliged and set up the tape recorder. From a heart overflowing with a new love for her own people,

Dayuma sent a personal message unconsciously reflecting her desires for them. After encouraging them to stay with Betty Elliot where they would "live well," she promised to come to them later.

"Maengamo, Mintaka, you two live there in another foreigner's house. In the same way I live here with lots of other foreigners. You two stay with the tall foreign woman. Follow her, do not go to another house. Stay with the tall white woman. She has one child, and is a widow. If you two go to another house it will not be good. I speak, and you two listen to me. My name is Dayuma.

"I lived in the house where you are now for three days. Now I live in the house of another who is like her relative. Here, far away, on the other side of the big water I live. Later, returning, I will come.

"Maengamo, why didn't you speak straight? I could not understand. You only said that long ago they killed. You spoke about my grandfather who was killed. Tell me about the ones who *live!* Tell me where they live. 'Here they live, here he lives'—tell me. Don't just tell me about those who were speared long ago. Does my mother live? I don't know. Did they spear her? I don't know.

"Now Umi, Wiñaemi, and Ominia live not far from where you two live now. Close by they live. Why don't you visit with them? I can't come now. I will come later.

"There where you live now they all sing, there in their singing-house. You two go there and hear about God who lives high in the sky. The Aucas say that long ago God created men and women. They didn't remember more. Where does God live? 'We don't know,' they said. Who created the water? 'God created the water. God created everything,' they said. They didn't remember any more.

"The Aucas don't live well. God lives high in the sky. Long ago His Son was born as a child. We did not live well, we sinned. We slept with other men. We shouldn't do it. It is not good. Don't you two live like that. It is true that I lived that way before, I did not live well. I didn't know about God, I didn't understand. Now I understand, and now I am happy. There was no one to tell me. I just lived. Now I understand, now I live well.

"When we did not live well God's Son came to earth. He in exchange died. After three days He came to life. Now He lives high in the sky. Very well He lives.

"When, returning, will He come? Maybe at night, in the day-time, at noontime—we don't know. Inside the earth lots and lots of fire blazes. Yes, it's awful. When He comes those who sin will live there. If we love God when we die we will go high in the sky where He is thatching a beautiful hut for us. Here in our hut we will die. Yes, our flesh will rot. Our souls will go high in the sky. It is very beautiful there!

"God's Son was born on the earth. His mother was an unmarried woman. His Father, God, lives high in the sky. Later, after God's Son was born, He became mature. He came to one who was blind. He touched his eye with His hand, and that one saw. Another had a lame foot and could not walk. God's Son touched him and he became better fast—then he walked rapidly! Another died, and God's Son said, 'Get up—stand up!' And he stood up! God's Son did very well. He loves everybody. He loves all of the Aucas. He loves them very much.

"Even though He did well some people said that He was a witch doctor. Some did not speak well of Him. He is not a witch doctor, He is God's Son. Do not be afraid of the devils. God's Son speaks to the devils. 'Go!' He says. And they flee! They are afraid of Him. The devils lived inside of a man's flesh. Seeing Him they were afraid. 'You are God's Son,' they said. 'Don't come here.' Then they said, 'We are many. In whose flesh will we live? We will enter the flesh of wild hogs!' Then they entered the wild hogs. They ran into a lake and were all drowned. The wild hogs died with the devils. God does very well. Don't you two be afraid of the devils. Now I love God and I am not afraid of the devils. I live very well.

"Maengamo, where is your son Kominkagi? Where is your son Ñamae? Why did you leave them behind? Why didn't you bring them? They will live well in the foreigners' house. Is your younger brother Dabu alive? Is your younger brother Kimo alive? They will live well with the foreigners. The foreigners will not be angry. They are very happy with the Aucas. If you keep spearing the foreigners, they are not angry in exchange. They just die, then they bury. Who killed the foreign man when they took Maruja? Who took her? Which of the Aucas came? Who speared? Tell me the truth. Why didn't you two call out and say, 'Don't spear! Come with us and visit. Here we two live.' Why did you let them come and kill? Why didn't you just come and get the machetes that the foreigners offered you?

"I lived with those same foreigners. They are like my relatives. I lived with them many moons. I went down the Napo and returned on the Curaray with them. When I was down there I thought of all of you. I said, 'When will my relatives come? I don't know.' I went on downriver to the mouth of the Grape Tree River, and then upriver on the Grape Tree River. Four days I lived there thinking of you all. I said, 'When, oh when will my relatives come? Where is the trail? When will my little sister come? When will my big brother come? Do they live? I don't know.' I was right there on the trail, but I couldn't come to you.

"Visit well with the foreigners. When they come to your huts, do not spear them. The foreigners who love God are good foreigners. There are others who do not know God and drink fermented drink. But the foreigners who love God are very good.

"Who speared my uncle and my big brother? Maengamo, is your husband Gikita dead or alive? Does Umi's mother live? You didn't say anything about her. You just spoke about those who lived long ago. Talk to me straight and give me the answers. Tell me who lives. I know that my father died long ago.

"When I first came out of the forest I lived in a foreigner's house. I just worked. I was hungry and hot. I said, 'When will I hear about God? I just live.'

"You live very well with a foreign woman. She does not understand the Auca speech. When she says, 'What is it? What is it?' you tell her what it is. Later she will understand.

"When you two came another woman came with you. Then she ran away. Who was it who ran away? Tell me so that I will know. You say that your younger brother ran back into the forest. Was it Kimo or was it Dabu? Why didn't you call to him and say, 'Come with us'? Why did you let them run back into the forest? Don't be afraid. The foreigners won't kill you.

"Does Wiñaemi's mother live? Does Wiñaemi's older brother Nimonga live? Does Umi's sister Wiña live?"

After inquiring about her relatives and pleading for further information about them, Dayuma began to ask about those whose names were new to her.

"You spoke of Mima. Who is Mima? Who is Boika of whom you spoke? Where did she live before? Who is Monga? Where did he live before?"

Dayuma made a final desperate plea for information about the location of her family group. For over ten years she had heard nothing from her own people and wanted a truthful report about them.

"Whose hut did you two live in? How many of you lived there? Long ago we lived on Palm River. Later the foreigners came there and shot Omaenga and she died. Then we lived on Fish River. Then Moipa did not do well and we fled. Now where do my people live? On what river do they live? You two speak to me. Do they live on Palm River? or on Fish River? I don't know. Where did you two live? Where were you living when you came out? When I heard that you two had come I had lots of fever and I could not go to you. That is all I speak."

February brought further breathtaking news. Betty Elliot had shown the two Auca women pictures from Palm Beach. While pointing to "Delilah" they had said "Imari." Betty relayed the word to Sulphur Springs.

"Gimari!" shouted Dayuma. "She is saying it is my sister Gimari!"

But what had happened to the initial "g"? In an earlier communication Rachel had noticed that the word for dog ginta was recorded by Betty as inta. "So your informants are probably not giving the initial 'g' much pronunciation," Rachel wrote Betty. Months later, however, it was discovered that Mintaka had a speech impediment and could not pronounce initial "g's."

Dayuma had not recognized the pictures of "Delilah" as Gimari when Rachel showed them to her at Hacienda Ila. She was therefore elated at the news that Gimari was living at the time of Palm Beach—but was she still alive? So far the tapes had not mentioned either Gimari or her mother. And did Gimari's presence with her Aunt Mintaka at Palm Beach mean she was an orphan and her mother Akawo was dead?

As the weeks wore on with no word of them, Dayuma's patience wore thin. Rachel wrote Betty,

"The girl is nearly crazy waiting to know if her mother still lives. She dreams almost every night that she and the two little sisters were speared. It is actually making her nervous to know that there is an answer available and she does not have it. She cries for her big brother—the tape gave all the details of his spearing and death. The smoldering fires of resentment would flare except for her desire to live as the Lord wants her to. But her anxiety holds me back in my work; I cannot work on the tapes without her. . . ."

Finally in late February a tape brought the word for which Dayuma had wept and waited: her mother Akawo was alive, and one daughter was living with her. But which daughter was it, Gimari or Oba? And had the other been killed? While Maengamo gave the welcome news about Akawo, Mintaka's voice was audible in the background:

"Your mother is living like a wild pig alone in the forest, just eating squirrels that are blowgunned and fish from the streams."

Why was her mother living alone in the forest? Was she fleeing from spearings and had to live alone with no one to protect her? If she was eating squirrels, who blowgunned them for her? Dayuma concluded hopefully that her brother Nampa must be living with her mother and one sister in the forest.

The same tape brought more sad family news. Aunt Wiika and Aunt Wiwa had been speared by Moipa long ago.

"Now the trees have grown tall in the place where they were speared, and the wind blows in their branches," Maengamo reported mournfully.

But a final shock was yet in store for the Auca girl whose spirit had been buffeted almost beyond endurance by the news of recent months. Rachel had sent Betty a picture of Dayuma with two toucan birds to be shown to Maengamo and Mintaka. Betty had set up two tape recorders, one to play Dayuma's questions, and the other to record the aunts' answers and comments on the picture.

When the picture of Dayuma was shown, Maengamo said,

"You say this is her picture? She is *dead!*"

When it was pointed out that it was Dayuma's voice on the tape, they said,

"Being dead she speaks."

The aunts had evaded the answers to many of Dayuma's questions. "Let her go herself and find out if she wants to know," was their impudent reply.

When Rachel had completed the translation of the last tape, she wrote Betty Elliot,

"Some day perhaps we'll have some pleasant subject matter to work on without the deep emotional reaction that this stuff causes Dayuma. But maybe not until there is a quorum who love the Lord. A cross section of the material shows a fairly high percentage of spearing so far—in Dayuma's work as well as in that of these two."

Spearings had, in fact, dominated most of Maengamo's conversation. At one point she had blubbered out,

"If your grandchildren grew up to be speared, and their grandchildren grew up to be speared, and their grandchildren grew up to be speared—you would cry, too!"

During the exchange of tapes Betty Elliot wrote Rachel,

"Maengamo's description of the murder of Moipa is a clear picture of the treachery of the people, isn't it? If they'd do that to one of their own number . . . Have you discovered what happened to Maengamo's husband? Or why her daughter died? Every time I ask about her husband I get a reply full of spears and killings, so I have always assumed he was speared. . . ."

Indeed the tapes only confirmed what Rachel had learned through several years of language work with Dayuma: the Aucas were ruthless killers, not only on their borders but among themselves. The prospects for reaching the tribe were, in one sense, darker than ever.

14

"WHAT DOTH HINDER ME...?"

WINTER in Sulphur Springs, though mild as compared with some parts of the United States, was brutally cold for a jungle Indian. Dayuma shivered and shook with the first frost of autumn which gradually chilled into winter. The colorful falling leaves had concerned Dayuma. Gaunt bare trees were a new sight for one who had known only perennial jungle greenness. Would the leaves ever grow back again? Yes, Rachel assured her, this happened every year, and the trees would be green again in the springtime.

The heavy warm clothing was like mail armor for Dayuma who had worn either nothing or a simple jungle dress. Even shoes had been a big adjustment—and now, bundles around her shoulders! She had easily carried loads of bananas weighing seventy-five or a hundred pounds, but weighty woolens were unbearable.

Other problems of living in the new environment were even greater. The girl missed her jungle fare, and the village offered few substitutes. One happy day she accompanied Rachel to the local butcher shop and saw before her wondering eyes huge juicy cuts to tempt meat-hungry customers. Her mouth watered. She hadn't seen so much meat since those days in the forest when her father and brother Wawae brought home all the monkey and wild pig that an Auca could eat. The pot would be emptied and filled, time after time, and meat cooked as long as anybody wanted to eat. Then the rest was smoked. Dayuma had never known the frustration of handling money, nor the cost of a heavy meat diet. The only price for fresh meat had been a trip into the forest with a blowgun.

"Show us quantity, not quality!" Rachel implored "Ben the Butcher," explaining her quandary. He, like all the other citizens of the village, was most co-operative, and the hungry Auca girl enjoyed plenty of meat.

Dayuma was disturbed one afternoon to learn that the fish she had been eating was not caught the same day. It had been frozen for a long time. Whereupon the neighbors brought her a freshly caught mess *with the heads on,* the "best part" according to Dayuma. She never forgot the kindness of those understanding friends.

A local lad, who heard that "the Indian girl hankered for the food of home," hunted squirrels for her.

Still another baffling matter: bananas had to be bought for ten cents a pound, while in the jungle one eats all he can hold for *nothing.*

This American way of life held many surprises. One day as Dayuma stood by the kitchen sink washing the dishes Rachel heard her cry out with wonder, "What is it? What can it be?" Rachel rushed to the scene and, upon looking out the window, realized that for the first time in her life the girl was seeing big white flakes of falling snow. She had flown over the snow-capped peaks of Ecuador, but was never this close to "frozen rain." The snow continued to fall to a considerable depth. Dayuma was eager to get into it. Rachel outfitted her with various warm togs and turned her loose. The enchanted girl wallowed in the white wonder, reveling in its fleecy softness. She stretched herself flat upon it and lay still so long that her favorite dog Spot came along and licked her face.

For months Dayuma had been praying that her eight-year-old son in Ecuador might join her in the States. She longed for him.

When Rachel and Dayuma had left the hacienda for the television program they expected to be gone only a month. Efforts were since being made to arrange the trip of the young boy to his mother. Now, with the thrill of snow, Dayuma was reminded again of him. How she would enjoy sharing the fun with her son! But as the weeks wore on and the child did not appear, the possibility of snow during his arrival grew very slim. Dayuma added to her daily prayers for the lad's coming an earnest petition for later snow.

Rachel wrote fellow workers in Ecuador who were trying to obtain the documents necessary for his departure,

"The Lord must answer her prayers for her boy—they are so spontaneous and precious!"

Dayuma, of course, could not understand all the paper work involved before the boy could leave Ecuador. Her impatience grew when the many phone calls and letters about her son brought no results. Then one day Capt. Larry Montgomery of Wycliffe's Jungle Aviation and Radio Service landed on a small field near Sulphur Springs. He was flying a Helio-plane donated by the citizens of Kansas City and designated for use of the Summer Institute of Linguistics in the Ecuadorian jungle. When Dayuma heard that he was headed for Ecuador she went to Montgomery with a special commission. When he got to Ecuador would he please get her small son and bring him to her as soon as possible? The Indian girl, accustomed to delivering messages orally in the jungle, had more confidence in a personal arrangement with a JAARS pilot than in the prolific exchange of letters which accomplished nothing.

Rachel was surprised at the request. Within two weeks, however, Man-of-Action Montgomery telephoned from Miami that he had just arrived by plane and had the small boy in tow. At the airport in Tulsa, Oklahoma, mother and son were finally reunited. In his report of aviation activities for the month, Montgomery included "delivery of small boy."

Rachel comments,

"I always knew that our JAARS fellows would willingly do many things for us beyond the line of duty, but I hadn't expected he would be able to carry out Dayuma's special commission so suc cessfully."

And Dayuma's prayer for snow was answered with abundance. This time Rachel dressed her two jungle Indians in warm clothes to sled and make snowballs and snowmen to their hearts' content. Once Dayuma made a church—a "God's singing-house." Later Rachel wrote to friends in Sulphur Springs,

"Perhaps you folks didn't know why there was so much snow so late in the season. We think it was because a young Indian mother asked the Lord to send the marvelous 'white' once more after her son arrived. So He sent three more snows in two weeks in early March!"

But there was something even more important to Dayuma than snow for her son—who was now being called "Sammy" by his American playmates. On the very first day of his arrival the joyful mother began to relate the wonders of God and His Son Jesus. The wide-eyed boy drank in the stories with as much eagerness as the mother poured them out. Rachel states that "in three sessions that first Sunday, amounting to about three and a half hours, she told her little lad all she had learned about God and Jesus during the months she had been separated from him."

Nor did her ardor cool. Each day she continued to teach Sammy in minute detail what she was learning from Rachel. The months of patient work with Dayuma had not been lost.

Dayuma also spent many days telling Sammy of other things she had seen and heard. There was the flight in the wood-bee over the big forest with Wallace Lindskoog. She mentioned the "trail in the skies" and the signals by which pilots guide the wood-bees, even when they cannot see.

One day Dayuma asked Rachel, "Where was the Captain's wood-bee made?" Rachel wondered if she was referring to the captain of an airline who had been very cordial to them on a recent trip. "Oh no!" objected Dayuma. "I mean *the* Captain!"

Dayuma was referring to Capt. Robert Griffin, chief pilot of JAARS in Ecuador, with whom she had flown from the hacienda to Quito. To her he was *the* Captain, who flew the Helio manufactured in Pittsburg, Kansas. Rachel arranged a trip to the factory one hundred and fifty miles from Sulphur Springs. It was a high peak in the visit to the States. While Sammy watched the welders surrounded by flying sparks, Dayuma inspected every detail of the Helio's "skeleton and skin and insides." "How the Captain's wood-bee was made" became a favorite conversation piece.

Sammy's presence was a balm for the girl who had passed through a dark valley, shadowed by death itself. Transparent joy in imparting her knowledge of the Lord to him was unmistakable evidence of a refreshed spirit.

Before Sammy arrived Rachel had questioned Dayuma, "If your son asks you what will happen when he dies, what will you tell him?"

"I'll tell him," Dayuma had answered, " 'If you die first, and go to God's house in heaven, I will come later and see you again. And if I die first, I will go to heaven, and you will come later, and I will see you again.' " Then, remembering her old Auca teaching about the termite, she added, "Having gone to heaven, you will not die again!"

As Sammy heard of heaven by day and by night Dayuma began to think concretely about transmitting the wonders of God's carving to her own people in the forest. "If I go to the Auca huts, what will they say? What will they do?" she queried. She had been away from her relatives for so long that she faced the possibility of not being accepted. One day she said determinedly to Rachel, "I'll go back—don't you go. If they are angry at me, I will die."

With her thoughts turned southward toward Mintaka and Maengamo and her tribe, Dayuma wondered how she might tell them the story. Perhaps the words of Grandfather's old song about "God created everything" might be applied to the Bible story of creation. She prayed that her people would not reject her message but that they would believe God's carving.

As news came from Señor Sevilla that Dayuma and her son were being released to Rachel for the Auca work, the girl seemed concerned. She asked,

"Who will feed us if we do not go back to the patrón?"

"We belong to the Lord and serve Him," Rachel told her, "and He will provide food for us. We will ask Him and He will supply."

It was a long step of faith for the girl who had worked from sun to sun in the field in exchange for food for herself and her little boy. Rachel saw that the girl was now ready to face the uncertainties of the future, including the dubious reception by her own group. They began to make plans for the trip homeward.

During the day Rachel analyzed the Auca texts. But not knowing when, if ever, she would have the same opportunity for teaching Dayuma the Word, she also spent many hours with her, reviewing the lessons taught, and covering new ground. One night as she was teaching her the narrative of the baptism of Jesus, Rachel noticed unusual interest. Dayuma listened carefully to all the details, and then repeated the story. Her interest was so great that Rachel cited two other examples of Bible baptism, the Philippian jailer who was baptized following his remarkable conversion, and the Ethiopian eunuch who asked to be baptized. Dayuma was impressed with the words of the eunuch, "Here is water. What doth hinder me to be baptized?" She fixed all the facts of the stories in her mind, and retold them practically word for word in her own language.

Fully two weeks later Dayuma startled Rachel with the question, "What good man of God can enter me into the water?"

Rachel had not expected the request so soon. She had thought that sometime, in Ecuador, the girl would be baptized. But the serious question and the earnest desire of the girl challenged Rachel into unanticipated action. As she prayed about "what good man of God" would understand the circumstances and perform a meaningful ceremony, she remembered Dr. Edman's vital interest in the girl from the first days of language work on the hacienda in 1955. One Christmas in Ecuador, Dayuma had met Dr. and Mrs. Edman in the Larson home. They had been most gracious to the strange Indian girl. As a personal friend he would surely be willing to have a quiet, private baptismal service for Dayuma. Rachel knew that his son lived near Sulphur Springs. Perhaps on a visit to Arkansas Dr. Edman could perform the ceremony. She wrote him a note at Wheaton College, and was amazed at the plan he suggested in reply:

"My heart was deeply stirred, Rachel, at your report of the tape that has gone from Dayuma to Mintaka and Maengamo, the first Auca testimony for the Lord Jesus in her own language to her own people. I shall be sharing this word with the whole College family, so we shall be trusting earnestly with you.

"My heart was likewise deeply stirred by the word of invitation to have her baptism. We shall be looking upward for the Lord's guidance and provision in that regard. It seemed to me there might be the possibility in the Lord's good will that the LeTourneaus bring Dayuma here some spring day, either a weekday or on a weekend; and we could have the baptismal service here. It would be most appropriate, it seems to me, to have the baptism in Wheaton, from which three of the five martyrs went on their way toward the gates of splendor. I shall be checking with the folk in Texas with recommendation for a date in May or April when the weather is warmer. (Our thermometer read 12 below this morning at daybreak!)

"Little by little the story of the past is being unraveled; and the pages of the future grow more exciting and wonderful!"

Rachel answered, "You folks take my breath away! I had thought only of a baptism near here somewhere, and presto! . . ." She concluded the letter giving consent to Dr. Edman's plan with the words, "Some day there will be other Aucas saying, 'See, here is the Curaray. What doth hinder us to be baptized?' "

The service was to be held in Wheaton on April 15, and industrialist R. G. LeTourneau agreed to pick up the trio in his private plane in Sulphur Springs. Very full days of packing and preparation preceded the big event. The baptismal service would mark the initial step in the homeward journey for the first Auca missionary to her own tribe.

Rachel learned in Wheaton that the ceremony had been publicly announced. It was consummated as planned on April 15 in the Wheaton Evangelical Free Church, pastored by Wilbur Nelson, Marj Saint's former pastor from California. Three languages, Auca, English, and Spanish, were used in the service in a thrilling review of how "Christianity came to the first member of one of the last Stone Age tribes in existence." Rachel had regretted that there was insufficient time to notify friends who would have had a special interest in the occasion. She had thought of the Larsons, the pioneers to the Oriente in Ecuador. She knew that they were in the States, but did not know where. It was a delight, therefore, when Rachel found they had been notified and were present. Mr. and Mrs. Fred Elliot, parents of Jim Elliot, attended, as well as his sister, Mrs. Jane Hawthorne. Mrs. T. E. McCulley, mother of Ed McCulley, was also there. Wycliffe was represented by Dr. Richard Pittman, Deputy Director, who accompanied the party in LeTourneau's plane.

Dr. Carl Amerding, professor of Bible at Wheaton and former missionary to South America, delivered the message. "I know of nothing else in my experience that compares to this," he said in a moving evaluation of the significance of the occasion. Then as a stirring climax Dr. Edman, the "good man of God," baptized Dayuma in a simple act of immersion. The first Auca Christian, smiling radiantly, gave witness to her faith in Christ. Sammy was dedicated to the Lord by his mother before her baptism. She hoped that he, too, would follow Him all the days of his life.

From Wheaton the Auca party traveled to the east coast for a farewell visit with the Saint family and to arrange documents for their departure. That the preparations for the return to Ecuador would require some delay was beyond the jungle Indian's comprehension. Finally by the end of May they were guests of Sam Saint and Cornell Capa in the Gold Room at Idlewild Airport, where thick steaks were served on gold plates. Later, when asked what Dayuma thought of the gold plates, Rachel replied, "The Aucas know nothing of the value of gold. The girl thought a lot more of that big juicy steak on the plates."

Rachel, Dayuma, and Sammy left New York City early one morning and the next day were at Limoncocha, Wycliffe's Base in the heart of the Ecuadorian jungle. The return trip had been as breath-taking as the sudden flight to California the year before.

As they flew over the Napo River from Shell Mera to Limoncocha, Dayuma looked down on Auca territory she had not seen since she fled. Rachel was amazed that as Dayuma studied the lay of the land she remembered the name of each river and ridge.

"Over there is where they killed my grandfather," she said, pointing to a ridge in the east. It was all very familiar. This country was home to the Auca girl.

Within a few minutes they would be landing at the Jungle Base. There Betty Elliot with Mintaka and Maengamo would meet them—perhaps today!

"Will my aunts recognize me?" wondered Dayuma.

She had recently dreamed that they thought she was a foreigner.

15

HOPE SPRINGS ETERNAL
—IN A MOTHER'S BREAST

IN a secluded corner of Limoncocha Base a small Auca clearing was readied for Mintaka and Maengamo. Dayuma knew what would make them feel at home and had given some welcome suggestions to Wycliffe personnel at the Base co-operating in preparations for the big event. Quichua workmen hurriedly constructed palm-thatched shelters where the Auca women could make their customary ground-fires. Dayuma and Rachel hung hammocks from the posts of the shelters overlooking the placid lake where Dayuma herself planned to go spear-fishing with them. An Indian had been sent to the forest to hunt the wild game that abounded. Succulent yuca grew plentifully in the jungle garden in another clearing connected by a shaded trail.

Rachel was almost as charged with anticipation as Dayuma.

"What shall I say to your aunts?" she asked, planning a greeting in Auca. "Shall I say, 'I like you'?"

"No!" Dayuma replied with vigor. "You say, 'I'm not angry with you!' "

Dayuma began orienting Rachel on how to receive her aunts and put them at ease. She selected the Auca name "Nimu," meaning "Star," for her. It had been the name of Dayuma's little sister who was hacked to death by Moipa's machete. One point of instruction was emphasized: Rachel was not to ask about the circumstances of Palm Beach until the aunts became well acquainted with her. They might think she was planning to avenge her pilot brother's death.

Suddenly word flashed over the radio that the plane bearing Betty Elliot and the two Auca women had left Shandia and would be landing at Limoncocha in half an hour. Dayuma immediately went to the airstrip and began to watch the clear blue sky above the giant trees. She paced up and down the strip which ran narrowly between walls of towering jungle from which it had been cut.

Dayuma's heart pounded and she rubbed her hands nervously as a distant speck growing larger and humming loudly moved toward her. Soon the plane was on the grassy strip, taxiing right for her. As it pulled up Dayuma saw her two aunts, and her eyes filled with tears. She was trembling with emotion. Before the plane stopped moving Mintaka's face was pressed against the glass and she was shouting, "Dayuma! Dayuma!" Maengamo recognized her instantly, too, and was talking and gesticulating wildly when the door of the plane opened. The two women tumbled out talking— especially Maengamo. In almost hysterically fast Auca she was continuing the harangue, begun on the tapes, about Moipa and the spearings which had thinned out Dayuma's family group during the last eleven years.

"They speared your brother Wawae . . ." were almost the first words that greeted Dayuma. In the burning midday sun at the door of the plane Maengamo poured out the details of her brother's death.

"It's hot here in the sun—let's go—" It was Mintaka who finally interrupted the recital of family spearings.

Rachel moved the knot of Auca speakers into the shade of the airplane wing. But Maengamo continued to go over and over the sad story. Dayuma had heard most of it on tape, but getting it firsthand, face-to-face with her aunts, was too much for her. She turned around, buried her face in her handkerchief, and wept. By this time a curious crowd of Quichua Indian workers had gathered.

Rachel's heart ached for Dayuma. She suggested that they go to their house and continue talking there.

The three Aucas settled quickly and naturally in their wooded haunt. Dayuma felt they might tell the truth only to her, so at first they were left alone to talk over the long years of family history since they had last seen one another. Around the fire they ate yuca, fresh fish, roasted bananas, and talked incessantly.

Rachel made her headquarters in a bamboo and chonta palm cabin, while Betty Elliot with her little daughter Valerie settled temporarily in another. At night Dayuma slept in Rachel's quarters and reported on the events of the day. She was hearing a great deal of family news, some of it good, but most of it punctuated with spears.

Rachel later hung her hammock under a thatched roof adjoining the Auca shelter where she could hear the fast nasal language as it continued all day and far into the night. Under her mosquito net at night she listened to questions and answers weaving the intricate design of the Auca way of life predominated by revenge spearings. One night Rachel heard the aunts tell Dayuma of spearing after spearing. When a killer was named Dayuma would ask, "And then who speared him in exchange?" Retaliation . . . spearings back and forth . . . always avenging the death of a relative. For more than a solid hour of "who speared in exchange?" Dayuma absorbed another tragic chapter of family history.

Uppermost in Dayuma's mind were questions about her mother: Where did she live? With whom did she live? This vital information should be had soon, in case Maengamo and Mintaka suddenly disappeared. It required many days of talking and eating around the ground-fire for the full story to unfold. And Maengamo was not given to logical narration. Essential facts about her family were often revealed to Dayuma as incidentals in the incessant flow of unordered sequence emanating from Maengamo. Eventually, by piecing the bits together, Dayuma learned the fate of all her family.

In the first days around the fire she found that Maengamo had left three of her children with Dayuma's mother. Mintaka's son was also living with her.

After Dayuma had fled the forest the family gradually migrated downriver, deep into the jungle and far from the outside world. It was so far in the interior that it took them two months of river travel and jungle trail to get back to their former location. By the time Maengamo and Mintaka left the forest so precipitously the family had returned and were living almost as near the outside as they had ever been. It was only a few days to Dayuma's mother's hut.

Dayuma recognized the hand of God in moving her family to an accessible place. If they had still been living in the deep jungle it would have been almost impossible to locate them. Rachel, too, saw the providential significance of the present location, for it was this new site that her brother Nate had spotted from the air. In the comparatively recent clearing he had dropped gifts from the plane preceding the contact with Dayuma's family at Palm Beach. And the knowledge that her mother was living nearby stimulated Dayuma's desire to return to her family.

Despite her anxiety to solve all the family enigmas, Dayuma could not resist the urge to communicate the wonder of God's carving to her aunts. Between the mouthfuls of delicious fresh-caught fish and gulps of banana drink, Dayuma regaled her aunts with bits of Biblical information utterly foreign to them. Although they were skeptical, the natural-born narrator held them spellbound by the abundant and fresh supply of Bible history which she had stored up, and which now overflowed.

"God lives high in the sky," she said. "He is the One who will never die. . . . Tariri used to say that the boa was God, but now he knows God. . . ." Dayuma drew from her acquaintance with the converted Shapra chief to emphasize her teaching about God. And of course she was desirous of making heaven as attractive as possible to her relatives. There would be no gnats in heaven—no bites to scratch. "And there we will not grow old and die. And we will never be hungry in God's house high up in the sky—"

Maengamo looked doubtful. Then, craning her neck and looking up to the clear sky beyond the thatch, she asked, "What will we *eat* in God's house? There's no yuca growing up there!" Food in quantity—yes, it was a chief preoccupation of all Aucas. Maengamo was not one to accept new information without question. She was a challenge to an alert teacher struggling to plant intangible, eternal facts in virgin soil.

Rachel occasionally joined Dayuma in the attempt to teach her aunts. One day when it was storming Rachel noticed that Mintaka was burning a wad of thick beeswax. The Auca woman was thus trying to avert the disaster of big trees blowing down on her flimsy shelter.

"Why don't you talk to God who *created* the wind?" Rachel asked her.

Talking to God was a new idea. Mintaka was struck by the thought.

"Talk to God? How do you talk to God—like this—?" and Mintaka stood up dramatically, threw her arms outward, turned her face toward the sky and began addressing God in fast Auca. Rachel turned her head slightly to conceal a surprised smile. She had been unable to guess what Mintaka's reaction to this new teaching would be—except that it would be refreshingly uninhibited.

Dayuma was a match for the unpredictable relatives. To Rachel's amazement, Bible narratives always came out in typical Auca settings, in characteristic Auca style. Dayuma applied the graphic storytelling technique used in tales of spearings.

One day Dayuma was describing an imaginary scene in heaven.
"Who comes now?" a voice says in heaven as someone approaches.

"Her name is Maengamo."

"She believed very well? . . . Who are you?"

"Mintaka."

"All right. Come on in. Here I have thatched your hut."

When the truth was presented too graphically for immediate acceptance and the aunts wore quizzical expressions, Dayuma would
comment, "I don't just say this myself. God speaks it!" She always
made it plain that the source of her amazing information was
God's carving.

One day as she was urging her aunts to receive pardon offered
through God's Son, she challenged them with the question,
"Whose heart will become like light?" Rachel was puzzled as to
the precise Bible passage that prompted the question, but she
thought it was a good idea.

The story of Noah and the ark pictured God in an animated
conversation with Noah.

" 'Now when you finish building it, let me know,' God said to
Noah. . . . Then when the people were all dead, it stopped raining." Daniel in the "jaguars' " den was a real thriller, even to
Rachel who had heard the account many times. With gestures,
spellbinding voice changes, and realistic sound effects produced by
the gift of mimicry Dayuma created suspense and excitement as
the aunts heard about Daniel for the first time. When the king,
who wondered if Daniel were still alive, called down into the den,
he heard the familiar Auca answer "Oo—oo—!" as the storyteller
imitated the response to a jungle call.

Dayuma tried to impress the aunts with God's power. He is the
One who rules over everything in the world. He speaks, and all of
nature obeys. "If God speaks, the rain doesn't rain," she told

them. "In stilling the storm on the big water He said to the wind, 'Why do you blow?' And the wind heard."

Even the parable of the fig tree came eloquently to life with Dayuma's colorful touch.

Jesus said to the barren tree, "Why do you not bear seeds? You are just selfish. You will *die!*"

Sometimes Rachel wondered just how far she would let the girl's interpolation go without some slight correction. One day when telling the story of the crucifixion Dayuma said that "the sun stopped shining and the day became like night so that God couldn't see them hitting His Son."

As Dayuma shared her knowledge of God with her aunts she was sharply reminded that her people had no basis for understanding this completely new truth. She knew it would take time—and patient teaching—to convince them. She thought of others in her family, and wondered how they would respond to stories Grandfather had never heard.

Her mother Akawo still lived, and quite near the outside world. Dayuma began to relive old scenes in the forest as her aunts reminded her of home. She wondered about her mother's attitude toward her, remembering with a twinge of pain that she had once threatened to strangle her. And there was no fond father to return to now.

"Does my mother want to see me?" Dayuma wondered.

"Of course she wants to see you!" exclaimed the aunts in unison. "She's been looking for you ever since you left!"

Dayuma looked at them incredulously.

"Your mother begged us to look for you and bring you home if we found you," assured Maengamo. "She said she would bring a whole mess of fish and we will have a feast."

"Yes!" Mintaka continued. "She told us to look for you at the foreigners' houses. She said that if you were married and your husband wouldn't let you come, she would understand—but she wants you to come home. 'If she is a widow and has children, tell her to come and bring the children,' that's what your mother told me to tell you."

Then her aunts, sometimes both talking at once, described in detail her mother's search for her down through the years. With no evidence that Dayuma lived but with an undying desire to see her again, she had never given up hope of her daughter's return. She commissioned Ominia, and Tyaenyae, Wiñaemi's mother, to find her. Ominia and little Wiñaemi had gone to the outside world and never returned, but Tyaenyae had retreated, frightened by the foreigners' guns.

"Tyaenyae came back and told us that the foreigners had probably killed Ominia and Wiñaemi—and had surely killed you, too," said Mintaka, recollecting the sadness of her sister Akawo when Tyaenyae had returned with only bad news.

"But I am alive—and Ominia and Wiñaemi still live at the patrón's house!" cried Dayuma.

"Yes, but Akawo doesn't know it," put in Maengamo. "She just lives out in the forest and knows nothing about those who have fled. We must go home and tell her."

"Your mother waited and looked for you for many moons after Tyaenyae returned," continued Mintaka. "Then one day she said that she herself would go to the outside and look for you. She said that she would take Gimari and Oba—they were still little children then—and look for you."

"But my husband Gikita wouldn't let her go!" exclaimed Maengamo. "He said, 'No, I will not let you go. You and the children would surely die.' "

Dayuma looked from one aunt to the other, hardly daring to believe it. Her mother, in spite of her great fear of the foreigners, had tried to search for her. And dear old Uncle Gikita had been caring for her mother after her father Tyaento was speared.

"Many more moons passed," the aunts continued, "but your mother would not believe that you were dead."

It was Maengamo who reminisced and reconstructed with Mintaka's help all the details of another search for the missing girl.

"Then one day your mother said to your brother Wawae, 'Go look for your sister Dayuma. Go to the foreigners and look until you find some sign or word from her. I must know about my Dayuma.'

"My brother Kimo went with Wawae to look for you—he was just a young boy then. Wawae and Kimo went through the forest until they saw a big trail that the foreigners had cut. Then they saw a foreign man. Kimo was afraid and ran and hid in the trees. Wawae, unafraid at first, began talking to the foreigner. Being afraid of the Auca man, the foreigner cried out and ran, too."

At that point in the story the two aunts and Dayuma laughed heartily.

"But Wawae stayed there and called and called," Maengamo resumed. "Finally the foreigner returned with a gift of a new machete. Wawae took only the workman's own small broken one. He was afraid that Moipa or someone else would kill him to get the other.

"Then Wawae asked the foreigner where you and the others lived on the outside. Where? and where? and where do they live? he kept saying. But the foreigner didn't understand.

"Then several foreigners saw Kimo hiding in the forest, and they were very afraid! But Wawae said, 'He's only a child,' and he called him to come out. Wawae wanted to go with the foreigners, but they only pointed to the trail back into the forest. They wouldn't take Wawae and Kimo with them.

"As they sadly started home, there on the big trail some Quichuas came carrying loads. But when they saw Wawae and Kimo they dropped their loads and ran.

"Wawae and Kimo wanted to see the foreigners' possessions, so they hid in the forest and waited. But two other foreigners came with guns and took all their possessions away. Returning, Wawae and Kimo told your mother that you were surely dead."

As Dayuma heard the story she told her aunts the other side of the incident which she had heard at Hacienda Ila. The Quichuas who had fled were carriers for the Shell Oil Company which was prospecting in the area. They had come out to the settlement on the Curaray, shaken and frightened at the sight of the Aucas whom they had seen on the trail.

"They said they stored all their things in an Auca hut," Dayuma related.

"Yes, the hut was very full," added Maengamo. "And our men said, ' "We must not take anything. There were lots of foreigners and they might shoot us with their guns." For a long time they didn't return and we said perhaps they left things for us. Then they came back and took everything except two axes, foreigners' fire sticks, and machetes, and we said, "Yes, now this is what they left for us" —and we took them.' "

The three Aucas enjoyed the joke as the story of Wawae was matched by the foreigners' side of the tale. Dayuma's laughter soon turned to tears, however, as Maengamo suddenly shifted the scene.

"Poor Wawae! Now he is dead—!" and she recounted how other Aucas, who he thought had come on a friendly visit, speared him in his hut instead.

"Our people fled and then returned to bury him, but they dug up his body and speared him again."

Weeping, Dayuma went to find Rachel.

"What is it, Dayuma?" asked Rachel. "Is it your mother? Is your mother dead?"

"No, she lives"—but the girl continued to weep violently. "It is my big brother—"

"But Dayuma, you already knew that he was dead."

"I know—but they dug up his body—"

"But haven't I told you that it doesn't matter what happens to the body?"

"Yes—I know that—but my big brother didn't know the Lord and his soul didn't go up to God's house in heaven!" Her body heaved with heavy sobs.

Rachel says,

"At that point I wept with her. I dreaded the day when the question about relatives who had never heard would come up—and this was the day. It was an agonizing heart cry of the first one in the Auca tribe to know the Lord."

Rachel was quick to remind the weeping girl that God had spared her mother and others of her family. Perhaps she would be the only one who could safely return to tell those who still lived about the Lord Jesus.

The next day Dayuma heard another installment of her mother's unceasing search for her.

Dayuma's half-brother Minkayi had escaped the spearings which took Wawae's life, and was determined to flee to the outside world. He promised Akawo he would look for Dayuma. For several days he went downriver looking for a place where he had heard many foreigners lived. He finally arrived at their big house where they received him kindly.

Minkayi would go blowgunning in the forest, and bring back meat which he shared with the foreigners. But the foreigners did not reciprocate. One day when they shot a tapir only a small piece was offered to Minkayi. Hungry and very angry, he watched the foreigners consume the meat. Shortly he left and returned to his forest home.

He decided to settle the injustice. Before long the spears were ready, and an armed expedition of reprisal went to the offending foreigners. The Aucas waited for them to come within spearing distance. Soon they heard voices nearby, and saw people moving among the trees. Amid savage shouts of anger the spears flew through the air toward the targets. Minkayi heard a startled scream and a muffled groan. Through the trees he saw two figures fall.

As the spearmen retreated into the forest they heard the buzzing of the foreigners' wood-bee overhead. It came closer, circled over them, and swooped down near the place where the spears had struck. Then the buzzing stopped. The big bee had come down to rest on the very spot! As Minkayi and his companions continued their journey into the forest they heard the loud buzzing again. Had the foreigners' wood-bee, like the buzzard, so quickly discovered the speared victims?

As Dayuma listened she questioned Maengamo and Mintaka further. What rivers had Minkayi followed? Where had he seen the foreigners? How long ago had this happened? As she heard the facts she began to make her own calculations. Yes, it was to the Quichuas at the army post of Villano that Minkayi had come. And she knew about the Indian man and woman who had been speared. So it was Minkayi!

But Dayuma knew something more. It was Rachel's younger brother Nate who flew the foreigners' wood-bee and who happened to be near the spot when the spears struck. And it was her brother who had flown the wounded Quichua woman to Shell Mera with a speartip lodged in her spine.

Dayuma looked thoughtfully into the fire as her aunts continued their long, involved story of a mother's relentless search for a missing daughter . . .

After Minkayi's failure to find Dayuma, there was more discussion around the Auca fires at night out in the isolated forest. Reports concerning foreigners had been unfavorable. They were stingy—and inhospitable. And more than likely the Aucas who had found their way to the outside and never returned were eaten by them. Yes, the outsiders were cannibals after all. Where was Dayuma? There had been no word of her for more than seven years now.

With a sigh Akawo admitted that it must have been so with Dayuma—but with no actual evidence she still wondered.

Akawo's daughter Gimari, who had miraculously escaped death in the big storm before Dayuma left the forest, was of marriageable age. She was maturing rapidly. Akawo planned that she would marry Dyuwi, a strong young man who was a suitable match for her attractive daughter. Oba, Akawo's younger daughter, was still enjoying a carefree, happy girlhood in the forest.

Akawo's young son Nampa, whom Dayuma had thrown clear of falling trees in the storm, was now a young man. He was old enough to know that he was a likely target for the spears of Naenkiwi, Moipa's successor. Naenkiwi had now mastered the technique skillfully used for many years by his teacher. His threats to other Aucas who would not follow his plans of attack generated the same terrifying power unleashed by Moipa. He was widely feared, and hated by many.

Like Moipa, Naenkiwi had taken several wives, to the consternation of the younger men soon to become eligible husbands. He had forcibly abducted his first wife after spearing her father. He had carried off his second young wife, still in early adolescence, from the home of her protesting brother. In a fit of fury he had spear-killed his first wife. Looking for still another he had decided on Gimari.

As soon as Naenkiwi showed interest in her young daughter, Akawo protested. He would not snatch Gimari away! But Naenkiwi had set his heart on the girl, and was not to be refused. The determined suitor had made his plans.

Naenkiwi had arranged a traditional wedding party where he would take Gimari as his bride. At the all-night dance the guests would place him and Gimari together in a hammock, thus signifying they were man and wife.

But Akawo, suddenly realizing what was going to happen at the party, grabbed Gimari by the hand and said, "Let's go"—and they fled into the forest. They built a shelter and stayed there all night. Late the next day they returned to the clearing.

Naenkiwi was furious. He came again for Gimari, sputtering threats to spear Akawo and Nampa if they wouldn't let her marry him. Again they said "No!" and Naenkiwi was really angry.

Meanwhile, Naenkiwi had won Gimari's heart. During the days of conflict she had become blindly infatuated with her persistent lover and wanted to become his wife. He continued to press his claims, now aided by Gimari herself.

There was also other excitement in those days. A foreigners' wood-bee that began to buzz overhead would sometimes swoop low over Akawo's clearing, make loud noises and drop foreigners' things from a vine hanging from its insides. One day as Nampa watched the bee circling overhead he saw a shining object coming down in front of his hut. It was a foreigners' pot, dropped right at his feet. Another day he watched as the vine dropped a strange bundle before him. In it he found a new kind of foreigners' birds, small winged creatures that had never appeared in the forest. He fed them daily, and proudly raised the foreigners' pets.

"If the wood-bee comes again I am going to send a parrot in exchange," said Nampa. Carefully, he wrapped the jungle bird in a housing of bark cloth, and fed it bits of banana. He began counting the days, and when he had used all the fingers on one hand and two on the other, the buzzing bee came again and swooped low over the clearing. He tied the parrot to the long vine hanging from the bee circling overhead. Then up went the big bee with the parrot.

Many times afterward the wood-bee came and dropped good and useful gifts in Nampa's clearing. Surely, thought the Aucas, there were other Aucas up there in the sky, sending down the gifts! "Who but Aucas would give us such nice things?" they reasoned.

And could it be that Dayuma herself—if perchance she lived—was giving good things to her very own family? Perhaps she was trying to say, "I am alive! I remember my mother, and my brothers, and my sisters!"

The possibility stimulated Akawo.

Nampa, too, felt that the wood-bee knew something about his sister Dayuma.

"The next time it flies overhead I am going to climb the vine and go find Dayuma," he announced one day.

"Don't go! You would only be killed," Akawo said. But when the wood-bee came again and dropped its vine, Nampa ran to the bamboo platform he had made for climbing to the bee. Then clutching the vine, he started up toward the circling wood-bee. With a sudden snap the vine broke, and Nampa went tumbling down to the platform in great disappointment.

"Now when will I find Dayuma?" he asked sadly as the foreigners' wood-bee flew off without him.

The visits of the big bee were the talk of the forest. Speculation ran high as the animated Aucas spoke far into the night around the fires. And hope revived in Akawo as she connected the buzzing creature with her long-lost daughter. It had dropped a piece of wood with five nicks carved on it. That was sure proof! Dayuma was sending a message to her family. Umi, Ominia, Wiñaemi, Aepi, and Dayuma must be alive. Perhaps she was saying, "Come! Come to me on the outside!" Old Akawo's imagination soared.

One day as several men from the clearing were hunting in the forest near the Curaray they heard the sound of chopping in the distance. It was like the noise of a big woodpecker hard at work. They followed the sound through the trees, out to the beach by the

Curaray. They crept closer, and peered between the big trunks.

There before their unbelieving eyes they saw the foreigners' wood-bee resting on the sand, and several foreigners chopping wood busily. Shocked by the unusual sight they hurried back to the clearing to share the news. What could it mean? Did the foreigners bring word from Dayuma?

Around the fire that night as the frogs croaked and the crickets chirped, all the Aucas in the clearing talked at once in loud excited tones. A plan was forming in Akawo's mind.

"Why don't you go to the foreigners on the beach and ask them to take you to Dayuma?" she asked Gimari, her eyes bright with excitement. Mintaka would go along with her.

The idea appealed to Gimari. It was a possible escape from her dilemma. She wanted to marry Naenkiwi but not at the cost of her mother and brother's lives.

"Nampa and I will come later," Akawo proposed. "If the foreigners are not angry you call us, and we will go with you."

There was little sleep that night as preparations were made for the trip to the Curaray. At daybreak Gimari and her Aunt Mintaka were on the trail. A short distance through the forest they heard someone coming toward them. It was Naenkiwi who had learned of the plan and was determined that Gimari would not escape. He joined the two women.

As they reached the river's edge they heard the sound of chopping. Curiously, they peered through the trees, and saw that the foreigners had built a small shelter and were still chopping wood.

"Let's cross the river," suggested Gimari. But Naenkiwi hesitated. He wondered if the foreigners had guns.

"I'm going," said Gimari, and with that she was in the water wading toward the sandy beach. Mintaka and Naenkiwi followed.

"Gimari wants to go with you in your wood-bee," said Naenkiwi as he approached the foreigners. "She is Dayuma's sister."

"Take me to my sister Dayuma," pleaded Gimari.

"I want to go too," added Mintaka.

But the foreigners did not understand. They took Naenkiwi alone up in the bee, circled around over Akawo's clearing, and came back to the beach. Still they failed to understand that Gimari wanted to go where Dayuma lived. The hours wore on and the mission was unsuccessful. The sun was sinking below the big trees.

"Dayuma is dead!" Gimari said in sudden disappointment. "That's why they don't want to take me!"

"They have killed and eaten Dayuma and the other Aucas. They will kill you, too," Naenkiwi added, ordering Gimari to leave.

Angry and disheartened, she turned around, waded the river, and started through the forest followed by Naenkiwi. But Mintaka lingered with the foreigners.

As Naenkiwi and Gimari returned on the trail they met Akawo and Nampa, with Dayuma's younger sisters Oba and Ana. They were planning to join Gimari as promised. Their old axes had been thrown away since they were expecting to receive new ones from the foreigners. Naenkiwi, however, gave them a bad report concerning the foreigners.

"They would only kill you," he told them, ordering the little family group to go home. "They tried to kill us."

When Akawo and her children arrived back at the clearing she found everyone preparing to follow her and go with the foreigners. She relayed Naenkiwi's news.

"How do they know that they are bad foreigners?" Maengamo challenged Akawo. "They couldn't understand what the foreigners were saying. They are young. I am older. I will join Mintaka on the Curaray and see for myself!"

Naenkiwi and Gimari arrived at dusk. The village was quiet. All had gone to rest in their hammocks and Gimari slipped quietly into her hut. Naenkiwi was still bent on taking Gimari. Silently, he entered his hut, picked up his spears, and, machete in hand, crept stealthily to Gikita's hut.

His sister Miñimo, who had discovered his plan, followed him secretly. As Naenkiwi lifted his spear to kill first Gikita and then Nampa, Miñimo grabbed him by the throat from behind and started to scream.

"Flee—all of you—run fast!" she called. Gimari's cousin Nimonga sprang quickly to his feet and grabbed Naenkiwi from behind while Gikita held him in front. The other men took his spears and broke them, and stole his machetes.

"Why do you spear?" Nampa shouted angrily. "Why don't you just ask for Gimari and not kill to get her? Now take her and go!"

Akawo objected. "No! you cannot take her!" and she grabbed her daughter.

But Nampa snatched Gimari away and gave her to Naenkiwi.

"Now take her and go to the foreigners and live!"

"I will not go to the foreigners," protested Naenkiwi. "They would only kill us. They have killed Dayuma and the other four girls. They are bad foreigners—and will kill the rest of us Aucas. They beat us and tried to kill us with machetes."

"I am going anyway!" exclaimed Maengamo. She had already made preparations for the trip.

"If you do, I will go myself and kill the foreigners," threatened Naenkiwi.

While the argument continued, Naenkiwi took Gimari and started off through the forest.

"Don't ever come back to us!" Akawo shouted furiously after them.

Naenkiwi's report was discussed by the men in the clearing, who became convinced that the foreigners had killed Dayuma and the other four. They were angry.

"Tomorrow we will go and see for ourselves!" they declared.

But the next morning Mintaka returned and reported on her visit.

"They were good foreigners!" she said enthusiastically. "They laughed a lot!"

"But Naenkiwi said they were bad—they tried to kill you," protested some of her listeners.

"He *lied!*" shouted Mintaka. "They didn't try to kill us—they were good to us!"

But Gimari had agreed with Naenkiwi, and the men were already making spears.

"If we don't kill them they will surely kill us," someone suggested. And all the ill treatment of the tribe at the hand of foreigners was carefully reviewed.

"Yes, they will kill us and eat us," another added.

"There are only five of them now, but more may come. They might kill us all."

The majority decided to stop them before they killed more Aucas.

"Let's make lots of spears fast!" Minkayi urged. The men began working feverishly. By the next morning they were savagely furious.

Maengamo's husband Gikita had made more spears than any of the younger men. Minkayi, Nimonga, Dyuwi, and Kimo had also whittled their own weapons.

"Let's go!" commanded Gikita finally.

Raging and yelling they set off at dawn for the Curaray.

"They spear-killed the five foreigners," Mintaka told Dayuma, "but your mother was very, very sad. They told her they had avenged your death and speared the ones who had killed and eaten you. But your mother still cried and cried.

"Then Minkayi dreamed you were still alive. He said he saw you in his dream."

Maengamo took up the story.

"After that your mother wanted to look for you again. Then one day the foreigners' wood-bee flew over the clearing again. Our men said they had killed its soul, but there it was buzzing again. It began to drop good gifts, and Akawo said you still lived. She went to the middle of the clearing.

"Flinging her arms heavenward like this"—by now Maengamo's arms were waving wildly as she re-enacted Akawo's conversation with the wood-bee—"she cried out to it, 'Where, oh where does my daughter Dayuma live?' As your mother watched, someone in the bee pointed to the west. Your mother said you lived there."

Maengamo paused, and then abruptly announced she was hungry. She blew up the dying fire and started to peel yuca to be cooked in the big black pot. As she and Mintaka busied themselves, Dayuma stared pensively at the fire now springing to life again.

Shocked and stunned by all she had learned in a few days at Limoncocha, Dayuma was facing some hard decisions.

It was just as she had thought. Her own people had killed Rachel's brother. The Aucas had not understood why the foreigners came.

"And my brother Nampa? He did not spear the foreigners?" Dayuma asked.

"No, Nampa did not spear on the Curaray, but after the foreigners were killed he went to the place where they were buried and shouted angrily, 'Why did you kill my sister Dayuma?'"

Then Maengamo reviewed the death of Dayuma's youngest brother, after the spearing of the foreigners.

He had been cruelly crushed by a boa while hunting in the forest. Black and blue and very ill, he lingered for a month. He had been cursed by the downriver Indians, Maengamo said, and finally died a horrible death.

Dayuma was beside herself. She had heard the details of her brother Wawae's murder. But she had expected to see Nampa again. Now he too was dead, she learned.

"If I had returned when I tried to run away from Ila, I would have seen Wawae again," Dayuma sobbed as she repeated the news to Rachel. "And Nampa tried to climb the vine of the wood-bee to find me. If I had returned then . . ."

As she finished weeping out her sadness, Dayuma said with finality, "I am never going back. My father was speared. Wawae was speared. Nampa is dead. Now I will never go back home. I won't teach you any more of my language—"

She poked a few belongings into her *shigra*, a small palm-fiber bag. Her son Sammy stood by, bewildered.

"Come," Dayuma said to him. "We are going."

Rachel watched as they walked down the trail and then off toward the Napo River.

For months Rachel had prayed as successive waves of sadness threatened to overcome the girl. Each blow seemed harder, and Rachel had asked for spiritual stability for Dayuma. Now the shock of hearing of her youngest brother's death, added to the details of the death of Rachel's brother at the hands of her people, was too much for the overwrought girl.

Rachel walked back to the thatched shelter, fighting tears. It was a quiet afternoon in the jungle. The clock ticked loudly. In the sultry stillness she was praying.

"Lord, I thought that Dayuma was the one to reach her tribe, but I have always counted on You. Reach the tribe, Lord, with or *without* Dayuma. . . ."

16

"FOLLOWING HIM, WE WILL GO"

As Rachel prayed, the minutes ticked away. She was facing the future of the Auca work without Dayuma.

Suddenly the stillness was broken as shouts of commotion rose from a jungle trail where Betty Elliot had been walking with Mintaka and Maengamo. Betty came running to Rachel, calling, "What is an *imiñi?* One has bitten Maengamo and she is in hysterics!"

Rachel could not remember what an *imiñi* was—"except that it was bad, and maybe a snake."

There seemed only one thing to do. Rachel started running down the trail through the big trees toward the river, calling to Dayuma, "A snake has bitten Maengamo! Come quickly!"

Dayuma wheeled around and shouted, "Why did you call me when I was running away?" But she quickly went back to see what had happened to Maengamo.

The *imiñi* turned out to be a scorpion which caused Maengamo pain and discomfort, but was not deadly. As Dayuma and her two aunts discussed the scorpion sting and sought remedies for it, they began to reminisce about various kinds of stings and bites in their clearing in the forest, and what was done for them.

During Maengamo's recuperation Dayuma forgot about running away as the three Aucas talked of returning to their forest home. For weeks they had watched the kapok tree down by the lake and already the big round pods were beginning to burst. Maengamo had told her family that if all went well and the foreigners did not kill her and Mintaka, they would return at the blooming of the kapok. The time had come for the homeward trek.

Dayuma, shaken by all the family tragedies, was not sure she wanted to go back to a home without father or brothers to welcome her. She wept for them occasionally. But one day she came to Rachel with a smile and tearless eyes.

"Now I have finished crying for my brothers." She began to talk about the trip into the forest with her aunts.

"If you don't return with us my brother will be furious," Mintaka had told Dayuma. Gikita had wanted Mintaka to go with the five foreigners on the Curaray and bring back a report from the outside world. Now after years of searching for Dayuma they would face certain death merely to report having seen her. They could not return to her family without her.

But Dayuma continued to wonder about many things. After an absence of nearly twelve years would her own people accept her, or regard her as a foreigner? What would they think of her clothes? Should she go all the way in to her family clearing? Would they let her return again to the outside world?

When the future of the Auca work had seemed very nebulous to Rachel several months earlier in Sulphur Springs, she shared some of her desires and questions with Dr. Richard Pittman, Wycliffe's Deputy Director. The steps leading back to Ecuador were clear, but how was she to enter the tribe?

"You do not have to know now," had been his calm reply. "When the cloud lifts, you follow."

The reminder of the cloud that had led the children of Israel through the howling wilderness strengthened Rachel's confidence in God's leading. Now, when Dayuma needed encouragement, Rachel told her the story of God's guidance by the lifted cloud.

The lesson of Christ as Shepherd of His sheep was also pertinent, but purely theoretical for Indians who had never known sheep and their habits. As a timely providence a mountain sheep was taken to Limoncocha by the United States Air Mission as a decoy for jaguar hunting and left in Dayuma's care. Rachel used it to illustrate otherwise obscure verses of Scripture. The sheep became attached to Dayuma and learned to recognize and follow her voice. It would not go ahead of her on the jungle trails, nor would it drink from the swift streams. One night it fell into a pit from which it could not extricate itself. When Dayuma passed near, it heard her voice and bleated. She climbed down into the pit and rescued it.

"When he putteth forth his own sheep he goeth before" was a Bible truth illustrated by the unusual provision of the sheep at the Base. "Following Him, we will go" became the Auca version of obeying the Good Shepherd.

As the time drew near for the three Aucas to leave Limoncocha for the Curaray trail, Rachel reminded Dayuma that she would soon be on her own with the Good Shepherd; she would need to recognize His voice, and follow Him. She reviewed the Bible lesson in preparation for the first missionary journey into the Auca tribe.

Eventually the little party set off on the trail leading away from Arajuno, heavy-laden with food for the trip, gifts for their families, and three "foreigners' pups."

As the three Auca women disappeared on the jungle trail, a missionary standing by remarked, "I wonder if we'll ever see them again?" Rachel recalls that as she said good-by to Dayuma she was confident of seeing her again, but that she didn't know whether it would be in two weeks or two years.

Rachel wrote praying friends on September 2, the day they left,

"Dayuma has a deep desire to teach her people God's Word, to see her family again, and to try to bring harmony within the tribe and with the outside world. On the other hand, she knows full well the darkness she is entering.

"By the time this letter reaches you, with God's blessing, all three may be back once again in what is left of the village where Nate started making gift-drops. Need I tell you that my heart has gone with her, and that I encouraged her to stay and teach her people without hurrying back if all goes well? Need I remind you that she is still a babe in Christ, and that the whole responsibility of introducing her people to the Lord Jesus rests with her? Pray for us as we continue our part in language study that will lead to a translation of His Word. Need I describe the darkness of heart and mind of a people who fear only what will happen to a dead body, but have no thought of what will happen to a living soul? Need I ask you to stand with Dayuma and me in prevailing prayer?

"Before they left, both Mintaka and Maengamo had begun to pray to the God in heaven as Dayuma taught them. Shall we not take this as a cloud the size of a man's hand and trust for the showers to come? . . .

"I am now so thankful He led me to give top priority to teaching Dayuma, for 'faith cometh by hearing, and hearing by the Word of God. . . .' "

A week later Rachel wrote to friends,

"I have had no word since they left, but it is the prayer of my heart that the Lord will demonstrate the power of His Word through this tribe which has been so publicized. The savagery has not been exaggerated—if anything, it has not yet been told. . . .

"All that I have been able to teach Dayuma of His Word she has committed to memory. Will you pray that the Lord Himself will protect the truths of it. I have been grateful to hear her retell Bible stories with great accuracy as I have listened to her teaching

Mintaka and Maengamo. Will you pray that she will be Spirit-led and kept free from the seething hatreds of the tribe."

Rachel also wrote her parents that there was no word from the Aucas. "No news may well be good news—and we walk by faith, not by sight."

A letter written by Dr. Edman from Wheaton College on September 12, 1958, breathed a contagious spirit of faith and hope:

"On every hand there is much intercession for Dayuma as she returns to her people. The principalities and powers of darkness will know in advance that the Holy Spirit is coming near, and there can be the same kind of opposition to her as the disciples experienced in the storm while crossing over to the shore of the Gadarenes. However, the Master of tempest brought them safely through; and on the morrow the demonized man was fully delivered. We trust for those who long have been in bondage to the evil one.

"How wonderful to know that our Lord's eyes 'run to and fro throughout the whole earth, to show himself strong in the behalf of them whose heart is perfect toward him.' He can give Dayuma understanding far beyond all the gracious and helpful instruction she has received, so as to make plain and pertinent the way of salvation. We trust there will be the same response as given by Chief Tariri years ago in Peru."

During Dayuma's absence, Rachel took Sammy along to the Cofan jungle tribe to visit Mr. and Mrs. Bub Borman, Wycliffe translators. Rachel stayed with Mrs. Borman and her small son at the isolated station while her husband and another translator made a survey trip on jungle rivers in search of other tribes needing Bible translation.

The Cofanes lived in the opposite direction from the Aucas and their customs were different. They wore the long loose-flowing *cushma* common to several jungle tribes of Ecuador and Peru. Instead of round balsa earplugs characteristic of the Aucas, the Cofan men plucked brilliant marigolds for their smaller earholes, or put a feather ornament through the hole in their nose.

While in the Cofan tribe Rachel stood by on the radio set twice a day for news that Dayuma might have come back out of the forest. But the weeks wore on, and there was no word. Anxiety mounted. Rumors were abroad that Dayuma had been killed, inasmuch as she was not spotted from the air. Rachel heard nothing of these rumors until she received cards of condolence from friends in the United States.

Then after almost a month the joyous radio message reached Rachel. Dayuma and several companions were in Arajuno. The same morning a Wycliffe plane was on its way from Limoncocha to pick up Rachel and Sammy and take them to Dayuma.

On October 3 Rachel wrote her parents,

"You have probably heard by now that Dayuma, along with Mintaka and Maengamo, plus one of Naenkiwi's wives and baby, three girls and two boys arrived in Arajuno last Thursday. Marj happened to be here, and she and Betty met them as they came in. Dayuma was in the lead singing 'Jesus loves me, this I know'—in *English!* By the time I got here she was pretty keyed up, and it has taken me a while to get the picture in focus. She brought an invitation for Betty and me to return with them, and has given orders about building a house for us.

"I had not heard anything definite about her for twenty-seven days, and had promised to fly over at the full moon if we could arrange it. My confident trust was put in the Lord. By full moon I was reunited with Dayuma. She just told me tonight about her trip in. . . ."

Dayuma, grown unaccustomed to forest trails, had become very weary and footsore as she traveled back to her old home. Her feet became swollen and thorn-pricked.

The three women took the old Shell Oil trail, thus by-passing the Quichua Indian village and building their own shelter the first night. The second day they traveled through the forest on the Auca side of the Curaray, a trail being cut as they went. But after hours of toil they found themselves at their starting point. They had lost their way and were chopping a wide circular trail.

At sunset they stopped by a small jungle stream. "Here there used to be lots and lots of fish," Dayuma remembered, so Mintaka and Maengamo took their nets and went fishing. Dayuma was delegated to build the shelter. Quickly, she cut off the leaves of the low yarina palm and hastily constructed a tiny shelter. She also built a ground-fire. Exhausted, she could do no more. By the time Mintaka and Maengamo returned with a mess of fish, thunder was roaring and lightning was flashing, and they were suddenly aware of a huge storm front of dark clouds moving downriver toward them. Maengamo took one look at the lightly-constructed shelter and offered to chop down a tipa palm for protection from the storm that was certain to come. By now it was late and getting dark, and Dayuma protested.

"Let's just ask the Lord to keep it from raining on us," she said. Maengamo and Mintaka assented, Dayuma prayed, and all three watched as the big black clouds retreated upriver.

The next day they continued through the trailless jungle. On one of the beaches they saw a huge jaguar lying in the sun, but it woke up and disappeared into the cane patch before they had time to be concerned. By evening Dayuma felt she could go no farther.

Tired and hungry, she began to talk to the Lord as Rachel had taught her.

"Shall we stay here?" Dayuma asked Him.

"Yes," came the answer.

As Dayuma took her bearings and talked with her aunts she realized this was the spot on the Tiwaeno River where she had lived as a young girl. The jungle had reclaimed the clearing when the family migrated.

"What shall we eat?" was the next question Dayuma put to the Lord. The yuca drink they had brought with them was long since exhausted. As if in answer to her plea, Maengamo remembered that years before when they lived on the Tiwaeno they had a sweet-potato patch growing on one of the beaches. They hurried upriver and found enough sweet potatoes to make a refreshing and satisfying drink.

The women cleared weeds and chopped jungle growth. They killed a big snake, and also saw the footprints of an oversized jaguar. They wondered whether they should stay temporarily on the Tiwaeno, or press on toward the family clearing. As darkness fell and they prayed and talked together, Maengamo decided she would leave at dawn and go to tell Akawo and the family that Dayuma was back in the forest. Mintaka would wait with Dayuma.

In the morning, after Maengamo's departure, Dayuma prayed. She asked the Lord, "What shall we eat?"

"Fish," came the answer.

So Dayuma and Mintaka made spears from cane that grew by the river and went spear-fishing, using the old jungle method. In a short time Dayuma had speared ten big fish.

By sunset of the second day, when Maengamo had not returned, Mintaka became apprehensive and said, "Let's flee back to the foreigners." Dayuma objected. If Maengamo did not return they must follow her footsteps in the morning to see what had happened to her.

It was now almost dark, and keen disappointment overwhelmed

Dayuma. For hours she had been looking downriver, listening for the tread of bare feet on the forest trail.

Had her mother died while Maengamo and Mintaka were on the outside? Or did Akawo not want to see her daughter after all? Perhaps by this time she was resigned that Dayuma and her aunts had been killed and consequently moved back downriver, deep into the jungle.

She thought of the bright shiny pair of foreigners' scissors she had brought for her mother to replace the sharp shells which Aucas used for cutting—and the big axhead. She was almost sorry now that she had carried it over the trail—it was so heavy. Perhaps her mother would never use it.

As the last patches of daylight fell on the trail by the rushing stream, Dayuma picked up the three pups she had carried in from the outside as a gift for her mother. She was sure her mother would be pleased. The Aucas had never had any dogs! She then walked down the beach for a last look around the bend before dark.

Suddenly the pups began to bark in quick shrill yips, straining to give a grown-up warning of an approaching noise. Dayuma's heart almost stood still as she listened. She heard voices, and then the thump, thump, thump of feet on the nearby beach. Was it Maengamo? And who was with her—Akawo? In the dim light Dayuma saw a bronze body round the bend. Could it be . . . ?

"Dayuma!"

She leaped with joy at the familiar voice of her mother.

"I thought my daughter had died long, long ago—and now I see you alive!" Akawo's voice broke.

Dayuma swallowed hard. "I thought you had died long ago, Mother!" she blurted out. For a moment she was awkwardly conscious of her clothes. And now she was much taller than her mother.

"I brought these foreigners' pups for you, Mother," she continued in a steadier voice.

Akawo chuckled with delight and reached out to take the little dogs, still yapping importantly. She lavished on them all the affection she felt for Dayuma.

It was quite dark when Kimo and his wife Dawa arrived. Maengamo and Minkayi found their way to the fire soon afterward. Everyone was laughing and talking excitedly as Mintaka flopped the smoked fish on the banana leaves spread on the ground by the fire. A hungry, happy family fell to devouring the delicious meat.

"The others will come tomorrow," Akawo said.

"Will my sister Gimari come?" Dayuma asked.

"Yes, she will come with your Uncle Gikita."

Dayuma was relieved. Maengamo had told her at Limoncocha that Gimari's husband, the terrible Naenkiwi, was brutally speared and buried alive. Akawo had been willing for Gimari to return to the family circle, but her sister Oba refused to have her. Oba had married Dyuwi whom Akawo originally selected as Gimari's husband before she ran away with Naenkiwi. Thus Oba feared the wiles of her sister. Gimari had gone to live with her mother-in-law Dyiko, who was related by marriage to Uncle Gikita. Dayuma was happy that Gimari would be coming with Gikita, for she was eager to see her.

"Gikita didn't want to come," laughed Maengamo, "but I told him that the foreigners would kill him if he didn't—so he will be here tomorrow."

Everyone laughed except Dayuma. Why didn't her Uncle Gikita want to come to see her? Did he think she had become a foreigner?

The next day others of Dayuma's family group continued to arrive on the Tiwaeno. Maengamo had sent word to all the Aucas surrounding the big clearing that Dayuma was back. Within a few days more than fifty grown-ups and children of the family group had hurried over the trail to see her. With Uncle Gikita and his family came Gimari carrying baby Bai in his bark sling. When the little boy saw Dayuma he began to scream. He was frightened by her clothes. Her hair style marked her as a stranger, too. Oba and Dyuwi came with their baby girl Adyibae who also cried in terror at the sight of Dayuma. This greeting was most humiliating for a fond aunt eager to see her nephew and niece. Dayuma's little sister Ana, born after she had fled the forest, was very shy at first. Very quickly, however, she accepted Dayuma into the family circle. Before many days had passed Dayuma was exercising the privileges of a big sister by spanking Ana with nettles for being lazy.

Akawo took over the family cooking in her big clay pot, as she had many years ago, only now it was little Ana who brought the water from the jungle stream instead of Dayuma.

Dayuma ate her fill of the delicious jungle food for the first time in many years. Minkayi had brought her "lots of monkeys," and her mother the big mess of fish promised upon Dayuma's return.

Tiny palm-thatched huts were hastily constructed close to one another as the Aucas cut back the jungle growth and hung hammocks around the log fires on the ground. Foreigners were a favorite topic of conversation as they retired in their hammocks at night. Dayuma's family had dozens of questions about them.

"We were afraid. We thought the foreigners would kill us and eat us," said some of the Aucas who inquired what they were really like.

"And that is just what the foreigners think about you!" laughed Dayuma.

Gradually the family group began to talk about the five foreigners whom they had speared on the Curaray.

"I was very sad when those foreigners were killed," said Dabu, who had not been present when the men of the clearing went to spear. "I cried when I heard about it. Later I went to the beach and cut down the big tree in which they had built their house. I felled it across the beach so that no more foreigners would come in and be killed."

As Dayuma told her people the other side of the story they said sadly, "Not understanding, we did not do well."

They still had questions about foreigners, however. A short time before Dayuma's return a foreign explorer had gone into their territory.

"Whenever we came near he tried to shoot us," they said. "After five days he became afraid. He killed himself with his own gun. Then we speared his body and burned the house he had occupied. His body rotted but the buzzards did not eat him. He was surely a devil."

Dayuma's people wondered what foreigners they could trust, and she assured them that "the ones who bring you gifts in the plane are good foreigners." She told of many good outsiders she had known and with whom she lived, and of their land far away where she had visited. For hours each night as they lay in their hammocks, warming their bare feet over the dying embers, Dayuma entertained them with stories of the many giant wood-bees in which she had flown. Her hands were constantly in motion as she described her long trip from Hacienda Ila to Quito in the Captain's little wood-bee, then the long, long flight over the big water in a huge one. She even told her people how the skeleton and skin of the wood-bees were created. She spoke of her trip to New York where she saw a mammoth canoe carrying many wood-bees on its back. All in all, her knowledge of the flying creatures impressed those who had seen them only high overhead.

Her family wanted to know what foreigners ate, and what kind of houses they lived in. Dayuma confessed she had often missed the meat of the forest, for foreigners did not have much meat.

They ate many other things, but even if she ate a lot she was still hungry for meat. She told them of the big houses where many foreigners lived together. Instead of walking on trails they sat down in "wood-bees that go on the ground" and went very fast. There were so many of these in big trails in the foreigners' land that one had to watch or he would be killed by them.

Many of the foreigners that Dayuma had known "carved" on paper most of the time. Why did they do that? the Aucas wanted to know. Dayuma explained that they were carving God's words for other people, like the Aucas, who had never heard about the true God. She then told them of what she had learned from God's carving. But her stories about heaven were more fantastic than those of the United States. Her mother and sisters laughed and said, "Why do you talk like that, Dayuma?" Everyone laughed derisively—except two. Old Mima listened carefully, and asked questions about God. Young Dawa, who had been captured from downriver after Dayuma left the forest, was eager to know more. She had become Kimo's wife and was now a part of Dayuma's family group.

As Dayuma told her people what she had seen and learned in almost a dozen years in the outside world they, in turn, told her all that had transpired since that fateful day when Moipa speared her father Tyaento.

Dayuma watched Gimari care for her baby Bai. She thought of Naenkiwi, Gimari's husband. When he had finally met his end, little Bai would have been thrown into his father's grave alive had not Gimari grabbed him and fled. And there was old Dyiko, Gimari's mother-in-law, who had come with her daughter Nombo and her children to see Dayuma. Nombo's husband Gaba had been speared by mistake by Naenkiwi a short time before his own death. Indeed many sad things had happened.

As the fires on the Tiwaeno burned low in the deep night and the Aucas slumbered in their hammocks, Dayuma lay awake and gazed at the same bright stars she had watched as a little girl. The rushing water sang nearby, accompanied by the loud chirping of crickets and the call of the forest night birds. The howling and chattering of many kinds of monkeys swelled the jungle jargon, sweet music to one long nostalgic for the sounds of home. And as she listened Dayuma reviewed what she had been hearing each day from the lips of old Uncle Gikita, and her mother Akawo, and all her relatives who had suffered and survived the many spearings since she left the forest of death. It all had a familiar ring. She closed her eyes and thought back to the days following her father's death . . .

When Dayuma left home Naenkiwi was a young boy living in Tyaento's hut with his mother Dyiko and his sisters Nombo and Omaenkiri, both of whom Gaba had taken for wives. Gaba had been born downriver, but as a small child was deserted by his father Awañita and brought upriver by his mother and raised with Dayuma's family. Naenkiwi's sister Miñimo was married to Akawo's brother Wamoñi and lived in another hut. After Tyaento was speared by Moipa, Naenkiwi fled to the forest with his mother and sisters. For months they wandered in the woods eating berries and palm nuts. Finally, when they returned to their clearing in the hope that Moipa had gone back to his own hut, they found instead that he had moved into their quarters and was appropriating all the food from their fields. In desperation Dyiko decided to go to Moipa and throw herself on his mercy. She would plead relationship with Moipa's household. She sent her children back into the forest with the instruction that they should flee if Moipa speared her. Moipa and his brother Itaeka were not home when

Dyiko arrived but their wives received her. She then summoned her children.

Gaba also came with Dyiko's family. However, when the men returned at sunset Moipa recognized Gaba as a member of Tyaento's group and moved to spear him. But Tamaya, Itaeka's wife, objected.

"Don't spear Gaba—he is my relative! If you spear him you will spear me!" Tamaya was Dyiko's younger sister. Moipa spared Gaba, who was permitted to live as one of the family group. Dyiko's son Naenkiwi was also accepted as one of Moipa's family. It had been through his association with Moipa and his aptitude for spearing that Naenkiwi was selected and trained by Moipa to be his successor.

Moipa and Itaeka had not settled their score with Tyaento's group. They soon made another attack on Akawo's family, spearing her sisters Wiwa and Wiika. Wiwa was the young aunt who had been Dayuma's favorite playmate during her happy childhood days in the forest. As Wiwa lay mortally wounded, she asked to be buried alive. When the grave was dug she climbed into it herself, clutched her arms around her knees, bowed her head and closed her eyes.

"Now I will sleep," she said, as they covered her over with strips of bamboo and tamped the dirt firmly above her.

Wiika also was suffering so acutely from spear wounds that she asked to be choked. Several refused, but Maengamo, moved by her agony, said, "I will do it." Thus Wiika joined her sister Wiwa in death.

Omaena, a cousin of Wiwa and Wiika whom Moipa also tried to spear at the same time, escaped and fled far downriver with his family.

Dayuma's brother Wawae and her uncle Wamoñi, bent upon

avenging Tyaento's death, were goaded by the added provocation of Wiwa and Wiika's deaths and the fact that their relative Omaena had barely escaped with his life. Wawae and Wamoñi started off on the trail through the forest, determined to kill Moipa and his brother Itaeka.

As they left the clearing Wamoñi's wife Miñimo called to them, "Don't kill my brother Naenkiwi, or my mother Dyiko, or my sisters!" She knew that the lives of all her family were in danger as part of Moipa's household.

When Wawae and Wamoñi arrived at Moipa's clearing they learned that Moipa and Itaeka and Gaba were off on a raid on their borders to kill foreigners. "Then let's kill their women—they killed our women," Wawae ordered. As they entered the hut with their spears the women and children fled and only Tamaya and her little child were killed. However, Naenkiwi, his mother Dyiko, and his sisters Omaenkiri and Nombo were all taken back to Dayuma's family group.

Wawae and Wamoñi cut a wide trail through the forest to make it appear that they had joined the foreigners, and a counterattack was averted. But Wawae knew that sooner or later Moipa would seek revenge. Wamoñi and he therefore moved the family group far downriver, out of reach of Moipa's spears.

When Moipa and Itaeka and Gaba returned from their raid on the outside, Itaeka found the rotting bodies of his favorite wife Tamaya and his child. Grief-stricken and angry, he tore through the hut and threw away beads and other foreigners' loot which he had brought home for Tamaya. Then he fled far downriver. Moipa found his wives hiding in the forest. Gaba discovered that his wives Nombo and Omaenkiri and his children had been taken captive by the attackers. Moipa, in the belief that the foreigners had joined forces with Wawae and Wamoñi, gathered the remaining group together and also fled far downriver with Gaba.

Meanwhile, Omaena and his group, who had previously fled, were discovered by the downriver Aucas and accepted without being speared. Omaena reviewed Moipa's killings and misdeeds and advised them to kill him, should he come downriver.

Finally, after several years of roaming the forest downriver, Moipa's group was located by the downriver Aucas, who had also found Wawae's group. A plan was devised to kill Moipa's group. Moipa, Itaeka, and Gaba were invited to join them at a party. Moipa, enthusiastic about the invitation, told Itaeka, "We will make an alliance with them and wipe out Wawae and Wamoñi and Tyaento's crowd." But Itaeka had seen Omaena in the forest and was afraid. Nevertheless, Moipa insisted they accept.

Feigning friendliness, the downriver Indians welcomed Moipa, Itaeka, and Gaba, and offered yuca drink to their guests. Awañita was among the downriver hosts intent on killing Moipa and Itaeka. When he heard the name Gaba he was certain this must be his own son whom he had not seen since a child. At a given signal, after the drinks were offered, the deceptive hosts fell upon their prey and started to spear.

"Don't kill Gaba!" Awañita shrieked. "He is my son!"

Gaba was spared, but Itaeka was hit on the knees with a heavy wooden club so he couldn't flee and then was speared. As Moipa was speared he tried to flee but was finally killed in the forest. Later, his skull, painted with the red coloring from the achiote fruit, was hung up on a pole before his wives' eyes. This was what Moipa had done with Miñimo's first husband Warikamo's skull.

After Moipa and Itaeka died, their wives were taken by the downriver Indians. One day one of the wives broke a large pot belonging to their captors. In anger the downriver group then killed all the wives.

After wiping out Moipa's family, except for his sister and her husband Tuwa, who escaped, they set off to kill the other upriver group. They found Wawae and his relatives in the forest, and started spearing. Wawae and Wamoñi soon fell, and the attackers began capturing the women. Nombo was one of the first to be taken.

In the fracas Nombo's two little girls Onae and Wato were separated from their mother. She called in vain for her children. Minkayi rescued Onae.

"They will only kill you," he said to the child. "Come with us." Onae's four-year-old sister Wato was lost in the forest.

When Gaba heard later that Nombo was taken to become a wife, he protested, saying, "But she is my wife. Give her back to me." She was released to her husband.

With the spearing of Wawae and Wamoñi the straggling survivors of Dayuma's family fled into the forest and were finally reunited. Akawo had escaped with her children, Gimari carrying little half-sister Ana on her back. Oba and Nampa had run into the forest with Wamoñi's daughter Ipa. Gikita, Mintaka, and Maengamo had also fled.

Gikita, determined to avenge the death of his nephew Wawae and his brother Wamoñi, called the men of the group together and instructed them. They were young—Naenkiwi, Kimo, Dabu, Nimonga, and Dyuwi—but eager to do their utmost in retaliation. Soon they started downriver and arrived at the clearing of their enemies. They fell upon one household, killing several members including a man and his wife, and taking captive their pretty young daughter Dawa.

The raid on the whole was unsuccessful owing to the inexperience of the spearers. Gikita was the oldest seasoned killer of the group. He decided to take his band back upriver and wait until they were more mature and able to do a thorough job downriver. Thus it was that Gikita and his relatives began their long trek through the forest upriver to their former location.

A young downriver mother, Miñi, with her small son Toña had escaped death and capture when Gikita speared. But her family were furious because she, a woman, escaped while her brother had been killed, and they threatened to spear her themselves. Terrified, she took young Toña by the hand and fled into the forest in the hope of joining the foreigners.

After almost a month of wandering, she saw footprints. To whom did they belong—the foreigners whom she sought or the killers of her brother? Whoever they were, they had food. She had seen where they cut the palm nuts and she and Toña were hungry and desperate. She must throw herself on their mercy. "If they kill me don't flee," she said to Toña as she left him in the forest. "They won't kill you. They will feed you." And she followed the footprints to the huts and entered the small clearing.

They were Aucas—the ones who had killed her brother! As Miñi approached Gikita's band, Naenkiwi lifted his spear to kill her. Dyiko protested, and they argued about whether or not to spear her. Weak with hunger, Miñi trembled with fright.

"I'll ask Gikita," Naenkiwi said finally.

Gikita's answer was "Let her live"—and Miñi and her son Toña joined his household.

As Gikita's group migrated back upriver they wondered what had happened to little Wato, younger sister of Onae who was now traveling with them. Then they discovered banana peelings and half-eaten fruit strewn along the forest. The trail led them to Wato who had been wandering alone in the forest for more than a month. She was thin and hungry, and most of her hair had fallen out. Like a frightened little animal, she clung to Maengamo as she joined Gikita's group.

Not all the children at the mercy of the virgin forest were as fortunate as Wato, who had been spared death by poisonous snake or hungry beast. When they lived downriver, Bibanga, a young girl in Gikita's group, was seized by a huge boa at the edge of the river. Before the others knew what was happening the reptile was thrashing the victim around in a thicket of brambles. No one dared get near enough to rescue her. She was mangled and crushed as her horrified family watched helplessly. Then the boa tried to swallow Bibanga, but failed because it could not disentangle her from the barbed thorns. Eventually the limp and broken body was freed from the thorns and buried.

Meanwhile, the revenge spearings continued downriver. The Aucas decided to kill Omaena and his family, who were originally from the upriver group. After killing them, the downriver group was torn by feuding and divided into two factions. Awañita heard that he was to be killed, and fled upriver with his wife Mima. Gaba and Nombo went still further to Fish River. Awañita's daughter Boika and her husband Monga had settled in the forest closer to the downriver huts.

While on their way to kill Awañita, the men from downriver attacked the hut where Boika and her brother Kipa lived. They killed Kipa and his wife, then pounced upon Boika and her husband Monga to kill them. One of the men grabbed Boika by the hair. She wrenched herself from his grasp and escaped, but not without leaving much of her hair in the hands of her attacker. Monga savagely bit the hand of the man who clutched him and thus freed himself. He was wounded by a spear in the back, but fled into the forest, in the opposite direction from Boika. Boika, with her small child on her back, ran through the forest as fast as she could to warn her father Awañita that his enemies were coming to spear him. In the darkness she lost her way.

Finally, Boika found a deserted hut where she decided to spend the night. As she entered she nearly tripped over something on the ground. She paused—and heard loud snoring. The party of killers en route to spear her father were also spending the night there!

She froze. Then the baby in her bark sling started to cry and she nearly choked the child to muffle her. Boika slipped out quietly and continued running through the dark forest.

By early dawn she had found the trail and arrived at Awañita's hut. "Flee!" she called out. "They are coming to kill you! They have killed my brother Kipa!"

As Awañita and his family fled through the forest they heard the downriver group approaching their clearing. They eventually reached the hut of Gaba and Nombo on Fish River, only to find they had gone downriver. Awañita pursued the pair until he could overtake them and sound the warning.

Another of Awañita's sons, infuriated that his older brother Kipa had been killed, tried unsuccessfully to find the enemy. He went to Kipa's hut where he learned that his brother had been brutally chopped up and that the survivors buried him. One of his fingers was still lying on the ground. Then as Awañita's son retraced his steps upriver, he was joined by Monga, who had been hiding out in the forest. The two men traveled together, and eventually caught up with the remainder of the family. They decided to search for the upriver group and throw themselves on their mercy, pleading the relationship of Mima to Akawo and Nombo to Naenkiwi.

Gaba and Nombo with their relatives built little shelters and slept in the forest in groups of twos and threes. It was the first night's sleep they had dared to take in many days.

After Gikita and his family group arrived back upriver, they had settled into their former routine of life. The only variation had been the months of excitement when the foreigners' wood-bee swooped low and dropped valuable gifts for the Aucas. And there had been the trip to the Curaray when the five foreigners were killed.

Dabu had married Miñi, and his brother Kimo took the captured Dawa for his wife. Naenkiwi had married several wives, but only Dyuwi's sister Ipa, taken against her brother's wishes, and Gimari, were living. Naenkiwi had speared one wife and had threatened to spear Gimari. When her baby Bai was a small infant, Gimari lay trembling and weeping in her hammock as Naenkiwi held the spear over her.

After Wamoñi's death Minkayi had taken his widow Miñimo. Three boys had been born to them. Then Miñimo became very ill. As she lay dying she lifted her hand in a final burst of energy, pointed downriver and said with a glassy-eyed stare, "I see them—the downriver people—they are coming to spear us—over there!" Minkayi buried his wife, and then gathered his forces for an attack on the approaching enemy. He did not question the prophetic warning of his dying wife.

Naenkiwi and several others of the family group joined Minkayi and went in search of the downriver people. Kimo alone refused to go. He had misgivings about spearing again. The second night they found hastily-constructed shelters along the dark trail. This was surely the group that Miñimo had envisioned. Shouts of fury pierced the night air as Naenkiwi and Minkayi, aided by Gikita and the others, began to spear. Screams of terror rose as some of the victims escaped, while others were pinned to the ground. At dawn the killers returned to see whom they had speared. Some of the survivors, certain that the attack had come from the downriver pursuers, also crept back to the spot to see who of their group had been killed.

To Naenkiwi's horror, he discovered his spears in the body of Gaba, his sister Nombo's husband. He saw Boika returning and lifted his spear to kill her. She called out to Gikita, her relative, for protection. Gikita, after learning she was Mima's daughter, told Naenkiwi not to spear her.

"Where is your husband Monga?" Gikita asked.

Weeping, Boika pointed to the forest where her husband was hiding. Gikita called out to Monga that he and Boika could come to live in his clearing.

Naenkiwi, very sad because he had killed his brother-in-law, returned to his clearing with Gikita and the others, joined now by Boika and Monga.

Later the same day Nombo, who had also survived the attack, went back to the place of spearing. She dug a grave and buried her husband Gaba, her father-in-law Awañita, and her own little child. Then she and her mother-in-law Mima, with other members of the family, wandered through the forest. One day Nombo discovered footprints along the beach. She recognized them as her brother Naenkiwi's. Her own brother had been in the group that speared her husband Gaba!

There were other footprints with Naenkiwi's, going now in the opposite direction. They were Monga and Boika's. Nombo turned to her children and said, "Let's go to your grandmother Dyiko's hut. Maybe she can tell us something about your sisters Onae and Wato." Mima and the others protested. They would all be killed. But Nombo took courage in that Monga and Boika had not been speared. Perhaps they too would not be killed. And she must find out about her two little girls, lost for years. It was worth a try. Finally her relatives consented to go and they began their journey.

As they neared Dyiko's hut Nombo approached the clearing alone and called to her. The old mother welcomed her daughter, then, after asking about other members of the family, summoned them to come from the forest. Nombo, in turn, asked about Onae and Wato: had they been seen? She learned that Minkayi had long since taken Onae to the outside where foreigners carried her off. But there was Wato, a grown girl now, peering shyly around a big tree at her mother Nombo.

Gikita welcomed Nombo into the clearing. He told her of the search for Wato, and of how they had found her with no hair after following her trail. Nombo was also happy to find her sister Omaenkiri, now Gikita's wife.

Naenkiwi, back in Gikita's group, was causing considerable friction. He could not forget that Nampa had never forgiven him for snatching away his sister Gimari. When Nampa had died of the boa's injuries, his family took consolation in the fact that Naenkiwi could not spear him as he had planned. But now Naenkiwi had threatened to spear Gimari. Dyuwi was angry at him for having taken his sister Ipa. The counts against Naenkiwi were mounting up. And the spearing of his brother-in-law Gaba had not helped matters. Naenkiwi, however, was brazen and fearless. He bragged he would kill them all.

His first victims would be Gikita and Kimo—and one day he lay in wait for them. But they returned to the clearing by another trail, although they were completely unaware of Naenkiwi's designs, and thus cheated him of his prey. Dyuwi and Nimonga had, however, discovered his plan and decided they must kill him first. At night they went to Naenkiwi's hut, and, upon finding him outside with Gimari, attacked him.

"What is that I see like a spear in front of me?" Naenkiwi shrieked.

Dyuwi and Nimonga speared him, but he tore himself loose and fled with two spears protruding from his body. Dyuwi, sure of his victim, left. But Nimonga waited nearby to see if Naenkiwi had really died. In the morning the mortally-wounded man returned and said he was dying. At his request, his own mother Dyiko and Gimari's aunt Gami dug the grave.

As Naenkiwi crawled into it he demanded that his children be thrown in with him. Gami tossed Ipa's and his little three-year-old girl into the grave, but Ipa fled with baby Tamaenta at her breast.

His other wife, Gimari, fled with baby Bai in the opposite direction.

While the bamboo slats and the dirt were laid on Naenkiwi and his daughter, Nimonga railed at him, "Why did you steal Ipa? Why did you take Gimari? Why did you kill Gaba? Why did you try to kill Gikita and Kimo?"

The earth was packed down hard. Nimonga waited until he heard no sounds. Then he returned to his own clearing.

Little Bai and Tamaenta toddled by the Tiwaeno. Dayuma was glad they had been spared. She knew, however, that unless they were taught about the Lord of love, they too would grow up to spear and be speared, to avenge and be avenged.

Around the fires on the Tiwaeno, Dayuma heard more unpleasant news. Gikita and the other men, now grown to maturity and seasoned in spearing, had readied the spears for another trip downriver. It was time to settle accounts with those who had killed Wawae and Wamoñi.

She pleaded with Uncle Gikita not to go, and prayed to God he would take her suggestion. Wawae and Wamoñi were dead. What good would it do now to kill those who had speared them so many years ago? The God she had come to tell them about wanted them to forgive their enemies and not spear in exchange.

Kimo quickly agreed. He was tired of spearings.

And as Dayuma's family settled in and built more shelters on the banks of the Tiwaeno, Uncle Gikita talked less and less of his trip downriver, and the spears were set aside.

17

HOME ON THE TIWAENO

WITHIN a few weeks Dayuma's people on the banks of the Tiwaeno had reviewed for her a twelve-year history of the Aucas, upriver and down. There had been a steady succession of spearings since she left, an uninterrupted march of unnatural, premature death. None of Dayuma's grandparents was living now, even though her mother Akawo was not very old. Her uncle Gikita, much younger than her mother, was the oldest man of the vanishing group.

But for Dayuma, the picture was different because she had changed. She was not the same Dayuma who had left the forest with hate and revenge. From the day Rachel had first communicated in faltering Auca the words of God's carving, life had taken on new meaning. For over a year Dayuma had been with foreigners like Rachel who "lived well" because they obeyed God. She had visited in their land far away where people did not spear one another. Could this ever come to pass here in her forest where people lived, apparently, to spear one another? Only God's carving could make a difference. It was God who had uprooted hate and planted love in her heart. She had found herself praying even for Moipa's surviving relatives, that they would hear of the true God. Months before in Sulphur Springs she had also begun to pray for those once hated enemies, the downriver Indians.

A plane flying low over the Tiwaeno reminded Dayuma that Rachel and Betty would be wondering what had happened to her. She was hidden by the big trees and the plane had not seen her.

They might think that her people had killed her. It was almost one full moon since she had said good-by to them at Arajuno.

As she talked with her aunts Mintaka and Maengamo about the return trip to the outside, Dayuma also talked to God about one matter very important to her. Upon her arrival in the tribe she had found Maruja, the Quichua girl captured by the Aucas, whose husband had been speared by them the year before when her aunts had gone to the outside. Maruja was living in Uncle Gikita's home. It was too late to help Maruja's husband but Dayuma was eager to return the captured girl to her mother Jacinta, who had been so kind in nursing Dayuma back to life.

Would Uncle Gikita release Maruja? Dayuma was troubled. One day she decided to make her request. Uncle Gikita thought a few moments and Dayuma tried to read his face. To her intense relief he said yes, Maruja could go back to her family.

Dayuma was grateful for something else as she planned her trip to Arajuno: the word from her people that Rachel and Betty would be welcome to hang their hammocks in the shelters being built for them overlooking the Tiwaeno.

Nights of wordy discussion around the flickering fire preceded the return trip to the foreigners' world. Who would go with Dayuma? It was plain that none of the men was interested. In spite of the good reports about outsiders they were unprepared to go. Kimo remembered the Quichuas' guns when he and Dawa had gone to the Oglán village with Mintaka and Maengamo the year before. However, the two venturesome aunts, nothing daunted, were ready for another trip. Mintaka's young son Gingata would go with his mother. Wato, now almost grown to maturity, was eager for the trip, as well as her companion Ñaeno of nearly equal age. Ipa, Naenkiwi's young widow, would go carrying her baby Tamaenta. Ipa's young brother Kinta joined the party. Gimari said that baby Bai was too big and fat to carry that distance over the trail. She would wait on the Tiwaeno for Dayuma to return with the foreign women. Mima's daughter Gakamo, the youngest girl of the travelers, would go along in spite of her mother's illness.

Dayuma was happy that Uncle Gikita did not change his mind about Maruja. As the Quichua girl left Tiwaeno with the group of Aucas, she wore clothes which Dayuma had given her. Mintaka and Maengamo also started out with the clothing they had brought from the outside world. It never occurred to the others that clothes were worn on such occasions.

The women and children, chattering delightedly and chuckling with excitement, were soon out of sight of the clearing and splashed with glee as they crossed the small stream. Happy children of the forest, they were in high spirits as they bounded lithely over the wooded trails toward Tapir River. Then another hilarious dip in the refreshing water—and with a yodel known only to Aucas they were off through the forest toward Grape Tree River. Dayuma and her aunts were gay leaders on the familiar trail as they climbed up hill and down the jungle valleys, clambering sure-footedly over fallen logs and through thorny tangles and slashing with their machetes when the trail was otherwise impassable.

After sleeping one night in the jungle, the Indian travelers finally arrived at the Quichua village on the Oglán River. There was animated discussion in the Quichua huts that night when Maruja rejoined her amazed family.

The party next followed the old Shell Oil trail, and finally emerged at Arajuno on September 25. With her usual exuberance Dayuma was singing happily when Betty Elliot and Marj Saint spotted her leading the little brood down the airstrip toward the mission houses.

It seemed a long time to Dayuma before Rachel and Sammy flew in from the Cofan tribe with Captain Griffin in the Helioplane. The young Aucas of the party were impressed with the foreigners' wood-bee about which they had heard so much. Veteran air-traveler Dayuma proudly showed them the inside and explained its operation.

There was hardly time in Arajuno to tell Rachel all she had learned during the month with her people. However, Dayuma reported some very important news. Two of the group who had come to welcome her on the Tiwaeno had not laughed when she told them about God's carving. All the others—including her mother and sisters—had laughed and said, "Why do you talk like that, Dayuma?" But two, old Mima and young Dawa, both women from downriver, had listened well. The night before Dayuma had left, Dawa said, "Now you are going. Tell me again about God's Son so that I won't forget while you are gone." Dayuma did so, and urged her to teach others while she was away. Old Mima had listened again, and had asked questions about Jesus.

Rachel says,

"Dayuma thanked the Lord over and over again as we prayed together that her people let her come back out, and that they invited Betty and me to go in with her."

When Dayuma had gone into the forest with her aunts, the germs of foreigners' colds traveled with them. With no natural resistance, a number of the Aucas had fallen sick with heavy colds. Mima and Akawo were among those most gravely affected. Dayuma was concerned about her mother's condition. But she thought too of Rachel and Betty waiting on the outside for news from the forest and therefore had decided to leave.

In Arajuno she told Rachel of Akawo's illness, and of her desire to return quickly. "Don't let my mother die before we go back into the forest," she prayed.

The group, augmented now by Rachel and Betty with her four-year-old daughter Valerie, prepared for the trip to the Tiwaeno.

The Auca members of the party needed little time for planning a return. The foreigners' things—clothes and cooking utensils—given them at Arajuno were ready for transport. But for several days Rachel and Betty pondered and pared their provisions down to a minimum load to be carried over jungle trails. It was a historic expedition that set out from Arajuno on October 6. For three of the members—Rachel, Betty, and Valerie—it would be an unprecedented experience. The Aucas were now wearing clothes, the gifts of Dr. and Mrs. Tidmarsh, missionaries in charge of the Arajuno station who for many months had participated in the gift-drops after the five men were killed at Palm Beach. The Indian women and girls proudly carried shiny new foreigners' pots, and one of the Quichuas bore a special burden, a little blonde girl, Valerie Elliot.

The cargo included equipment for two-way radio contact, lifeline to the outside world. However, Rachel and Betty relied more heavily on the volume of prayer ascending around the world for the outcome of the venture. Concerned friends kept their radios tuned or watched the incoming mail for news of the unique missionary journey prefaced by widespread intercession for safety and success.

The travelers said farewell to a small group of missionaries and Quichua Christians as they walked to the end of the airstrip. There Dayuma gathered her party together and prayed in Auca, asking God to go with them on the trip and protect them from snakebites and jaguars on the trail. She prayed earnestly that her people back in the forest would receive the two white women well. Then they disappeared on the trail that soon merged into the tall grasslands beyond.

For several hours they followed the fairly level, narrow, but solid road that had been paved with stones by the Shell Company for its trucks. It was the trail originally traveled by gold prospectors and rubber men, but long since fallen into disuse as enterprises one by one had been forced to retreat from Auca territory. A good distance down the trail they found a lonely abandoned dump truck which for years had been rusting in isolation. Dayuma explained the phenomenon to Indians who had never seen a "woodbee that goes on the ground."

After hiking through open forest that showed signs of former clearings the travelers crossed the Dayono River, halfway between Arajuno and the Oglán. The river had been named for Dyuwi's grandmother Dayo who fished downriver with *barbasco* poison. One day while fishing she had been bitten by a snake. She was pregnant at the time and had returned home in great pain. The child that was born prematurely soon died, and shortly thereafter, the mother. All the Aucas knew the course of the Dayono River which flowed from that point on the trail deep into Auca country, and were now reminded of their family history. Here also the Aucas reviewed an attack upon explorers who used this water gateway to venture into the forbidden land.

Without changing pace, the Aucas crossed the river in water well above their knees, followed by the Quichua carriers and the foreigners. As they left the more level land surrounding Arajuno they ducked under branches of big trees and climbed over fallen logs across the trail. At times they waded through shallow swamps on felled trees to keep from sinking into the rich mud. There were scenic views down deep valleys where the racing stream below tossed up billows of white foam. Occasionally they heard bird songs, the celestial flutelike call of the *wiiwa* bird, or the squawk of a flamboyant macaw as it screeched overhead. They crossed deep ravines with tall jungle trees rising majestically. At the halfway mark the group reached the winding course of the Oglán.

They picked their way through the huge rocks of the riverbed and continued on the trail now leading through steep and hilly forest.

In spite of the exotic beauty of the trail Rachel began to tire. "Just two more big hills and one little one," Dayuma encouraged. "It won't be long now."

By late afternoon the weary travelers finally spotted the planted fields of the Quichuas high above the village on the banks of the Curaray.

After a welcome night's sleep on the ground of an Indian hut and with a replenished supply of yuca and bananas some of the Tiwaeno-bound party set out down the Curaray in two small dugout canoes. The others took to the trail that followed the river or crossed it here and there. Dayuma accompanied Rachel and Betty and Valerie in the heavy-laden dugout canoes. She was tense with her new responsibility but happy that this day had finally come. The polers skillfully guided the canoes over occasional rapids and were soon rhythmically shifting their weight from the back to the forward foot. On one side of the river a sheer rock wall dropped down to the water. Overhanging trees or logs that had been carried downstream by strong current had to be carefully avoided, particularly by the poler in forward position whose job it was to steer the course. They poled the heavy canoes in the current's full flow, although at times the passengers were soaked to the skin as they rode through splashing rapids. The jungle sun soon dried them out, however.

After passing the series of rapids on the Curaray the party traveled downriver to the mouth of the Oglán, marked by several large sandbars and wide sandy beaches. Dayuma pointed pensively to a small shaded spot on the bank where her husband and baby boy were buried. She reminded Rachel that there she herself had had a battle with death.

Sharp Indian eyes were ever alert for birds or animals that might appear at the edge of the forest bordering the beaches. Occasionally a wild turkey or other game would be sighted and shot with the guns which the Quichuas had brought along.

The Aucas who had gone on foot were often visible through the trees, and could be seen wading along the beaches or gayly swimming to the opposite shore. The clothes with which they proudly started from Arajuno had long since been set aside as the unhampered Indians once again enjoyed the freedom of the open forest. At mid-morning everyone stopped on a beach for nourishment. Balls of yuca dough were unwrapped from banana leaves, mixed with river water in gourd bowls, and consumed by the thirsty group.

The travelers were aware that they were penetrating deeper into Auca territory. "Let your long hair down," Dayuma advised Rachel. "Then if the other Aucas attack they will know you are a woman. Our people always spear the men first." The Quichuas frequently checked the guns lying in ready position near each poler.

They soon pushed on down the spacious, spreading Curaray toward the mouth of Grape Tree River. Along the beaches were occasional abandoned shelters built by Quichua fishermen. Rustic platforms for smoking fish were falling unused in the sand. For months now the river had been practically deserted for fear of the Aucas. By four o'clock in the afternoon the canoes were anchored to the navigators' poles that were firmly planted in the solid sandy bank by the river. Experienced Indians fell immediately to constructing lean-to shelters on the beach, with stalks of wild cane to support roofs made of the long arching leaves. A few well-aimed strokes of machetes and the encampment was ready. Driftwood bleached in the jungle sun made a roaring fire. And by dark the canny hunters were back with birds and small game to be roasted and eaten before the campers retired in the shelters surrounding the glowing coals. Quichuas and Aucas, who in years past had attacked and counterattacked, communicated with smiles and gestures, and shared their meat as they ate on the sandy beach.

Early next morning the dugouts headed up Grape Tree River, a smaller stream pushing its way through crowded jungle. Poling was slower as they bucked the current in the narrow channels, and occasionally it was necessary to chop a way through trees that had fallen over the stream. Often the party would get out and walk the beaches while the polers pulled the heavy-laden canoes over the shallow rapids. Branches of fragrant flowering trees arched gracefully across the rushing stream, or beautifully colored jungle birds would dart in front of the canoe or dip across the water in their happy flight.

The Aucas were irresistibly drawn to quiet waters at the bends of the river where fish abounded. The young boys were now carrying long thin chonta spears as they waded into the deeper waters, eyes alert for fish, and encouraged by the others. Ipa and Maengamo stood by and called to Kinta as they sighted the fish, and Mintaka was spurring her young son Gingata on to action. The younger girls flanked the fishermen to catch the fish as they were tossed over. Dayuma suppressed her desire to fish and stayed in the canoe with the foreigners.

The journey upriver was a memorable one for Rachel as Dayuma reminded her of tribal incidents recalled by the familiar jungle landmarks. And with every stroke of the polers Rachel was aware that she was coming close to the fulfillment of a hope that had been deferred for many years.

"There is the beach where Moipa attacked the gold hunters," Dayuma said. The men had crossed over to the Tiwaeno, stolen the Aucas' yuca and cooking bananas, and returned to camp on the Grape Tree River. But they were volleyed with spears in the night, and had abandoned the camp in the darkness. The next morning Moipa and his men had helped themselves to the foreigners' possessions. This was the world once ruled by Moipa's spears.

At the mouth of the Tapir River the Quichua polers hesitated, looked to Dayuma for direction, then guided their dugouts up the smaller river. By the unwritten law known only to forest men, they were well aware that this was the river marking the point beyond which foreigners never dared to go.

The Tapir River was now fringed with exquisite palms of many varieties and stately bamboo bending with the breeze. The swift water that became shallower as they approached the end of their canoe trip forced them to stop and laboriously chop a passage through a huge fallen log. After tying the dugout canoes high on the beach with strong jungle vines, the Quichuas adjusted their packs once more and followed the Aucas and the foreigners on the tiny stream leading off to the forest trail.

Maengamo took the lead in search for the almost invisible trail and cut the overhanging branches as she went. This was virgin forest, and the animal trails to the water holes were more clearly marked than those of man. All followed slowly up the steep hills and across the narrow ridge.

Dayuma pointed out a cross path known to the Aucas as Moipa's trail. They were on the homestretch.

"We are almost there," said Dayuma as she heard the stream playing over the rocks around the bend. She was unable to suppress her excitement. She chuckled contentedly while she pointed out the old sweet-potato patch that her father had planted years ago, and the site of the old yuca field. The trail entered the Tiwaeno and followed the crystal-clear stream.

"That is where Gimari was born," she said as they left the river and climbed the bank.

She led the way over the trail on the bank around the bend of the stream. Trees overhung the path to the clearing and a wild cane patch curtained the huts from view. Then the trail entered the Tiwaeno again and after following the stream they came to the Auca huts nestled in a new small clearing cut out of high forest.

Rachel recalls,

"It surely was a sweet picture to me to round the bend and see the buff roofs of the little thatched huts—and the lovely copper-colored bodies gleaming in the sun!"

Kimo rose serenely to welcome the party and stood watching, arms folded, as they filed up the trail. He seemed like a handsome statue as the afternoon sun played on his well-developed muscles. A pleased expression betrayed his curiosity. His young wife Dawa smiled a welcome as the foreign women approached her. Gimari, holding her baby, laughed shyly and spoke to Dayuma as the travelers gathered in the clearing.

Rachel's first letter to her parents from the Tiwaeno clearing was written in the late afternoon of October 8 and taken out by the returning Quichua carriers. In it she said,

"The welcome could not have been more friendly. You'd think these bronze girls were debutantes entertaining, and that this happened every day. They are really charmers. Kimo's wife has no children yet. Gimari has a darling fat baby, Bai, who is another of Naenkiwi's children.

"The little huts are so low I can hardly get into them. . . . It seems the most natural thing in the world to me to be here, a thing I felt the Lord was leading me to over five years ago. Do pray that this situation will be workable and will accomplish the Lord's purposes. . . .

"Kimo's wife Dawa is from the downriver group. Although the natural situation would never take her back to them, I pray that she may be one of the contacts that will lead them to Him, too. It is a larger group than this one, and they speak the same language."

Kimo with his wife Dawa and Dayuma's sister Gimari were the only ones on the Tiwaeno clearing when Dayuma returned with the foreign women. Kimo proudly showed them the big shelter he was constructing.

"All alone I built it," he said with a boyish smile. It had been slow work to fell trees and haul them in alone. The shelter was not finished, but Kimo had fulfilled Dayuma's parting instructions.

"Where are the others?" asked Dayuma.

Kimo said they had returned downriver for a new supply of food, but that he had stayed behind to wait for the foreigners he hoped would come.

He did not add the fact that the other relatives had left in fear. As they faced the possibility of outsiders entering their land they had become apprehensive and returned to their former clearing.

18

"WHAT IS HIS NAME?"

THE almost deserted Tiwaeno clearing had come to life with the return of the Aucas accompanied by the foreigners. From the cluster of thatched huts the young boys, trailing their long fishing spears behind them, hurried off to spear-fish upriver. Maengamo hung her hammock, and was off across the river to bring back yuca for her family. The younger girls went to the stream with their clay pots for water. Ipa, shadowed by her tiny son Tamaenta, went to the forest to bring firewood.

Young Gakamo did not seem to know what to do with herself. As soon as she had arrived on the clearing, Dawa informed her of her mother Mima's death caused by the foreigners' colds. She had been buried downriver. Dayuma, too, felt her loss, since Mima had listened eagerly to the stories of God's Son.

Betty with her little daughter and her few possessions moved into the empty shelter adjoining Maengamo's hut. Dayuma decided to sleep with the young girls in their hut nearby, and Maengamo offered Rachel three long pieces of bamboo to make a bed on the ground beneath her palm-thatched roof. There were no corners for privacy until the curtains of night were automatically drawn. On the other hand, the jungle moon was clearly visible, enhanced by its reflection in the swift waters of the Tiwaeno which played melodiously on the rocks. It was a sociable life, and the Aucas were a gregarious people. Huts were close enough to permit hammock-to-hammock conversation.

At dawn the day after the arrival of Dayuma and her friends, Kimo took the forest trail to the old family clearing to spread the tidings. He had seen the foreign women for himself and wanted to persuade the others to return to the Tiwaeno.

Rachel and Betty spent the day becoming acquainted with their Indian family. Rachel noted in her diary, "Dawa is a real charmer. She looks like an Oriental princess—graceful, smiling and well-poised. Gimari looks older than her Palm Beach pictures, but she still has those beautiful long dark lashes framing shiny black eyes. As I sat on the log beside the girls you would have thought this happened every day. . . . They would be perfectly at home in the White House, I'm sure, and just as socially acceptable with a bit of clothing on."

Dayuma had warned Rachel that the speech of her people in the forest would be fast, and difficult for a foreigner to follow. Communication on a simple conversational level was possible, however.

"Dayuma lived at my house," Rachel said to Gimari as they sat sunning themselves on the balsa log. "She is like my little sister. Now we are happy to be here."

Gimari was a pitiable figure on the buoyant Tiwaeno scene. No longer was she the winsome Indian maiden who had gone to the Curaray to see the foreigners. Disillusioned and listless, she lived alone with Bai in a tiny dark hut which she had thatched down to the ground and which sufficed for her hammock and fire. Only necessities for herself or her son drew her out of gloomy seclusion. Rachel watched for opportunities to chat with Gimari.

"Kimo left this morning to go downriver," she told Rachel in a conversation inside her hut.

"Where is your mother Akawo?"

"She is downriver. Perhaps she will come . . ."

Ordinarily, one day was required over the trail to arrive at the family clearing downstream. However, at sunset of the day Kimo left there was a shout on the Tiwaeno, "They are coming!" With Dayuma in the lead, everyone ran to the riverbank. Among the Auca girls there had been speculative questions: Would Akawo come? Would she be wearing the dress that Dayuma had given her when she first came in from the outside? She will put it on when she reaches the river, just before coming here, they concluded. Their prediction was right. Dayuma's mother Akawo was the first to arrive—and there were unmistakable signs that the wrinkled dress, wadded in a ball as the old mother fairly flew over the trail to Dayuma, had just been put on. And she was carrying the three pups.

Again Rachel noted,

"Dear old Akawo was trembling from sheer joy and excitement. Her wrinkled face has a permanent smile—and she talks constantly, as though we understand every word. How I wish that my mother could have seen her joy! She was older than I had expected her to be—but evidently a character and a personality in her own right."

Her delight at Dayuma's return with the foreigners was transparent, and Rachel did not "expect to see any greater joy on that old wrinkled face until the day she knows Christ as her Savior."

Akawo was immediately at home in the new clearing. She soon hung her hammock and reclined in it as she stirred the boiling pot on the fire within easy reach. She chattered contentedly with Rachel.

"You are Nimu. You came down from the sky. You must call me Mother." Akawo was pleased that her little girl's name had been given to Rachel by Dayuma.

The old mother quickly laid aside the outsiders' dress. Her only apparel was the costume jewelry Dayuma had brought her. Rachel later described her as "having no eyebrows left (the custom is to pluck them out entirely), and, wearing big splashy bracelets on bare arms and with her neck wrapped in strings of huge beads, Akawo looked the part of a bored society dame."

Although Akawo had heard Dayuma tell of God's carving, and of how His Son came to earth, this new information brought little response. Her life continued almost as it had through the years. But as Rachel and Betty became a part of the Auca settlement, visiting and conversing with the women was a daily routine. After a few days with Akawo Rachel wrote,

"Yesterday I saw the first glimmer of light on Akawo's circumscribed horizon. I went over to visit and sat in one hammock while she, sitting in her own hammock, fed the dogs, parrots, and smaller birds, and cooked the dried corn on her little ground-fire. Peeling the scorched husks down, she gripped the ears of corn with her toes, broke off the parched kernels and ate them. We talked about common, everyday things—ancestors and spearings and the birds in the sky. Presently she looked up to the blue sky towering with white clouds and asked, 'Does God owuka—stay in His hammock—away up there in the sky?' Well, as far as I am concerned, she may think of His throne as a hammock. It is certainly the functional equivalent in this culture. We all live in them—cook, work, play, rest, speak, or what have you. Why not think of hammocks in the house God is thatching for them up there? But God's furnishings will surpass either the hammock or overstuffed furniture and Oriental rugs."

Dayuma's younger sister Oba and her husband Dyuwi soon followed Akawo, with their baby girl Adyibae. "Oba has all the charm of the other girls," Rachel observed, "the same gracious smile and poise." Dyuwi had all but lost his life when the foreigners had attacked the Aucas. A big gunshot scar was visible on his back.

Young Monga made an overnight visit. He was not as openly friendly as the others and kept eying the guns of the Quichua carriers who were still there when he came. He was "pale and pathetic-looking" and ill-at-ease. Very early in conversation with Rachel and Betty he pointed out his spear wounds received down-river when his brother-in-law Kipa had been killed. He made it plain that he had not gone along when the Aucas speared the five foreigners.

Uncle Gikita arrived next with his young boys Komi and Koni. Jolly and good-natured, Gikita talked to the foreign women with a snaggle-toothed grin. Although not aged he was the patriarch of the group. Out of curiosity he had come to see the visitors Dayuma had brought.

Dayuma's half-brother Minkayi and his wife Ompora arrived a few days later. Rachel observed that "Minkayi is an extrovert. He is lanky and broad-shouldered. Friendly, he smiles most of the time.

"He made *pogantas*—crowns of palm fiber—and woven arm bands for us. I put them on and did a few of their galloping dance steps until Gimari just about collapsed laughing. I told Minkayi I wanted lightning bugs for the arm bands. Afterward he said that when he went home he would catch a lot of toucan birds and make feather head bands for Betty and me."

Nimonga came later with his wife Wiña, and her mother Gami. He was short and stocky and his "dark and foreboding" expression was accentuated by the black *huito* dye which he had smeared on his face. Even the talk about his sister Wiñaemi and his sister-in-law Umi—both of whom still lived at the hacienda—did not seem to soften his evident dislike of the newcomers. However, old Gami, Dayuma's aunt, listened eagerly to news of her long-lost daughter, and her eyes filled with tears. She showed the foreigners the spear wounds she had received downriver when Wawae and Wamoñi were killed. It seemed natural for Auca conversation to center on spearings and scars.

The shelters on the Tiwaeno were ideal for observing Auca life and for hearing the language day and night. Without walls, they were actually no more than corner posts and a ridge-pole supporting a palm-thatched roof.

Lessons in language and anthropology continued without interruption even after dark, as described by Rachel in a letter entitled "Night Life among the Aucas":

"At dark everyone turns in—unless there is a pot of monkey meat on the fire, or bright moonlight, or rain that blows in the wall-less huts. Long-legged Uncle Gikita stretches out crosswise in his hammock, his huge bare feet hanging over the fire, sometimes pulling his little boy in on top of him. Little Tyaemae lies on her stomach in her hammock swung on the other side of the fire and I can see her dainty little feet, toes down, in the lighted smoke of the fire. Maengamo burned her hammock before she went to the foreigners' houses last year, so she plunks down on another side of the fire on an old piece of a dugout canoe. Her teen-age son swings his hammock high between the next two posts and curls his growing legs up. That leaves me to put down the bamboo boards, blow up an air mattress, hang a mosquito net, and enjoy both a blanket and the fire. Someone keeps the fire whipped up most of the night.

"When Dabu, Kimo's brother, came to visit, he slept on a piece of canoe under one of the hammocks. His long tousled hair was not a foot and a half from mine. At 4:30 A.M. I had a nightmare and screamed loud enough for Dayuma to hear me in her nearby shelter.

" 'Nimu—Nimu!' she called, but the moans continued. 'Rachel!' she switched to English and woke me—and everyone else.

"Dabu sat bolt upright and said, 'Nimu, what is your name?'

" 'My mother calls me Rachel,' I said. From that moment on Dabu and his sister Maengamo carried on an animated conversation about the foreigners' houses.

"Another night the dogs barked at 10 P.M. I awoke just in time to hear Gikita say, 'Jaguar!' and in no seconds flat he sprang to his feet from the horizontal position in the hammock as if he were a jaguar himself.

"One night when the pups began to bark Maengamo decided that the downriver group had come to attack. She hurried out to a big log and for fifteen minutes called out to the unseen foe: 'You all watch out! Don't spear us! The foreigners are with us here. We are learning about God and we want to live well.'

"Under the reciprocal law of the Aucas these groups have accounts to settle. This, too, is an effective device of Satan for wiping out a heathen tribe before it ever hears of a Savior. Recently the downriver group did come looking for these Aucas, but their search was in vain though they came close to the old village where some of Dayuma's relatives still live. Our faith reaches out to the downriver group (a few of whom live with us here), but even Dayuma does not see how this dreaded foe could be reached for the Lord.

"Dayuma's dear old mother through the years has seen the spearkilling of her father, two sisters, a brother, husband, son, daughter, son-in-law, plus many other relatives. 'Sin when it is finished bringeth forth death.' It has brought much death here. Practically all of the men and some of the boys who live here on this clearing have taken part in spearings. And all—men, women, and children—have felt the effects of sin and its pattern which were slowly wiping out this primitive tribe. May the standard of God 'whose we are and whom we serve' be raised against it."

Long after Rachel and Betty would retire for the night, Dayuma often talked around the glowing log fires with her people. Sometimes, however, there were interruptions in a night's slumber.

Rachel states,

"One night after I was sound asleep I was awakened by Dayuma: 'Nimu! Minkayi says he wants to believe in the Lord!' Blessed interruption to a night's sleep. She had been talking to him at her mother's blazing fire as they swung in their hammocks. 'I told him Jesus is coming again someday and he must be ready to go with Him.'

" 'Fine,' I said. 'Now you must teach him more about who Jesus is.'

" 'I did—I told him how He was born, how He lived, how He died, and how He was raised again . . .' Thank God for this open heart.

"Back to sleep. Came the soft pattering of bare feet.

" 'Nimu!' and a proffered gift of monkey meat from Ompora. Another blessed interruption, an acceptable sign of friendship and interest. Minkayi had killed the monkey with his blowgun.

"Asleep again—and called once again.

" 'Nimu!' I sat up and without a word Nimonga's wife Wiña handed me a cooked monkey leg, hairs half burned off, skin and toenails on! Without a word I took it and thanked the Lord for this further sign of friendship on the part of one who had seemed so unfriendly.

"The night's sleep was further interrupted when Maengamo sat up in the dark (as she often does) and began to sing the strong nasal chants of the tribe. Nor do I fully understand the motives and emotions that prompt them—anything from war cries to pretty little songs about the birds. Someday there will be songs of praises to the living God rising as a sweet savour to Him during the long hours of the night. . . .

"They say the very best way to learn a language with the proper intonation is to hear it subconsciously, even when one is doing something else. This night life ought to do something for me. I rejoice at the opportunity to hear the Auca language the last thing at night, the first thing in the morning, and many hours in between. . . .

"There is a rhythm and melody to this language that Dayuma has lost through the years outside the tribe. One of my favorite sports is trying to imitate it, which sends Dayuma's sisters into gales of laughter. Nothing ventured nothing gained!"

As the foreigners settled in to Auca living they learned to eat, as well as speak, with the forest people. "The more men there are here, the better the food supply," wrote Rachel. Monkeys and birds were blowgunned in quantity when several men were on the clearing, and fish were speared in the river. Some fish were hand-caught in the nearby streams by women and children. Sometimes Rachel and Betty were invited by the Aucas to go hunting wild hogs or other animals in the forest.

One day Gikita's son Kimo came back to the clearing and announced that he had killed an *amunga* monkey carrying its young. But alas, the prize had fallen into the hollow center of a high tree. He was recruiting help to fell the tree and extract the monkey. Dayuma invited Rachel to join the fun. Soon the group of young hunters along with Dayuma and Rachel were off to the forest. Wato, the young girl of the expedition, carried embers for making smoke to ward off the swarms of insects that were sure to attack unprotected bodies.

When they arrived at the tree where the monkey had fallen the boys surveyed the situation first and chopped down several smaller trees to make a clearing through which the huge tree could fall to the ground. The young Indians took turns with the ax, and finally the giant of the forest crashed to the ground and the woodsmen retrieved the monkey. To their delight they found two porcupines inhabiting the same hollow trunk. Although the attempt to smoke them out failed, the effort was great sport. Swarms of bees molested the party but Wato and Dayuma drove most of them off with their smudge. They found the beehive in a small tree nearby. After the search for the porcupines was abandoned, the small tree was felled, the bees smoked out, and honey enjoyed by all.

On another occasion the lively Tiwaeno young folk went to the forest for a honey-feast. They felled a big *wipita* tree which held a huge hive. When the tree hit the ground the enthusiastic Aucas dug into the honey with their hands, scooped up the exotic jungle nectar and, licking their fingers and smacking loudly, consumed as much as they could of the sticky delicacy.

When the Indians had eaten their fill they dipped gourd bowls into the honey to be carried home for the older folks and children. They also chipped off pieces of the colorful *wipita* wood to make medicine for foot itch or to be used for extracting dark red dye for fishing nets and hammocks. The heart of the fresh-hewn tree was a glowing deep rose color.

For the foreigners, living with the forest folk was a liberal education in adaptation to one's environment. The ingenious tribespeople fully exploited the forest not only for food but for many other useful commodities. Supplies from cultivated crops still came from the former clearing. Bananas and yuca were brought by the women and girls over the rugged trail in heavy-laden baskets resting against their backs and supported by bark tumplines across their foreheads. Crops were well under way on the Tiwaeno, however, and as the forest was cleared more yuca was planted.

From time to time there were special gifts of food from members of the family desirous of expressing their satisfaction with the new settlers. Rachel wrote of Dabu's return trip to the Tiwaeno several weeks after his first visit,

"Dabu, tall and broad-chested, arrived last night with a gift for his cousin Dayuma, a huge basketful of smoked wild hog which he had carried all day over a rough and steep trail. Dabu lives further away than any of Dayuma's relatives. He had been to visit us only once before. From the first he seemed impressed with the fact that we had come to tell the Aucas about God. The MAF plane was due to make a supply flight so Dabu decided to stay over a day and see it again. It has been three years now since he first saw that little yellow plane piloted by Nate. . . .

"Toña, a young Auca lad from downriver, came with Dabu. This was his second visit. How well I remember the first one. His young face, with the thin and handsome straighter features of the downriver group, had been filled with sadness, seriousness, and downright fear of us. He had sat down on a log and refused to come near.

"This time he evidently set aside his fears, and went all out to see what the foreigners were like. All morning he watched us write, cook, and swim, and he listened to us trying to talk his language. He said nothing until he could contain himself no longer, then he threw back his head, laughed heartily, and said something about me. I simply could not understand.

" 'What did you say, Toña?' I said. 'I just don't *hear*.'

"With that he repeated something, laughing uproariously, which made it still harder to understand. But I was determined. I came closer and asked him to tell me slowly. Then all the Aucas went into gales of laughter. I finally gave up, wrote what I had caught of it in my notebook, and found out later what he had said. Then it was my turn to laugh.

" 'Nimu, if you just had your hair cut in bangs over your ears you would be able to *hear* us!' had been Toña's comment.

"Traditional hair style here (cut with sharp clam shells) for men and women, young and old alike, calls for bangs halfway around the head to a point behind the ears. This makes a pretty frame for the balsa ear plugs, leaving the ears free to *hear* the Auca language clearly. But it will take a lot more than an Auca haircut to enable me to understand all I hear in this Auca clearing."

As Dayuma readapted quickly to the forest she took her place clearing weeds for crops, planting yuca, bringing firewood, or spearing fish. Consequently "there is no such thing as regular hours for either study or teaching," Rachel wrote. "It just doesn't work out that way. As for teaching her the Word, or reviewing with her a lesson for the coming Sunday, I just have to take whatever opportunities that come, when the others have gone off to fish or swim and she is more or less alone." Although Dayuma did gather her people together on Sunday mornings for a very informal time of instruction in God's carving, most of her teaching was offhand and unscheduled. Rachel tells of such a "lesson" when Dabu was visiting:

"Early in the morning after Dabu's sister Maengamo and some of the others had gone off to clear the forest for planting, Dayuma began to tell Dabu about God's Son Jesus. We were all sitting around the ground-fire on 'pews' made of old split canoes. I watched Dabu as he sat shaving darts for his blowgun, scarcely ever looking up at Dayuma. Was he listening? It was hard to tell. I noted the ways Dayuma sought to make the story clear.

" 'The foreigners were watching their "pets" at night—"pets," something like deer,' she began, trying to describe sheep for an Auca who had never seen one. Then she went on telling him of the birth of Jesus:

" 'Those watching their pets said, "Let's go fast to see." Then they came to a tiny thatched hut where Joseph and Mary were—'

" 'Was He already born?' interrupted Dabu. How well he had been following every word! Dayuma finished her story with a brief résumé of Jesus' life, death, and resurrection.

"In conclusion she said to her cousin, 'Now, Dabu, you teach this same thing to your children.'

" 'I shall teach my children,' Dabu replied."

Dayuma was grateful that her people were listening well to her now, without laughing, as they had at first. Gradually they began to understand why the five foreign men had come to the Curaray, and now the two foreign women with Dayuma.

"Not understanding, we killed your men," some said, and others added, "Now we will hear from God." Each week Dayuma gathered her little brood under a thatched roof and taught them God's carving. Although, according to Rachel, most of the members of the congregation came in their "birthday clothes," some of them wore "furs"—live pet monkeys wrapped around their necks or squirrels perched on their heads.

"First Dayuma instructs them not to laugh, then she teaches them little by little about God, the Creator, and His Son Jesus. In telling of Jairus' daughter the other day she explained, 'When someone dies in the foreigners' houses, they cry. They don't laugh as the Aucas do'—and then she proceeded with the story. As she prays she asks the Lord to throw out the witch doctors and the devils. Tyaenyae, the mother of Wiñaemi, the youngest Auca girl still living at the hacienda, is known as a witch doctor here. (She hasn't come to see us yet.) Whenever someone is sick they say she has bewitched that person, and threaten to spear her if he dies."

On October 12 Rachel noted a meeting typical of those early gatherings in the clearing:

"Today I had the joy of hearing Dayuma teach God's Word to all the Aucas on the Tiwaeno clearing. Nimonga sent little Ana to call me, then they called all the Aucas together in mother Akawo's hut.

" 'Sit there on the log—or over here,' directed Dayuma as the informal meeting got under way.

"Dayuma called again to the others in their huts, and finally all came to hear. She chose to tell the story of Joseph. The young Aucas laughed, but all of the others listened well. After she had Joseph's bones ordered back to his father's land she told her people to shut their eyes, that she was going to talk to God. She prayed for her people, that they would come to know Him so that when He returned and called they would 'following Him go up to heaven.' She prayed for Mother and Dad, and for Betty's folks, and for Sammy in school in Quito. She prayed for those who are leaving to go downriver today, that the snakes would not bite them. She prayed that Jesus would command the devils to go out of the bodies of the Aucas, and that they would live well. When she prayed there was not a sound out of anyone—all were respectful, although they had seemed a bit embarrassed at the story."

On another Sunday Dayuma told of the birth of Christ which Rachel had reviewed with her during the week. Rachel noted, "She even included the fact that Joseph was of the house of David—a detail that I hadn't mentioned for weeks. The Lord certainly has blessed her with a keen memory, and the Holy Spirit seems to bring things to her remembrance. . . . Omaenkiri, one of Uncle Gikita's wives, didn't seem to pay much attention, nor the young girls. The young boys saw a bird in the forest and interrupted the story a bit. There were other interruptions, too, but all in all the meeting went well. Then Dayuma prayed: 'All close your eyes now, we're going to talk to God. "Keep Uncle Gikita and the others on the trail, don't let the snakes bite them. Throw out the witch doctors and the devils." Who will be the first to love and obey God and live well?' "

As Rachel listened to Dayuma teaching her people about God and His Son, she marveled that "in God's planning Dayuma was the first one to carry the name of Jesus to her people." Three years before when she began to teach Dayuma at Hacienda Ila no one in the Auca forest knew His name. Now in telling Bible stories, Dayuma would begin her narration in good Auca fashion by first introducing the name of the main character: "Jesus, His name is Jesus . . ." Gradually her people were learning His name.

Omaenkiri, Gikita's other wife and sister of Naenkiwi, was the first of the older generation to respond to the teaching about God's Son. In making her daily rounds, Rachel often visited Omaenkiri in her separate thatched hut.

Rachel recorded,

"Omaenkiri's mother Dyiko came over the trail to visit us. She and her other daughter Nombo came with the rest of the Aucas out of curiosity to see the foreigners. One day when I arrived in Omaenkiri's hut old Grandmother Dyiko was nursing her grandchild, and squatting beside her, her daughter Nombo, also in her 'nothingness,' was nursing her baby.

"That day as Omaenkiri sat in her hammock, with her little children, stirring up her fire and talking to her mother and sister, she began to tell them that I had come with Dayuma to teach them about Jesus. It was a big thrill for me to listen to Omaenkiri telling her family what Dayuma had taught her about the birth of Christ. I was amazed at the details she remembered. But as she told the story she turned to me and said, 'Now what was His name?' The name of Jesus was strange to her and she couldn't remember it. Suddenly it occurred to me that I was now hearing an Auca from the forest itself—not Dayuma—telling still other Aucas about Jesus!

"Shortly after I heard her tell the story Omaenkiri came down with the fever and colds which had been going around since the initial contact with the outside. But carrying one little child and leading another, she had left on the trail to go back to her home.

"A day or two later Monga, his body wet with the recent rain, appeared on the other side of our little river before the sun was very high in the sky. All of the Aucas knew that he was a bearer of 'ill tidings.' Only one who had run all the way over the jungle trail could have arrived at that hour. The message, which he breathlessly called out across the stream, was for Uncle Gikita who was tying palm leaves with vines to the framework over our heads."

Omaenkiri, Gikita's wife, was dying. "Tell my husband to come quickly. Who will bury my dead body?" was the message. Monga, who was from downriver, distrusted everyone, his own people as well as the foreign women toward whom he had been hostile on his first visit to the Tiwaeno.

Gikita finally persuaded Monga to cross the river and give a few details. Then Gikita shinnied down the bamboo post, picked a few green bananas out of a basket, and prepared to leave immediately. Betty and Rachel wondered if either of them should go to help the sick mother, but it seemed out of the question to do more than send some pills with Gikita.

As he set off on the trail with Monga Dayuma called after her uncle, "If Omaenkiri dies, don't choke the baby! God doesn't want us to do that. Let the baby live!"

Several days later the Indian women returned with their heavy loads of yuca and bananas, and the word that Omaenkiri had died. But her baby had not been choked. Her niece Wato, the bashful young girl who was rescued by Uncle Gikita after she had wandered alone for weeks in the forest, stated the facts of her aunt's death without the faintest semblance of sadness. Maengamo gave more details. Dayuma alone, her heart softened by love for the Lord, wept openly as she swung in the hammock and listened.

On the way home Omaenkiri had felt a hard blow on the back of her head. Her son denied dealing it. From that moment on she was sure the devils had hit her and she would die. Later, when the fever had taken its full toll and cough wracked her body she ran outside from her hammock, crying, "Mima is calling me—I must go!"—and fell dead.

Omaenkiri's little children were a part of the family on the Tiwaeno. One day Rachel noted that "the three children had their fire burning merrily at 5:30 A.M., and seemed perfectly capable of carrying on without their mother." Widows and orphans found their niche in group life, and each did his share of work by hunting, fishing, or clearing weeds in the yuca patch.

Rachel says,

"Dayuma and Gimari would sometimes go fishing for themselves, taking the younger ones with them. During her first days on the Tiwaeno Dayuma had still felt some resentment toward Gimari for the way she had gone off with Naenkiwi, causing such heartache to the family. Upon her first arrival at the Tiwaeno when she greeted Gimari she had not even asked the name of her baby. Gradually forgiveness replaced Dayuma's initial anger.

"I think if it hadn't been for little baby Bai, Gimari would have pined away." She was lazy, and lived in her hammock. Although she no longer laughed at Dayuma's teaching, there was no spark of curiosity.

Rachel continues,

"As I tried to make friends with Gimari I began to see in her the same possibilities there had been in Dayuma. After a little while in spite of herself she began to listen. I started teaching her as I had Dayuma, line upon line, precept upon precept, very simple truths. Finally I got her to respond to questions. At first she would whisper the answer very quietly.

" 'Gimari, where does God live?' and she would point up to the sky in her bashfulness.

" 'How many sons does He have?'

" 'Aroki—just one,' she whispered.

" 'What is His Son's name?'

" 'His Son's name—I don't remember,' Gimari said softly.

"I taught her the name of Jesus over and over again until she could remember it. Then to my great joy I found that Gimari would not only whisper His name, but she was teaching baby Bai the name of the Son of God. In fact, Jesus was one of the first words that baby Bai lisped."

In that name lay the hope that Bai would not grow up to avenge the spearing of his father Naenkiwi.

19

"JUST LIKE KAPOK, RISING WITH THE WIND"

As the "Explorer VII" streaked through space and settled into orbit in the autumn of 1959, another conquest was in progress on a tiny clearing back on the earth's surface. Occupation of the Auca settlement by the bearers of Good Tidings for earth dwellers had been quiet and unspectacular. But like the launching of the rocket, it was an historical incident.

"You are making history here on earth—and in eternity," wrote one interested friend to Rachel.

"If we are," was her response, "the Lord has chosen this tiny spot to highlight for the world many tribes being reached by missionaries, unseen and unsung, too busy with the job at hand to write home about it. . . ."

For those who had hoped and prayed many years that the untamed tribe of the forest would be possessed for Christ, the Auca advance was conquest in a new dimension. Fear of foreigners, the chief obstacle to progress, was being overcome by the love of God through human channels. Dayuma, who now taught her people God's carving, oriented them also in their relation to a larger world. She was drawing aside the forest curtain and expanding their limited horizons.

As her people stood around—in their natural nakedness or in various stages of dress—Dayuma told them about the rest of the world. She wore a cotton print dress which she had made herself, but for Aucas in general the wearing of clothing was as yet a custom of outsiders.

"Our Auca country is like a drop of spit on the back of my hand," she said to them, realistically suiting the action to the word. "The land is small, the water is very, very big. The land is like this"—she picked up a gourd bowl, turned it upside down, and pointed to the imaginary continents—"and all *this* part is water." The improvised world globe was amusing to some and incredible to others, but at least the rudiments of physical geography had been taught.

The foreign women were closely observed in their first months on the Tiwaeno. From the time of their grandfathers the Aucas had referred to such people as "like *bogi* monkeys" whose palms are white. With only one Auca word for "outsider" it was convenient to compare the white foreigners to the well-known monkey. Rachel was called a "red-skin" because of her fair, sunburned skin upon arrival at the settlement. To the dark-eyed Aucas the blue eyes of the foreigners were "like rain." And the foreigners spoke their queer language "with crooked teeth," or with "a dry tongue."

Lessons in mutual understanding continued as Dayuma told of other Indian groups and their customs. There were foreigners in Rachel's land who still spoke their own languages. She told them that long ago in that land to the north there were no people speaking Rachel's language, only other groups of foreigners. Then the white foreigners came from across the big water and planted their corn there. It was very hard for them to live at first, for there was little to eat. But God helped them and their corn grew. Then they made a feast to thank God, and the Indians and the white foreigners ate together.

The people in Rachel's country still have a feast every year in remembrance of their ancestors who almost starved before God made their corn grow. They also learned how to kill wild turkeys and use them for food. Now, in Rachel's land, a tame variety of turkey is eaten on the day of the feast. Dayuma had been to one of these feasts. They had lots and lots to eat, much more than just corn and turkey. Then the foreigners thanked God, and sang to Him.

"Why can't we do like that and thank God here on the Tiwaeno?" Dayuma asked. Why not, indeed. And the little clan was gathered on heavy hardwood logs and comfortable hammocks for an unscheduled lesson from God's carving.

The session "was not exactly orthodox." Dabu was sitting on bamboo planks and leaning against a post; Maengamo was stretched out on her back on the old overturned canoe, and Wato was sitting over in the corner nursing the sting of a vicious mañi ant. Rachel says,

"Perhaps there were nicer Thanksgiving services somewhere—but not for me. I raised my heart in praise to God for bringing us here—and for a whole lot more."

For the special occasion Dayuma chose to tell the story of David in good Auca fashion. As a noisy macaw squawked nearby she narrated the spellbinding tale:

David was a handsome young man "with hair the color of the red iyatai ant."

"Take my machete to kill the giant," said Saul to David.

"It is too heavy," answered David. "Carrying nothing I will go."

When David approached the giant an interesting Auca conversation followed:

"Who is this?" Goliath sneered. "You are just little!"

"My God is the only God," answered David. "High in the sky he lives."

"We have lots of gods," bragged Goliath.

The later spear-throwing scene came alive with Auca reality. David dodged the spears that Saul meant for him. Saul persisted in his search, but each time missed his mark.

"Moipa pursued us. Like that Saul pursued David," said Dayuma, bringing the story very close to home. "If you love God, you don't do that," she emphasized to her Auca audience. "You don't try to kill your enemy."

Later when David was surrounded by the enemy he spoke to God and said, "Now what will we do? Now they will kill us. Now where will we flee?"

Then Dayuma went on to tell how a messenger from Saul's house came at that time and called, "Saul, Chief, the enemy has already come to your houses! Hurry and go home! They have already taken your possessions and they will capture your wives. Hurry—hurry—hurry!"

The narrator's comment was, "God had just told the enemy to come and do that." Then as David called his soldiers together and left he was happy and said, "Now God has done well for us." And he went free.

Later, when Saul was cornered in a cave, he could have died at David's hand.

"Now you can kill him," said David's friends.

"No," answered David, "God will kill him. I will not."

Again, when David did not use the power of death in his hand as he found Saul asleep, a lively conversation between David and his friends ensued:

"David, you foolish man, why don't you kill him?"

"No, believing in God I will not kill him. I will not spear." David tiptoed, carefully stepping over the men sleeping with Saul, and refusing to avenge himself.

When Saul awoke and realized that David could have killed him he said in amazement, "He didn't spear me!"

In addition to the strong moral against the spearing of one's enemies, Dayuma drove home another point: do not dabble in witchcraft. By picturing the sad end of Saul as he consulted the witch, she used the Bible example for teaching against similar practices among her own people.

In her closing prayer Dayuma beseeched the Lord that her people would go with Him and not go with the devils; that they would let Him avenge their enemies and not spear for themselves.

Young Monga had refused to join the informal circle of attentive Auca listeners. His youthful face always wore a dark expression, reflecting a fearful, distrustful attitude. Shadowed by the disapproval of some like Monga, the new colony formed by Aucas and foreigners was an innovation on trial. One day when unfriendly glances had been cast her way Rachel rejoiced in a particular comfort from Psalm 46 where God is set forth as the One who would be exalted among the heathen, and the one who "cutteth the spear in sunder."

In spite of the resistance of a few there was a heartening reaction of several to the new way of life. From the beginning Dawa had been eager to hear, but at times the things taught by Dayuma and reiterated by Rachel seemed incredulous. One day when the lesson had been about Jesus' walking on the water "just as if it were beach," Dawa objected.

"That couldn't be—no man can walk on water!"

"But Jesus *did*," Dayuma insisted. "He is the Son of God—He made the water, and He walked on it." Dawa began to accept the teaching concerning the miracles of Christ as she realized that He was the Ruler of all nature.

Lessons taught in the daytime were often continued at night around the fires, or in the hammocks. As the Aucas reviewed the amazing truths of God's carving, the foreign women absorbed more of the language of the forest. At that time Rachel wrote, "I asked the Lord for that which would help me most with the language, and I guess I got it. Maengamo's open-air hut, with Ipa and baby Tamaenta, is a perfect setup for learning Auca. And the fire where the meat is smoked is a comfort as it dries the damp bedding. . . ."

Pet monkeys rustled the palm leaves overhead at night, or tame birds stirred on their roosts. Occasionally a sudden, pitiful cry signaled the distress of a night victim. Once when Rachel was awakened by the half-human cry of a suffering animal she woke Dayuma and asked what it was. At first Dayuma said it was just a jaguar killing a *paenae*. But as she listened to the prolonged cry she said no, it was a boa attacking its prey. "If it squeals a long time, a boa is crushing it," she explained.

During the day pets were a source of amusement—and sometimes consternation—to Rachel. She laughed when Dayuma's monkey grabbed a banana from the pet parrot, but a little while later the picture changed. Unnoticed, the thief sneaked down the rafter and snatched away a cooked bird-thigh that Rachel was about to eat. Then after devouring the juicy morsel in front of Rachel, it ran high up in the peak of the roof.

Sometimes the "juicy morsel" was a relative of the pet *iwa* monkey itself. "The *gamunga* monkey is peeking out of the pot, head and torso," Rachel wrote as she observed a meal in the making. "I have really gone into neutral on such things. I believe I could even eat a monkey head now—though I wouldn't want to deprive the Aucas of a delicacy. The smoked ones still remind me of the shrunken heads of Tariri's tribe."

Once in awhile when monkey hunting had been good there was a feast of monkey heads. All ate to the full of the delicious meat as soon as it was cooked, but the heads were saved for tomorrow's feast. Mother Akawo would pass out the delicacies, the largest heads being given to the oldest men, and the smallest to baby Bai. As they squatted on the ground around the fire they would noisily lick and suck the grotesque skulls. It was a unique experience for a foreigner, and something of a psychological adjustment to food fashions. According to Rachel, the biggest hurdle was to witness the "mouth-to-mouth" sucking of monkey heads.

One day Oba arrived with a collection of charred monkey limbs poking out the top of a basket. She presented Rachel with "all the appendages as a very special gift, topped by two blackened monkey heads. I am getting over some of my prejudices. I finally consumed some of the brains myself, but left the sucking of the eyes to Akawo. The effect was a bit eerie—reminded me of that grave-digging scene from *Hamlet* that I saw in Stratford-on-Avon. The grave-digger stuck his fingers through the inside of the skull to make eyes that twinkled and a tongue that wiggled."

As Christmas approached, a brief recess on the outside was suggested. Dayuma was desirous of visiting her son Sammy in school at Limoncocha. Jim Elliot's parents would be coming to South America and Betty was eager to see them. So the foreign women packed a few belongings and made their way with Auca companions through the forest and up the rivers to Arajuno. They came out as quietly as they had gone in. Their first stay of almost two months in the Auca settlement was brimful of rich experiences. If the Aucas had learned much, the foreign women had learned more.

Rachel and Dayuma took Sammy to Quito for the holidays. While there they entertained a special visitor. Miss Marguerite Carter of Gospel Recordings, Inc. in California had come to Ecuador to help make records in the Auca language to be played later for Dayuma's people in the forest. By diligent work and with Dayuma's co-operation material for four records was successfully taped. Each of the records, three minutes on each side, contained in concentrated Auca a succinct summary of Scripture stories. Two of the records were prepared from material taped as Dayuma had first taught Mintaka and Maengamo about God. The content of the four records would give an uninitiated Auca a fair idea of what God's carving said, from the creation of the world to the death and resurrection of Christ. The tapes were flown to Los Angeles to be processed and then pressed into records.

In late February Dayuma and Rachel returned to the tribe. Betty and Valerie were delayed and would follow in March. The trip in alone with Dayuma was an intensive lesson in jungle travel for Rachel—with an experienced private guide. As they left their Quichua carrier at Tapir River, Dayuma put Rachel in the lead on the trail. It was time she learned the ways of the woods. But in the virgin Auca forest Rachel would stray and follow the path of the tapir or deer. Dayuma would then laugh, or even scold, "Can't you see where the Aucas have bent the sticks on their trail?" Bent or broken twigs and sticks had to be recognized. And Dayuma cautioned Rachel against snakes. The leader on the trail always kept his eyes peeled for them.

Finally, after arriving and settling again, Rachel wrote on February 20,

"Dayuma and I came over the trail carrying a minimum of equipment. We knew before we arrived that there would not be many Indians around. Dayuma's forest-trained eyes had failed to find footprints, and the trails were overgrown. They had to be opened up, though we had been gone such a short time. There was no one on the clearing when we arrived, but the logs were still glowing in Kimo's hut. Soon Dawa, followed by her pet wild hog, came splashing across the river in response to our call.

"This was the second time that Kimo and Dawa had waited for the foreigners. The first time the others had waited awhile, and then left when their long-established fears of foreigners got the better of them. This time, when the new moon appeared and we had not returned, the witch doctor began the refrain that the foreigners will not return. But Kimo waited—Kimo who just three years before had gone with the others to kill the five foreign men on the Curaray.

"At twilight Kimo came back from hunting, poison-dart-holder swung around his neck, blowgun and fishing spear over his shoulder, but alas—empty-handed. Kimo hung up his dart-holder, carefully slipped his blowgun across the thatch in its accustomed place, sat down in the hammock and warmed himself by the fire in the tiny shack. He drank the ripe banana drink his wife offered him in a gourd. Then, as the sun sank behind the high trees, he and Dayuma started to talk:

" 'Nimonga and Monga said you wouldn't come,' Kimo began. 'Dreaming, your mother saw you come back with Nimu . . . Omaenkiri's baby is so thin . . . Boika's new baby was a girl. She wanted to step on it and kill it . . . Returning, Uncle Gikita will bring Maengamo at the next full moon . . . Dabu is planting a new yuca patch downriver. Later, bringing his food by canoe, he will live with us here . . . Returning from the foreigners' houses, everyone was sick . . .'

"Soon it was Dayuma's turn: 'The Quichua carriers who brought us were old and tired. They brought our things to Tapir River and returned . . . We heard that the downriver Indians killed a foreigner over on the big river and lots of foreigners went looking for them with guns—foreigners who don't love the Lord . . . Gikari [the Auca name given to Betty Elliot] and her little girl will be coming later—we came first because we didn't want to keep you waiting any longer . . . We saw a big anteater on the trail . . . Did you know we would be coming when our wood-bee flew over? The man in the wood-bee thought you were Dabu . . .'

" 'Did he?' asked Kimo. 'The wood-bee just went round and round. We heard it coming—*wuu, wuu, wuu*—and then it went round and round . . . Who is his wife, the wood-bee man? How many children does he have? . . . No, we haven't killed anyone since you left. We have not been over to the Curaray . . . Tomorrow, I will go to Tapir River and pick up your things. Alone I will go the next day over the trail to your mother and the others. I will tell them you are back . . .' "

Twilight turned to darkness, moonbeams filled the open shelter, stars became brighter. Soon the conversation faded with the dying fires as they all fell asleep.

Before Kimo left for the family clearing downriver he and Dawa were speculating with Dayuma about the others. "Why haven't they come? Who would tell us if the downriver Indians had speared them all?" Later Dayuma informed Rachel of the predictions: The enemy would take Ana and she would become the wife of a downriver man. Bai would be killed because he is a small boy. Adyibae would be speared because her mother couldn't escape with her; Dyuwi, because he is a man, and Mother Akawo because she is old.

It was a grim picture Dayuma and Kimo were painting, and Rachel prayed that someone might come soon with word.

Several days later at twilight Rachel heard the glad shout "Kimo has returned!" Again, Kimo warmed himself at the fire, and pulled his strong muscular legs up in the hammock beside Dawa as he told the news.

"Your sister Gimari is still sick. She almost died, but she is better now. Akawo told baby Bai that if his mother died she would hit him over the head and kill him. She said she would put him in the hole with Gimari. Then little Bai cried and cried . . ."

Rachel was shocked. She knew of Akawo's threat to kill Dayuma when she was a small child if Moipa speared her father. But baby Bai was so small he could barely say a few words.

Kimo continued,

"All of them were very sick. They are better now. Uncle Gikita nearly died with bad skin sores. He said he was bewitched by the Quichua Indians when he went to the outside. He saw a fellow with 'rotted feet' in their village and said he was cursed in the same way. He was so sick he sent for Dyuwi to come and bury him. Akawo had a sore toe and couldn't go over the trail to see him. Gami went, but she wasn't much help. When he was almost gone—he was so weak he couldn't talk—Maengamo made a paste of hot peppers and rubbed it on his sores. That really brought him to. It burned so much that he rallied. Gami gave him hot water mixed with something else, and he began to get better.

"All of them were angry at Dayuma—even Akawo—for bringing in the sicknesses from the outside. Two have already died, Mima and Omaenkiri, and now these sicknesses. Nimonga said he would spear us all if Gikita died."

"Who—me?" asked Rachel.

"Yes."

"And you, Kimo?"

"Yes."

"And Gikari—and her little girl?"

"Yes."

"And Maengamo?"

"No . . ."

Then Kimo recited more family calamities:

"Minkayi was bitten by a stingray and nearly died. His mother said she would bury one of his children with him if he died. He is better now . . . Mintaka has gone to live with Nimonga . . . Maengamo said the bugs were bad here on the Tiwaeno. She has built another hut downriver . . ."

One day Rachel heard Dayuma teaching Dawa about God's carving—a welcome relief from the sad family news volleyed repeatedly from hammock to hammock. She said of Adam and Eve,

"If they hadn't sinned, we wouldn't get sick and die—and we wouldn't have to clear weeds now. You see how it is when we are gone only a short time. We have to cut through the trail in places. God said to Adam, 'Adam, clearing weeds and planting yuca stalks you will live.'"

Later Dawa was overheard relaying a lesson to Kimo. "God cre-

ated *everything* . . . We know the names of two stars, *gagai*—
'evening star'—and *wanimu*—'morning star,' but God knows the
names of all the stars."

It was evident that Dawa pondered well all that she heard.

"Dawa does a lot of thinking," Dayuma said. "She isn't like the
others. Laughing Kimo says, 'Before, we used to eat dirty. Now
that Dayuma has taught you, you have listened." And Dayuma
added, "Now Dawa keeps her hut clean. Being careful, she serves
the food."

By the first week in March when Betty and Valerie rejoined the
Tiwaeno family, none of the Aucas from downriver had yet returned. It was a desolate scene, compared with the vibrant activity
a few months before. But a week later Akawo finally arrived with
Dyuwi and Oba and little Adyibae, and Maengamo appeared with
Tyaemae and Wato. The clearing soon began to echo once again
with the merry laughter of young voices and the friendly chatter
of older women.

And once again there were gay expeditions into the forest. One
day the Aucas and foreigners went in search of delicious *awaemae*
fruit growing high in the big trees. When they located a
fruit tree Kimo quickly wrapped a strong jungle vine five times
around his ankles in a support for shinnying up the tree. He was as
nimble as a "monkey-on-a-stick."

"What a subject for a sculptor!" Rachel thought. "Leg muscles
that the Academy of Fine Arts knows nothing about—at least, not
in that strength and intensity."

Kimo soon pulled himself to a height of about one hundred and
fifty feet. He clung to the trunk of the tree, barely reaching
around it. Then, machete in hand, he started lopping off the
branches which held the tasty fruit and tossed them to the ground

for Dayuma and Rachel to place in the palm-leaf baskets they had made. Between strokes he picked the fruit and ate as fast as he could. Then Kimo slithered gracefully down the trunk.

"His muscles are like steel straps," Rachel thought again. "His toes are stronger than most fingers, and more supple. No wonder Kimo has conquered the huge trees of the forest!"

Another day the party went to the forest for juicy jungle omu-yaemae fruit. As Kimo shinnied up the big tree a sudden storm struck. Dayuma made a palm shelter for the ground party, but Kimo was pelted with torrents of water. Finally he reached over to a tall palm, whacked off several leaves, and made himself a shelter in mid-air. He braced himself on the smooth bark of the tree which he gripped with the vine supports around his ankles. When the worst of the storm was over he cut the limbs bearing the succulent fruit and dropped them to the hungry hikers below.

Another day while traveling alone in the forest Kimo saw a huge boa. He was without his weapons, but heaved stones at it to stun it. Then he returned home for his machete and spears. Rachel recorded,

"We followed Kimo on the trail and saw the immense ugly creature almost twenty feet long. Kimo first speared its head, and we watched the contraction of its strong muscles as it slowly wrapped its body around the spear. Then he and Dayuma quickly made more rough chonta spears and jabbed the creature, pinning it to the stream bed to which it had slithered. Kimo speared again, and all watched and yelled as the boa wound around the spear. They jabbed it several more times, then he and Dayuma began pulling the spears out and rejabbing until the stream flowed red with blood. Finally, when they had pulled all the spears out the beast stretched itself in fury to its full length and advanced, mouth open and head up. With a mighty yell Kimo speared it right down the throat.

"I was so impressed with the strength of the boa—you could see it in the tightening of the muscles. All I could think of was poor crushed Nampa, and little Bibanga. The spearing technique made me shaky as I watched; people were killed by the Aucas in just this same way.

"When Kimo got back to the clearing Dawa gave him a strong pepper drink to prevent a boa growing in his stomach."

Sometimes there were fishing sprees, or a wild hog chase. As other young Aucas from the former clearing joined the group the activities were pursued with greater spirit. One afternoon a simple fishing trip turned out to be a greater success than anticipated. The Indians encountered a herd of hogs at the edge of the river, and immediately gave chase. Young Kinta speared one. It was probably his first wild hog, and Rachel says "he was one proud little Indian as he climbed up the bank with a big smile, his white teeth shining in the afternoon sun, and his brown body displaying maturing muscles." Fortunately they had taken the canoe to spear fish, so it was a simple matter to dump all the fish and hogs in the canoe and bring it home.

The extra food supply gave Dayuma the opportunity to call them all together to begin the long-envisioned clearing of an airstrip on the Tiwaeno. There were huge trees to be felled, and heavy stumps to hack and heave and haul away—but Dayuma inspired her people to tackle the tremendous task.

Little Bai carried off the first root to clear the strip. Rachel remembered that her brother Nate had tried to tell Bai's father Naenkiwi—or "George" as he called him—that he wanted a strip made. "God's ways are past finding out," she wrote in her diary, "but we have had the privilege of seeing the little son actually start it."

One day when the work was barely under way a plane was heard overhead. An impressive knot of Aucas waved greetings to the large plane of the Ecuadorian Air Force on its way east to the border. The plane made a turn and circled back over the Auca field.

"Look!" shouted Dayuma lustily. "Flying low, the big wood-bee of the chief of the land comes to see! All hands to work!"

On the same exciting day the JAARS plane flew over unannounced on its way back to the Limoncocha Base. Still later that day, the MAF plane passed overhead unexpectedly on its way home to Shell Mera. After awhile the government plane circled again on its way back to Quito. There was almost too much excitement for one day, but it gave impetus to the airstrip project.

After each day's work the Aucas relaxed in the hammocks around the fires where they swapped stories or sang. The exotic song fests are described by Rachel:

"As the daylight fades and the moon rises in the east, the Aucas pull their feet up into their hammocks, or stretch them out over the dying embers of the burning logs of the fire nearby. Then one or another of the men will break out in the rhythmic, nasalized, oft-repeated stanzas of an Auca 'song.' Perhaps it should more aptly be called chanting, but whatever it is I have come to enjoy it. Sometimes a grandmother will sing as her grandchild tugs at her breast. Sometimes several sing all at once—each a different song. That really adds to the effect. The seven huts in this clearing are mighty close together.

"At dawn it is often the same thing. I never know which will wake me up first, the rooster that was dropped as a little chick in a bucket by Nate, or Kimo or Dyuwi. Their hammocks are not twenty feet away, though they each have separate thatched roofs. The songs may be anything from 'I have worked hard all day like a leaf-cutting ant,' to a little ditty about 'Floating, floating in our new canoe.'"

As Aucas joined the settlement the songs became more varied and frequent, and the volume greater.

By April when all of Dayuma's family had arrived on the Tiwaeno clearing, those who had been hostile were more tolerant—even friendly. At that time Rachel observed,

"Dyuwi is visibly softening toward us. Occasionally he is actually hilarious about my attempts to imitate his wife's speech. He used to be sullen, so I am delighted to be laughed at. But we still have our problem child Monga who tells so many lies it's hard to keep the picture straight. I think he is trying to be a 'big shot' and make up for the fact that he is an outsider. Dayuma has 'lectured' him about 'talking wild.' Both Nimonga and Minkayi seem to have gotten over any fears they had.

"Dawa and Gimari are wanting to know more of the Lord. Last night Dawa got out of her hammock to sit up and listen to Dayuma telling a Bible story back to me after dark. In fact, from the comments coming from different directions I judge there must have been at least a half dozen other listeners in various hammocks. Then Dawa prayed aloud to the Lord.

"A few do not come to the Sunday gatherings, but we are encouraged as we see the answers to prayer here and the general response."

As Easter approached Dayuma drilled her family class on the death and resurrection of Christ. The story of the raising of His dead body had never ceased to thrill her, and she emphasized it to her people, most of whom were still fearful of what would happen to dead bodies.

Gimari and Dawa listened attentively as Dayuma's animation carried her audience along with her. They hung on to every word.

"Then the followers of Jesus came and looked into the tomb—"

"Ndae!—There was no one!" shouted Dawa, her eyes shining with triumph. Dayuma beamed her approval, then continued with the sequel of the disciples' walk to Emmaus with the risen Christ.

"They two returned fast at night. They called out to the others, 'We have already seen Him. He is awake. We came back to tell you. He spoke to God—He is alive! We saw Him!'

"Then the others said, 'You must be talking wild. How can those who have already died be raised?'

"Then the two said, 'Why don't you understand? It is true what they said about Him long ago. They said He would live again.' Then another said, 'One moon and one-half moon He lived there, being raised.'

"Afterward He went high up in the sky. 'Now I will go away,' He said, 'and when I go away, I will go to be beside my Father, God. Now I am going up. Afterward, in the same way, returning I will come,' He said.

"He will come again, not as a child. He will come again in the same way He went—as a Man. You say that kapok being light goes up? Like that He went up, just like kapok, rising with the wind. Higher, higher, higher. Just like that. Going up, the wind takes the white fluff higher—like that, He went up. Up to the other side of the pretty clouds. Then He was not. Where did He go? They didn't see.

"Then the ones God sent, the ones who live high in the sky with God, came. 'Why do you all stay looking?' they said. 'You all in the same way will go up.' When will Jesus come? He is the One who said, 'After I go up high, I am going to come again.' Those who died long ago, believing in God, Jesus will call. Hearing, fast they will be raised. All of them, those who believed in God, will go high up in the sky.

"Now we do not know just when He will come. Day, night, sunset, midnight, dawn—we don't know. But He will come. When God says to His Son, 'Yes, now You go,' fast He will come.

"All of those who do not believe in God, all of them will be thrown out. You throw worms out of the corn. Like that God will throw them out. Do you all understand? That's how it is. Those who do not believe, the devil will take. It will be bad for all of them.

"That is how God's trail is—like that ravine over there on the other side of the river. You won't be able to cross over. Here is the devil's trail, and there is God's trail. It is a very, very beautiful trail as you go up there."

On Easter Sunday Dayuma reviewed the story. Then she challenged them directly,

"Who, and who, and who will say, 'Yes, I love God, I want to live well.' Dawa, will you?"

"Yes," said Dawa.

"Kimo?"

No reply.

"Gimari, will you?"

To her expression of consent Gimari added, "Tomamoni!—All of us!"

Dayuma explained that those who love God often sing to Him in remembrance of good things He has done. One refrain in an old Auca song about the God of creation would be appropriate. Thus the simple gathering ended with the Auca chant, "God created, God created everything." Then as if inspired by her own message concerning a risen Lord, Dayuma added original Auca words to the old tune:

> "We say the stars shine, He created all . . .
> Seeing, we will love Him in our hearts . . .
> Following Jesus, to God's House we will go . . .
> We will say 'No' to the devils, we all will love God."

Old and young quietly followed Dayuma's lead as each line was repeated many times.

Rachel wrote in her diary,

"It was the very first 'congregational singing' in Auca! I'm sure it rejoiced the heart of the Lord who heard from heaven. May it be true that 'all of us' will believe in Him before another Easter Sunday in Aucaland."

20

"OUR ANCESTORS WERE TALKING WILD"

OLD Akawo sat in her hammock rolling the strands of *chambira* fiber with her wrinkled hand against her bare thigh. At times as she chanted an Auca tune or called to her grandchildren as they played in the clearing, she would look down the path toward the stream. Two moons had passed since Dayuma and Rachel returned to the outside.

"Will Dayuma bring her son or not when she comes with Nimu? . . . Will he look like an Auca? . . ."

Her family did not really believe Dayuma had a son until Dabu went once to Arajuno and saw Sammy with his own eyes. Ever since then the others—especially his grandmother—had been eager to see him.

Finally the big day arrived and the glad shout "They have come!" rang through the Tiwaeno clearing. Akawo hastily pulled on her dress and waited in her hammock to welcome her family.

Sammy looked from one to another as Dayuma, speaking to him in Quichua, explained who his relatives were. Akawo was grinning from ear to ear.

"My grandchild he is!" Akawo could hardly believe her eyes. "He looks like Wawae."

Dika and Gingata looked Sammy over and decided he would be a good playmate, even though he spoke only a very few words of their language. For Akawo, lack of a common tongue was no barrier. From the moment she saw Sammy she chattered with him in Auca which she assumed he understood.

Sammy, who was immediately at home in his new environment, was soon learning from Uncle Gikita or Kimo or Dabu how to whittle fish spears. And almost immediately he began to follow his relatives into the forest to learn the exciting secrets of blowgunning. From his hammock he would watch Kimo make the poison from the bark of the *oonda* vine for darts to be used in hunting. On his return from trips downriver or into the forest he would join the others who were hungrily dipping into the family meal of fish or monkey spread invitingly on banana leaves on the ground.

Akawo was proud of her grandson. She cooked special pieces of fish or meat for him, roasted his bananas and made his yuca drink. She wanted him to be a good Auca, so she made him a *komi* from jungle cotton and wound the thin cord around his hips, as she had done for each of her own children. Akawo announced that soon it would be time to start making holes in his ear lobes for the big balsa plugs.

In addition to hunting and fishing Sammy had a very special job: he played the Auca phonograph records which had arrived in time to be taken to the Tiwaeno with the returning party. To the amazement of the Aucas, Dayuma's son could wind the "foreigners' thing," place a disc on it, and make it talk in their language!

The first time the group heard the box speaking about God they were stunned into complete silence. Rachel had learned long before from Dayuma that Aucas said the least about the things that impressed them most. Dyuwi and Oba followed every word. Kimo stopped making poison darts and came closer to see the records turning. He folded his muscular arms, leaned against a post, and riveted his eyes on the talking box. Akawo forgot her work, squatted down on the ground beside the phonograph, and listened closely. The four records were played over and over again.

"Now listen, all of you come. Come and sit down and listen," was the message from the box. "Listen, and then believing, live. Long, long ago God created. The sun, stars, and moon He created . . . then the wild hogs and the jaguars. . . .

" 'Now what shall I create? I will create a man. I will take dry earth and breathe into it and create a man who will live. . . .' "

After the temptation in the garden of Eden and the entrance of sin into the world God said, " 'Now what will I do that they may live well? Now in exchange I will send my Son. Yes, He will become like a child and be born.' Then He died high on a tree, His very good blood dripped.

"This is the way God speaks. Our ancestors just said, 'God created'—then they didn't remember any more. . . ."

Uncle Gikita paid little attention to the foreigners' thing with its new message. "When I die I will just become worms," he said. His interest lay in "stuffing himself on wild hog" rather than hearing God's carving. But Akawo listened as long as anyone would wind the box.

Sammy taught Dyuwi how to operate the machine. Then when no one else was around Dyuwi would often listen raptly. One day he heard the record say, "If we don't believe in Jesus our hearts are black like the blackest night. If we believe in Jesus our hearts become like light. Do you understand?"

"I understand!" Dyuwi answered vigorously.

Gimari liked to listen, and she too learned to operate the foreigners' thing. Clumsily at first, she changed the needles and beamed with great satisfaction when she could make the box talk. She always brought baby Bai to hear. As he squatted on the ground, his eyes would brighten each time he recognized the name of Jesus spoken on the records.

In the evening when the men came home from hunting they would gather around to hear the records over and over again. They seemed never to tire of the repetition of the messages.

The story of the Gadarene commanded great attention. Dayuma's version of the miracle held her people spellbound, just as Rachel's account had moved her when she first heard it.

"The devils are afraid of Jesus," the machine said. The listeners hardly moved a muscle.

The owner of the pigs that were drowned by the devils was "very angry." He said to Jesus, "Jesus, why did you come here? You said to all of my pigs, 'Die!'—and they *died!*"

The Aucas always broke into a hearty laugh when they heard how the pigs ran down into the water and were drowned. But the lesson of the power of Jesus over the devils often provoked serious discussion around the fires afterward.

A summary of the Ten Commandments covered one side of a record, and gave them something new to think about.

"God says that you should not spear people," was the solemn message. "Even if you don't spear them yourself, but tell others to spear, that is sin."

Kimo and Sammy became close companions, especially as the Quichua-speaking lad quickly began to speak the language of his forest family. Sammy was able to tell his relatives much about the outside world. As the time drew near for Rachel to go to Limoncocha, he told Kimo of the foreigners there. Kimo and Dawa had wanted to go to the Base ever since Wintaka and Maengamo returned with a favorable report.

It had been almost two years since Kimo attempted a glimpse of the world beyond the forest. At that time the guns of the Quichuas had frightened him back when he reached the Oglán. Dawa had actually gone out with Mintaka and Maengamo for a few brief hours, but ran back into the forest to join her husband.

Even when Dayuma went to the Tiwaeno the first time alone with Mintaka and Maengamo, before the foreign women had ventured in, apprehension still filled the forest. Kimo and Minkayi had been wary of the contact made with the outside world. However, after hearing from Dayuma about the outside as well as about God's carving, Kimo had resolved to receive the foreigners peaceably and to build a shelter for them. He had believed Dayuma's words that the white women would bring good and not evil to the Auca forest. However, others had warned him of bad days ahead.

"The hut you build will become your grave," they had predicted morosely. But Kimo was not to be dissuaded. He had promised Dayuma that he would build a hut for the newcomers—and he did.

When Rachel and Dayuma and Sammy began to make definite plans for Limoncocha, Kimo and Dawa decided to accept Dayuma's invitation to accompany them. She had been encouraging them to see for themselves how the good foreigners lived. Aucas would be welcome, she said.

In September when the party started for Limoncocha, Betty Elliot and her daughter Valerie left for a visit to her parents' home in the United States.

Rachel and the Aucas flew from Arajuno to Limoncocha in the JAARS plane "just like the wood-bee I saw being made in Nimu's country," Dayuma explained. Kimo and Dawa were glad to be on the ground again. Kimo admitted that his first ride was a frightening experience. He flew very high and the jungle trees below seemed far, far down. He saw the long, winding Napo River with clusters of huts or Quichua Indians along its banks.

At Limoncocha Kimo saw many amazing foreigners' things, including a tractor and a motor scooter. His first view of the tractor at work was an awesome sight. He heard the roar of the "wood-bee on the ground" and ran out to see what was happening. He kept a safe distance under big trees at the edge of a clearing as he watched the mechanical monster pushing huge tree stumps and logs before it, and even knocking down small trees. The strength of the tractor driven by the foreman of the Base impressed Kimo.

In a few minutes the tractor had accomplished more than a complete day's work for an Auca. He said with a hearty laugh, "I wish that the man pushing that wood-bee would beat me. Then I could work like that on the Tiwaeno!" He was remembering when Grandfather Karae often came back from a full day of chopping trees or clearing weeds, and, following an Auca custom, would pick up the leather thong and beat the bare backs and arms of the youths. In this way they too would grow up to be good workers.

But Kimo's chief delight was to watch the JAARS pilots and mechanics in the hangar working on the "skeleton and skin" of the wood-bees. He marveled at the ability of the men to "create" the bees that flew so high.

Rachel wrote at that time,

"Kimo went to the Base with certain misgivings. For the first three weeks he would not walk alone the short distance from our house to the hangar, though he very much wanted to see the airplane 'created.' There were too many Quichua Indians around. Although they had no firearms, he was afraid. But before the month was up, Kimo would stay at the hangar alone with our pilots and mechanics and even carried on quite a monologue in Auca."

Dayuma proudly escorted Kimo and Dawa around the Base, where they shared the happy life of the foreigners living there. They went canoeing and fishing on the lake, and ate contentedly around their ground-fire outside Rachel's thatched hut. They even learned to play the hilarious game of volleyball which the foreigners enjoyed each day at sunset. Awkward at first, Kimo quickly learned to co-ordinate his strong muscles to the unfamiliar sport and send the ball over the net.

But the high point for them was the teaching from God's carving, held each evening under the thatched roof. Dayuma and Rachel would lead in Auca, or Catherine Peeke in Quichua. Catherine, who had enjoyed working with Rachel at Hacienda Ila, was now visiting her and the Aucas at Limoncocha. When she taught Dayuma and Sammy in Quichua, Dayuma would interpret the message into Auca for Kimo and Dawa.

For the first time in their lives Kimo and Dawa observed the habits of foreign men who loved God. They heard them pray. They watched them gathering also to hear God's carving in their language.

After a moon at Limoncocha the day came for the Auca group to return to the Tiwaeno. An hour before take-off time Kimo and his friend Sammy were at the hangar, standing by the Helio-plane laden with their blowguns, dart-holders, and small bundles of foreigners' things acquired at the Base. Kimo wore a broad, happy smile as he said good-by to the foreign friends who surrounded the plane as the party left.

From Arajuno the party again took to the now-familiar forest trail. When they arrived on the Tiwaeno a few days later all fifty-six of the Auca family group were on hand to hear Kimo's report. Many things had impressed him, but one observation especially gripped Kimo: the difference between "foreigners who loved God" and those who did not. When traders from the Napo River or Quichuas from surrounding villages had come to the Base for medical treatment or on business, Kimo asked curiously, "Do they love God?" Very often the answer had been negative. He had watched the handful of Christian Quichuas who worked at the Base, as well as other outsiders.

"Those who believed in God were happy—you could tell by

their faces," was Kimo's conclusion. "Those who did not believe in God had sad faces. They live 'black.'"

"They looked like bats!" Dawa added.

"The Quichuas who live on the Napo River heard God's carving a long time ago," Kimo told his people. "But they have not all believed. We have just heard God's carving. If we had heard long ago, fast we would have believed."

Kimo had made another observation as he flew over the vast jungle. "We cannot hide from the wood-bees that fly over us," he told his people. "From the sky the smoke from the fires is clearly seen."

Kimo had noticed at the Base that on Sunday the Quichua Indians first went to hear God's carving, and then hunted for food in the forest. Back on the Tiwaeno he followed the same practice and encouraged others to do likewise. One Sunday Dabu was more eager to hunt than to listen to the early morning lesson. Kimo said he would listen to God, then go hunting. He asked God to help him find meat quickly. After the gathering he took his blowgun and went into the forest. Early in the afternoon he came home with a happy smile and a collection of toucans, wild cranes, and gata monkeys. Dabu returned later with nothing. Kimo had a simple explanation for his success:

God said to the toucan, "You go sit on the tree by the trail and wait for Kimo"—and the bird did. The animals were just waiting to be carried home by Kimo for hungry mouths in the clearing.

Happy-go-lucky Minkayi listened with interest to Kimo's view of God's carving. And even Nimonga was saying that he would "plant lots of yuca and live for a time on the Tiwaeno." Although friendly, he had little interest in the new way of life which Kimo and others wanted to follow.

As Rachel listened to the Aucas around the fires at night, or in the hammocks during the day, the typical pattern of conversation was being varied by talk about God's carving. References to attacks from the downriver people bore a new emphasis.

"If they spear us," Rachel heard Dawa tell Dayuma one day, "we will just die and go to be with Jesus."

Dayuma often agreed with the gloomy predictions concerning the fate of the Tiwaeno group. In fact, she told Rachel that when she would be speared she wanted her to take Sammy as her own son. One day Rachel felt impelled to channel Dayuma's thoughts in another direction.

"Dayuma," she said, "why do you always talk about being killed by the downriver people? Why don't we ask God to keep us from being speared until we finish God's carving for your people?"

Dubious at first, Dayuma began to include this request in her prayers. God *could* protect them. In fact, He could make a way for His carving to reach the impossible downriver people who were still angrily throwing spears at wood-bees that chanced to fly overhead.

"If God says 'No,' they won't be able to touch us," Dawa chimed in one day.

Foreigners good and bad were always a topic of conversation. Once when Rachel joined Dawa and Dayuma, she realized they had been talking about the foreigners killed on the Curaray. At the Tiwaeno Rachel had heard that Dawa and Mintaka and Akawo were with the five Auca men who killed the foreigners, but she had never interrogated the eyewitnesses. Now Dawa was recalling impressions.

"After the first one was speared the other foreigners shot their 'things' into the air," she said, "but they did not shoot our men. When all their shots were gone, our men just speared the rest of them."

Now Rachel knew how the bullet hole was made in Nate's plane.

Dawa's recountal later encouraged Rachel to ask Akawo about the death of her brother Nate.

"Mother Akawo, you saw my little brother killed. Would you tell me about it?"

With tears and many gestures the woman began to describe the agony of her son Nampa who was crushed by a powerful boa and later died.

"Crying with great pain, 'your little brother' Nampa died," she sobbed in conclusion.

It was then that Rachel realized Akawo was speaking to her as Dayuma's big sister. "Your little brother" meant acceptance into Akawo's family. She inquired no further concerning her own brother's death.

As part of the family circle Rachel learned more about Auca beliefs and legends. She filled in many details of stories Dayuma had told her through the years. One day she asked Dayuma for further information about the Auca creation and flood story. "Ask Uncle Gikita," she replied. "He knows the stories better than anyone else."

Indeed Uncle Gikita proved to be an excellent storyteller. He seemed glad to repeat the story for Rachel, who handed him the microphone. Uncle Gikita seemed amused as he examined it and wondered if the midget machine could really "hear" him. He was elated when he heard his own voice coming back from the box.

"The big rain came and covered the land," he began. "Then the Aucas heard the flood waters coming. 'Watch out!' they called. If they had not lived well, the water fast took them, then they didn't live.

" 'We have lived well,' some cried, and the big water flowed around them on one side and the other. There they just stood on a little piece of land.

"A man and his wife said, 'We will cut off a rotted log,' and they hollowed it out. Then they took beeswax and put it on the ends, patting and patting it on. They put in all their food, yuca stalks, banana cuttings, sweet potatoes, corn, peanuts. Then they took their fire stick and crawled in. They closed the hole with beeswax. The waters carried them far, far downriver. Swirling with the current, they floated to where 'downriver' ends. Then the log got caught in the underbrush, and they could no longer hear the bumping against it. 'Let's make just a tiny hole. If the waters come in and drown us, we will die.' They made just a small hole. There was no water! The sun was shining. They opened their log, and took out their food. They began to clear weeds to plant their fields.

"Then two others said to them, 'Who are you?'

" 'We are Aucas,' they replied. 'We were about to be drowned upriver, then we came here.' "

At this point old Uncle Gikita stopped to laugh heartily.

"Then two red-headed woodpeckers came," he resumed. "Flying right straight through the big tree trunks, they left holes in them. 'What do they do? They are strong,' the Aucas said. In the morning, waking up, they saw the two red-headed woodpeckers swooping down and pulling up the earth with their beaks.

" 'The big woodpecker is creating the mountains and the hills,' they said. That's what our ancestors said, Nimu. They were talking wild," chuckled old Gikita.

"Talking wild? What do you mean, Uncle Gikita?" asked Rachel.

"Now we know better," he laughed. "Dayuma has come and told us that God created everything! Now we know the straight story."

PUBLISHER'S NOTE: The following epilogue was sent by Miss Saint from Ecuador after proofs of the preceding chapters had been air-mailed to her to check for accuracy.

EPILOGUE
by Rachel Saint

As Dayuma and young Sammy and I trudged along the trail near the Tiwaeno clearing we began to wonder what we would find after being away two months. It was February 19 and we were returning to Aucaland after weeks of intensive work with Ethel in Quito on *The Dayuma Story*. While there, Sammy had broken his leg, causing a further delay in our return.

On the trail we came to Dawa's yuca patch and heard the Aucas laughing and talking as they worked on the airstrip. Dayuma called to them but they were having such a gay time they didn't hear her. So Dayuma said to me, "Yodel—in the Auca way!" I tried. It was a poor imitation. Immediately there was an answering shout "Nimu!" The Aucas knew that nobody else would yodel quite like that, and the whole gang came running out to meet us.

What a sight to see them streaming across the big fallen log bridging the last ravine before the clearing! The men had been digging stumps and the women and girls clearing brush away. They had done a lot in our absence. As we entered the clearing we could see that several huts had been closed in with bamboo. There were signs of "settling in" on every side.

The whole group was there except Nimonga and Minkayi, who were harvesting their crops at the old village (Terminal City). Akawo was especially happy to see Sammy—and Sammy was mighty glad to see his grandmother again. She clapped her gnarled hands together, fingers spread wide apart, and said, "This many days I have been here waiting for you." She had come from the old village just ten days before, hoping that we would return.

As everyone gathered in Kimo's hut where we live we gave news about our trip to Quito and back again. Then the Aucas gave us their report. It was all good news. No one was sick, no one had died. Boika's baby had not been born yet.

Then Kimo looked up quietly and said, "We counted the days while you were gone, and on God's day we spoke God's carving." He and Dyuwi had gathered the group together each Sunday and taught them.

"And the talking-thing got better all by itself!" Dawa added.

This indeed was good news. When Dayuma came to Quito just before Christmas (she had stayed out with her people on the Tiwaeno for a month after I left) she reported that the phonograph which we had left in Dyuwi's care was not working. For some reason it wouldn't go. I prayed that somehow they would get it working again, for we had counted heavily on the Aucas' use of the four Gospel records while we were away. What a thrill to hear that it got better "all by itself"!

It was so good to be back with all the Aucas. As I sat in my hammock in Kimo's hut I glanced across the river and saw a big new hut on top of a hill. Uncle Gikita had built his hut there. He had become tired of having the crickets eat everything down by the river where we were, so he moved across the river to higher ground. Monga had also built his hut over by Gikita after the

Tiwaeno flooded him out of his little hut. Trees had been felled on every side, and now we could see much farther in every direction.

And everyone had new pets! You never saw so many pets in all your life—monkeys of all sizes and shapes, and many beautifully colored pet birds. Dayuma's big pet monkey was tied with a vine to a tree. She had dreamed that he had died, but there he was. And Sammy's little *gata* monkey was fine, too. All the small children had pet monkeys. And of course the Auca mothers were obligingly caring for the monkeys. Nombo's little girl Dyiko had a tiny *miimo* monkey perched on her head, and Mintaka and some of the other women were fondling their pet birds as we talked.

After we had been there a few days Nimonga and Minkayi came with their wives, children, grandmother, hammocks, fishing nets, blowguns, spears, and a few "foreigners' things" to live permanently with us. They brought a *buyuga* for me, a tiny rodent that I could hold in the palm of my hand. They very kindly dug a hole in the ground beside my hammock for the little pet. Nimonga also brought a pet macaw for me, a long-tailed scarlet, blue, and gold one. I had told him that I wanted one, and he remembered. He had caught it up in the hills and was raising it for me.

As I sat there watching all the pets and listening to the happy voices of the children that rang through the clearing I thought back to last year at this time when Dayuma and I had returned. There were only two who had dared to wait for us, Kimo and Dawa. This time we found practically the whole crowd.

It was chonta season, and the Aucas brought us heavy branches of the brilliant orange-colored fruit. Komi and the young boys shinnied up other wild fruit trees, some of them two hundred feet high, and lopped off the huge branches bearing delicious smaller fruits. Sometimes several went up a tree at the same time. They seem to be as much at home climbing trees as we are walking on the ground.

The thing that interested me most, however, was the spiritual fruit that we found on our return. There was the thrilling night when Kimo came home from the day's hunt, slipped his blow-gun off his shoulder and into its vine loop holder, then relaxed lying face-down crosswise on his hammock, dressed only in his komi. The whole crowd had gathered around to hear the Bible story which Dayuma usually tells at sunset. The nine hammocks in our hut were full of Aucas—children and older folk—who were in the habit of coming to hear that evening story. But this night Kimo stretched out and said, "Now I will talk about Jesus." He began to talk face-down to the ground, and to nobody in particular.

"Lift your head, Kimo," I said, "so that all of us can hear what you say about Jesus." He did, and we had the joy of hearing, for the first time, an Auca man give a message about Christ. It was a most amazing dissertation beginning before the birth of Christ, then telling of His birth, and how He healed the lame and the blind, and raised the dead. He concluded with the death and resurrection of Christ, and of His coming again to the earth —all with great accuracy. He talked for at least half an hour. It was an overflow of all that Kimo had been fixing in his mind about the Lord.

Dayuma had started to prompt him, but soon found that it was not necessary. Dawa quietly filled in from time to time when he slowed up. As Kimo talked dusk turned to dark, and Dawa stirred up the fire once in awhile. The flickering firelight played on the swarthy bronze muscles of his strong back. What a picture —and what a message! Dyuwi left his hammock and came over and squatted nearby to listen. Dyuwi's keen interest in God's carv-ing had not wavered one bit, but had increased in our absence.

He gladly listened to Kimo. As he squatted there in the moonlight he repeated softly some of Kimo's phrases, as if trying to memorize them. When Kimo finished talking Dyuwi prayed out loud, then all went to their own hammocks and their own fires for the night.

That night we went to bed satisfied that the Seed was beginning to take root, and to bear fruit.

The following Sunday it was Dayuma's turn to teach. I wanted to make sure that the men knew what the forgiveness of sin meant. Dabu was going to be there for the meeting and I wasn't sure how much he understood, because he hadn't lived with us for many weeks at a time. That Sunday at our early-dawn meeting Dayuma made clear the fact that, as we believe in Christ, God buries our sins in the deepest "big water." He throws them behind His back, and He will not remember them. She closed by telling about Tariri the Shapra chief living in the wild jungle to the south of us who has believed in Christ. She told them that when I was living in Tariri's tribe years ago he had insisted that the boa was greater than God. Finally Tariri had understood God's carving, and believed in the living God. She told how he had killed many people and shrunk their heads (the Aucas were horrified!), but that now he teaches his people about God.

After the morning meeting I had a radio contact with Reggie McClendon at Limoncocha, reporting in as I do each morning. Then I turned on my little transistor radio and "happened" to hear Chief Tariri speaking. I recognized his voice and some of the Shapra words. Dayuma recognized him, too, and called to all the Aucas that Tariri himself was now speaking. He was talking from his home on the Pushaga River to one of his kinsmen at the bilingual school at Yarinacocha. Tariri is a commanding personality, and he sounded like a chief as his voice boomed out. All the Aucas listened, impressed with the authoritative tone of his voice. This was Tariri who used to spear-kill, Dayuma said, but now he is teaching his people about God. It was a wonderful climax to a lesson on forgiveness.

After that message about Tariri, Dawa said to me one morning, "Talking, Uncle Gikita goes to the forest."

"What do you mean, Dawa?" I asked.

"Uncle Gikita is like Tariri now. Talking to God he goes to the forest."

Then I remembered that Dayuma had told the Aucas that Tariri prays as he goes out to hunt in the jungle.

"That's what I told you," Dawa continued. "I told you that we Aucas would not take a long time to believe in God. Just as soon as we hear we believe."

And Dawa did believe as soon as she heard. Now she was rejoicing that Uncle Gikita talked to God, too. Not long ago Gikita had been saying that he would just die and turn into worms.

Another day when Dayuma gave the lesson she finished by saying,

"Now the foreigners do it like this: Those who know for sure that God has cleaned their hearts just say so. They say, 'Before, I did this, and this and this. But now Jesus has washed my heart clean with His blood.'

"Now who, and who, and who will say what God has done in your heart?"

Dawa spoke up immediately and said, "Before, I did not live well, but now I love God with all my heart."

She had scarcely finished speaking when Dyuwi was heard. It must have taken a lot of courage for him to speak up as he did in front of the other men with whom he had killed at Palm Beach. They were all there listening. He started counting on his little finger and said, "I killed this one," then holding up the next finger, "and I killed this one, but that was before I knew about

Jesus. I did not do well, but now Jesus has 'erased' my heart."

Dyuwi is a young fellow, the youngest of the five who killed at Palm Beach. That was his first killing, and Naenkiwi was the second. I believe that that will be the last.

Kimo very seriously followed on when Dyuwi finished, and started counting on his little finger.

"This one I killed was an Auca, and the next one I killed was an Auca. After that I killed a foreigner, and after that another foreigner." He counted four and then said, "But I did that when my heart was black. Now Jesus' blood has dripped and dripped and washed my heart clean. I don't live like that any more. Loving the Lord I live."

Gimari quietly added that she too loved God and now lived happily.

There was no further outward response from any of the others, but the other men, especially Nimonga, listened very carefully. When we had first come to the Tiwaeno, Nimonga was antagonistic toward us. We have seen his attitude change. He listened intently as Dayuma spoke about the forgiveness of sin. She was teaching graphically, using illustrations understandable to Aucas.

"As my *gata* monkey is tied by that vine to the post over there, so we are tied by sin. We cannot get away by ourselves."

When Dayuma told how God frees us, "just as we untie the *gata* monkey," a very sweet smile crossed Nimonga's face. I knew that he was beginning to understand. That afternoon he came over to my hut, sat down on a log with his little girl on his lap, but apparently with no special purpose in mind. He didn't seem to have anything to say.

"Nimonga, did you understand what Dayuma said this morning about forgiveness of sin?" I asked.

"Yes, I understand."

"You won't say no to God?"

"No, I won't say no to God."

Shortly after that Nimonga had a very narrow escape. He was out in the forest and a deadly poisonous snake bit him on the foot. He waited for his foot to swell, expecting to become faint and die. But nothing happened and he came home.

The Aucas were convinced that God had heard their prayers that they would not die from snakebites. Gikita went on a fishing trip with his family down the Tiwaeno. When they returned a week later, they reported that he had been bitten by a very poisonous snake. He reached the clearing the next day, his foot was still badly swollen, but he got better.

Gikita said nothing about what God had done in his heart the morning Dyuwi and Kimo talked, but one day I had a very good visit with him. He was weaving some Auca arm bands to my measure, the kind of ornament the old folks used in their dances. He had set up a little stick frame and was weaving the bands with hand-spun cotton and human hair. Red toucan feathers were stuck in as the final touch. Big, broad-shouldered Gikita was telling me with some pride that he was making the bands for me, and that this is just the way the "dorani—the ancestors—did it." He is the only one left in our group who knows how to weave them. I had been making tape recordings of legends of the dorani with Gikita. He never ceases to marvel at that little machine. When he had finished one story he said, "Does it really understand? Does it hear?" I told him that the little foreigners' thing did understand —and I let him hear for himself, much to his delight.

Gikita was open and talkative, and he began telling me about his family. He never knew his father who was speared before he was born. If he had been a girl he would have been killed at birth. Then he started talking about spearings. I knew that Gikita was a seasoned killer, and that he had been on many spearing raids. But this day he started counting on his fingers. He used all the fingers of one hand and the little finger of the other to count the raids—and he had speared at least twelve men.

"I did not do well. That was before I knew God," he said. There were tears in his eyes.

"Amaewo—for the last time—I have killed. We did not understand that your men wanted to help us. I killed the first one . . ."

Then Gikita told me exactly what had happened on Palm Beach. Dawa had already given me her version as an eyewitness, but now Gikita was confirming what I had already heard.

Gikita killed the first foreigner on the beach, then the other foreigners began shooting into the air. As they fired, one bullet grazed the head of young Nampa, who was hiding behind the plane. There was no way for the foreigners to know that he was there, for he did not participate in the spearings. Dawa was crouched on a hill across the river watching it all, and a bullet went over her head.

All the young Auca men began to run when the foreigners shot, but Gikita called them back to kill the rest.

"Being older, Gikita was not afraid," the Aucas had said.

Then one of the foreigners ran to the wood-bee, got in and shut the door. He looked around toward the beach, opened the door, and went back to join the others. Then the Aucas speared the rest. One was killed on the beach and the others in the water.

Later, when Dayuma had told the Aucas that the foreigners had good motives and did not come to kill them, they checked back on the events of Palm Beach. They were convinced that the men had not come to kill, nor did they flee in the face of death. These facts had affected Kimo especially, and eventually made possible an entry to the tribe.

Gikita said that he also helped to spear one of the others.

"It was bad, bad, bad," he said.

Later Dayuma made a trip with the Aucas to Palm Beach and

found that it had washed away completely. It no longer existed.

Another day when Dayuma was talking with her people the matter of spearings came up. She had heard through some Quichua Indians that Aucas went to Villano in her absence, and were seen hiding in the forest to kill.

Minkayi immediately objected, "We told you that we were through spearing. Since you came to tell us about God we do not spear. We did not go to the foreigners' houses. Those who said that are deer, talking wild. What God has spoken we believe."

Monga, who is from downriver and was our problem child, is opening up to us. Sometimes he just comes and sits in the hammock. One day after sitting for a long time saying nothing he finally asked me to wash his shirt. His little wife doesn't know much about washing clothes. One day he was watching Sammy "carve" on paper as I was teaching him his lessons from his Spanish schoolbooks. Monga said that he wanted to carve like Sammy, so I gave him a paper and pencil. He made a series of loops on the paper.

"What are you carving, Monga?" I asked.

He told me that the big loops were the mother and the father, and that the little loops were all of their children. Then he started naming the members of a downriver family, his relatives. I told him to wait till I wrote them down. I had to ask which were men and which were women. How did I know whether the person with the name of a monkey or alligator was a man or a woman? As I took an interest in his drawings he made more for me, and before we finished he had drawn some twelve families for me, making all the big and little loops. And I had written the names of more than a hundred downriver Indians. Two and a half years ago when Monga had come to our group all of them were living.

I had long since memorized the names of the men of the group against the day when the Lord gives us the longed-for peaceful contact, but somehow hearing the names of the women and children—all growing up, the men and boys being taught daily to come and kill us—did something for me. These were names of Aucas, many of them related to those in our own group—still using their stone axes, still hating all outsiders, still trained to revenge within the clan, and still living "without God and without hope . . ." The other day on a canoe trip Minkayi was poling in front of me, and Nimonga in the back, and Minkayi's wife Ompora was squatting right in front of me with her baby in a bark sling. I began thinking about the little fellow's name— Ñiwa, the name of the downriver leader, the killer so much feared by our group—and I learned that day that the little lad is a grandson of Ñiwa! Our group is so closely related to them—but only a miracle of the Lord will make possible a friendly contact without further killings.

By the end of March we prepared to leave for Quito again where I was to read proof on *The Dayuma Story*. The night before we left I made a tape recording with Dyuwi in which he told what he believed about Jesus. The best part of it was his enthusiasm. When he finished he looked up with a big smile and said, "Nimu, tomorrow when you and Dayuma go I will teach our people about Jesus."

"Yes, Dyuwi," I answered, "you and Kimo call all of the people together and teach them God's carving." This is what they had done before in our absence.

As we left Dayuma said, "When the moon is cut in a slight round sliver we will return."

"Meat I will smoke, come and eat," called Minkayi as we took to the trail.

GLOSSARY

(S., Spanish; Q., Quichua; A., Auca)

ACHIOTE (S., ah-chee-oh-teh)   This decorative shrub, the urucu or bixa (*Bixa orellana*), has a pink blossom and a fragrance akin to that of the apple blossom. The Aucas paint their faces with the soft red pulp which coats the spicy seeds.

AMUNGA (A., ah-moon-gah)   The musmuki (*Aotus infulatus*), a nocturnal monkey. A foot in length, it has a very long tail, and eyes encircled in black. The Aucas hunt the amunga in hollow logs, where it sleeps by day.

AUCA (Q., ah-oo-cah)   The name "Auca" is used interchangeably in Ecuador with the term "Aushiri," also of Indian origin (possibly Cofan or Záparo). It is a term used by the Quichua Indians to designate savage, pagan, or barbarian groups of Indians. In Spanish and English the term has been narrowed to indicate the one savage tribe or group of tribes which controls the southeastern jungle of Ecuador, the area between the Napo and the Curaray Rivers.

AWAEMAE (A., ah-wam-a)   The *walis* (Q.) fruit, similar to the wild cherry.

BALSA (S., bal-sah)   The balsa or corkwood tree (*Ochroma piscatoria*, etc.), whose light-weight wood is used by the Aucas to make earplugs and other objects, especially the balsa raft for river transportation.

BARBASCO (S., bar-bas-coh)   Barbasco (*Lonchocarpus nicou*). A shrub whose roots are pounded and cast into a dammed-up stream to drug the fish, so that they are easily caught by hand or with spears.

BOA (bo-ah)   The boa constrictor, an anaconda which is said to attain to the length of 39 feet in Auca territory. Connected with witchcraft in Auca beliefs; antidote after killing a boa is to drink an infusion of hot pepper. The water boa is more feared by the Aucas than the land boa because of its greater size, and they rarely attempt to kill it because of the disadvantage of its being in the water.

BOGI (A., bo-gee)   The machín (S.) monkey. The Aucas referred to white foreigners as "like *bogi* monkeys" whose palms are white.

BUYUGA (A. boo-yoo-gah)   A rodent, the *chambu* (Q.), smallest variety of agouti (*Dasyprocta*). Has the appearance of a tail-less squirrel and lives in the ground.

CHAMBIRA (Q., cham-bee-rah)   The tucuma (*Astrocaryum tucumá*) fiber, taken from terminal tender leaf shoots of this palm.

CHONTA (Q., chon-tah)   The chonta or pejibaye palm (*Guilielma gasipaes* or *G. speciosa*). This palm is planted for its prolific (though seasonal) vegetablelike fruit, called *chontaruro* (Q.). The especially hard cortex of the chonta palm trunk is considered the best material for Auca spears; was formerly the material used for making heavy, tooth-studded clubs, and for creating a substitute *machete* (S.) or long bush-knife. The latter was given a sharp edge by cutting and filing with a stone. Of all the palmhearts available, only the heart of the chonta palm is appreciated by the Aucas.

COCUYO (Q., coh-coo-yoh)   A light-bearing snap beetle. One inch or longer, bearing light cells on abdomen which emit a large red light when the beetle is in flight, and small light organs on either side of the thorax which may produce green lights when the insect is crawling among the bushes. Both lights shine constantly rather than intermittently, and both seem to vary in intensity or become extinguished at the will of the creature.

CUSHMA (S., coosh-mah)   A loose-fitting, full-length robe worn by the men of several Amazonian tribes; made simply of one or two lengths of cloth joined at sides and shoulder, with a slit for the head.

GAGAI (A., gah-gah-ee)   The evening star.

GAMUNGA (A., gah-moon-gah)   The kinkajou or honey-bear (*Cercoleptes caudivolvus*). A carnivorous nocturnal mammal with prehensile tail.

GATA (A., gah-tah)   The woolly monkey, a favorite for pets.

GIKARI (A., gee-car-ee)   The Veracruz ivory-billed woodpecker, scarlet crested.

GIMINIWAE (A., ghee-mee-nee-wa)   The *uchu putu* (Q.) or "peppei kapok" tree, which bears a dark-colored, worthless kapok. The giant tree is anchored by great buttressed roots which fan out to form natural booths. Orioles customarily hang their long nests from the high arched branches of this tree.

GYAEGYAE (A., gyag-ya)   The challulla (Q.) river fish of Ecuador and Peru.

HUITO (Q., wee-toh)   The edible fruit of the genipa (*Genipa americana*) tree yields a clear juice which is colorless on application to the skin, but soon turns black. Used for decorative body painting.

ILA (Q., ee-lah)   The *ojé* (S.), a giant among jungle trees (*Ficus anthelminthicas*). Hacienda Ila takes its name from a small stream which runs through the property; the stream presumably bears the name of the formerly abundant ila tree.

IMIÑI (A., ee-meen-yee)   A scorpion, whose curved abdomen is terminated in a poisonous sting.

IWA (A., ee-wah)   The howler monkey (*Mycetes*).

IYATAI (A., ee-yah-*tah*-ee)   A slender, red-gold ant of about three-fourths of an inch in length. A member of the household of the leaf-cutting Atta ants.

JAGUAR (S., *jag*-war)   A carnivorous, spotted "Great Cat," one of several large varieties known in Spanish as *tigre*.

KAPOK (kay-pahk)   A tropical tree of the Bombacaceae family (*Bombax ceiba*), source of the cottonlike kapok fiber. The tall tree grows along the rivers, bears its seed in a dark pod surrounded by the kapok fiber. Since the tree is thorny, trees are often cut for harvesting the fiber, but some trees are scaled by the Aucas.

KOMI (A., *coh*-mee)   A "belt" of loosely twisted cotton strings worn around the hips by the Aucas—men, women, and children.

LEAF-CUTTING ANT   The "sauba" or parasol ant (*Atta cephalotes*). This refers to the worker caste, whose business it is to cut and carry large leaf fragments to act as fertilizer in their underground fungus gardens.

MACAW (mah-caw)   Refers to one of the large blue-backed *guacamayos* (S.) of the parrot family, especially the scarlet macaw and the golden macaw.

MAÑI (A., *mahn*-yee)   The *Dinoponera gigantea*, one of the world's largest ants, about an inch and one quarter in length. The sting of this giant mañi ant causes severe discomfort for several hours, comparable to that produced by the sting of some scorpions.

MIIMO (A., me-ee-moh)   The *chichico* (Q.), tiniest of the monkeys found in this jungle. Body not over eight inches.

MU (A., moo)   The *macana panga* (Q.), a low-growing leaf which the Aucas use to intersperse rows of a larger palm leaf in thatching. It is also used to spread on the dirt floor of the Auca huts to serve as tablecloth, serving dish, and plate.

NIMU (A., *nee-*moo)   The Auca word for "star."

OCELOT (ah-se-laht)   A carnivorous "small cat," which is here used to refer to any of the number of varieties known in Spanish as *tigrillo*.

OMUYAEMAE (A., oh-moo-yam-ma)   A jungle fruit similar to the peach. The Aucas call this fruit the *moipa omuyaemae*, referring to the time when Moipa and Gikita found a tree of the ripe omuyaemae fruit, ate several, and Moipa suddenly got a seed stuck in his throat.

OONDA (A., oh-ohn-dah)   The curare poison, made from *pala wasca* (Q.) or "flat vine," the *Strychnos toxifera*. The tips of blowgun darts are coated with curare for killing small animals.

ORIENTE (S., oh-ree-en-tay)   The popular name for the eastern jungles of Ecuador.

PAENAE (A., *pan-*na)   The agouti (*Dasyproctus aguti*). Edible rodent which attains to almost two feet in length. Accused of being a great manioc thief.

PATRÓN (S., pah-*tron*)   Landlord or employer of Indians. They work for, owe their allegiance to, and claim protection from this landowner.

PIRO (S., pee-roh)   A member tribe of the Arawak language family. The main concentration is located along the Urubamba River in Peru, and there are other widely scattered villages of Piros in other sections of southeast Peru and possibly in Bolivia and Brazil.

PITOWAE (A., pee-*toh-*wa)   The *Euterpe edulis* palm, whose giant pinnate leaves are used by the Aucas as thatching; this was the common roofing material used on the large Auca huts when the tribe was more numerous. This leaf is used in conjunction with another, the *mu* (A.), which is doubled over the pitowae to make an especially tight roof. The oily fruit has the appearance of a ripe olive, but a milder flavor and less flesh. Used by the Aucas for food and for hair oil.

PLÁTANO (S., *plah-*tah-noh)   General term embracing the banana (*Musa paradisiaca sapientum*), or the plantain (*Musa paradisiaca normalis*), one of the real staples of the Aucas, which is cooked as a vegetable, whether green or ripe; the ripe fruit is also the basis of an unfermented drink.

POGANTA (S., poh-*gahn-*tah)   A simple headband, formed of one strip of the cream-colored fresh leaf-shoot of the *ramos* (Q.) palm. The headband is often decorated with spots of red *achiote* (S.) paint.

QUICHUA (kee-choo-ah) The most numerous Indian group in western South America; the dominant Indian language, handed down from the Inca conquerors. Dialects of Quichua are spoken in jungle as well as highland areas.

SHAPRA (shah-prah) A member tribe of the Candoshi or Murato group of head-shrinking jungle Indians; north Peru, in the region of Lake Rimachi.

SHIGRA (Q., shee-grah) The carrying net, made in varying sizes, is woven by jungle Indians from tucuma palm fiber. It is interlaced in one piece with an elongated strap of closer weave, to serve as a tumpline.

SPIDER MONKEY According to the *Encyclopaedia Britannica*, "a group of tropical American monkeys known to zoologists as *Ateles*. They take their English name from the slimness of the body, the elongated limbs, and the long tail, the under surface of the prehensile extremity of which is naked. The thumb is rudimentary or wanting. Their long coarse hair and the broader partition between the nostrils distinguishes them from the woolly spider monkeys (*Brachyteles*). The species are arboreal."

TAPIR (tay-per) A hoofed, herb-eating mammal (genus *Tapirus*), called "jungle cow" by the Quichuas, for it attains to the proportions of a small cow.

TARIRI (tah-ree-ree) A contemporary Shapra Indian chief, region of Lake Rimachi, northern Peru.

TIPA (A., tee-pah) The *tarapoto* (Q.) palm (*Ireartea ventricosa*). The fruit borne is a tiny coconut, not eaten by human beings, but is one of the chief foods of the jungle deer. The broad pinnate leaf is used for temporary shelters. The trunk is commonly used for uprights in Auca huts; it is also flattened by splitting, utilized as wide springy boards for flooring.

TOUCAN (too-cahn) Tropical perching birds (*Rhamphastidae*). The species to which most common reference is made here, boasts of a large curved beak almost as long as its body, black with light blue pattern.

UVILLA (S., oo-veel-yah) The uvilla (Spanish for "little grape") fruit has a single stone, but is much like the grape in flavor, consistency, and skin. It is borne in great clusters on the crown of branches spreading high on the slender trunk of the uvilla tree.

WANIMU (A., wah-nee-moo) The morning star.

WIIWA (A., we-ee-wah) The *pingullu* (Q.) or "slender bamboo" bird. A tiny brown-black bird, its whistle is like that of a melodious flute.

WILD PIG   The peccary (*Tayassuidae*) of tropical America. Two varieties are recognized here: the collared peccary and the white-lipped peccary. The latter is the larger variety, and customarily runs in bands.

WIÑATARA (A., ween-yah-*tah*-rah)   The name given by the Aucas to another Auca group who speak a slightly different dialect.

WIPITA (A., wee-pee-tah)   The *mintal* (Q.) tree, whose red wood is grated and boiled in water to form a brilliant red lacquerlike liquid. This is used to paint areas of the foot affected by a fungus which resembles interdigital ringworm. The red paint is also used to dye tucuma fiber cords in preparation for weaving hammocks.

YARINA (S., yah-ree-nah)   Edible, refreshing fruit is borne at eye-level, enclosed in a mass of hard, bristly shells. Its rather fine pinnate leaf is woven for a durable thatch by the Aucas. Unsuitable for a quickly-constructed, temporary shelter.

YUCA (S., yoo-cah)   The manioc or cassava (*Manihot palmata, utilíssima, esculenta,* etc.). The several varieties cultivated by the Aucas are all edible upon being cooked. After boiling, a staple is made by pounding and masticating the root to form a mass which is mixed with water as desired, and drunk unfermented by the Aucas. It is wrapped in leaves and carried on trips.

ZÁPARO (Q., sah-pah-roh)   A near-extinct language family of jungle Indians, scattered along rivers in northern Peru and southern Ecuador. Known by various family names, river names, and dialect names. The Quichua name "Záparo" designates a certain type of covered basket, woven by the Záparo Indians.

LIST OF NAMES

Adyibae   (ah-dyee-ba)   baby daughter of Oba and Dyuwi
Aentyaeri   (an-*tyar*-ree)   Dayuma's relative who initiated mass spearing
Aepi   (*ap*-pee)   young captured Quichua girl living with Dayuma's family
Aka   (*ah*-cah)   one of Moipa's wives
Akawo   (ah-*cah*-woh)   Dayuma's mother
Ana   (*ah*-nah)   younger half-sister of Dayuma
Awaenga   (ah-*wan*-gah)   relative of Miipu
Awaengai   (ah-wan-*gah*-ee)   father of Nombo
Awañita   (ah-wahn-yee-tah)   father of Gaba
Bai   (*bah*-ee)   Gimari's baby
Biba   (*bee*-bah)   young daughter of Gikita
Bibanga   (bee-*bahn*-gah)   young girl in Gikita's group, Itaeka's daughter, killed by boa
Boika   (*bwee*-cah)   Awañita's daughter and wife of Monga
Dabu   (*dah*-boo)   brother of Kimo and Maengamo; relative of Tyaento
Dawa   (*dah*-wah)   arrived with Dayuma's mother Akawo at first meeting with Dayuma after twelve years; married to Kimo
Dayo   (*dah*-yoh)   Dyuwi's grandmother
Dayuma   (dah-yoo-mah)
Dika   (*dee*-cah)   son of Gikita
Dyiko   (*dyee*-coh)   Gimari's mother-in-law; mother of Naenkiwi, Nombo and Omaenkiri
Dyiwanga   (dyee-*wahn*-gah)   mother of Moipa
Dyuwi   (*dyoo*-wee)   strong young man Akawo hoped would marry Gimari, Dayuma's sister; married Oba, Dayuma's sister, instead
Gaba   (*gah*-bah)   husband of Nombo and Omaenkiri
Gakamo   (gah-*cah*-moh)   Mima's daughter
Gami   (*gah*-mee)   Dayuma's aunt; Akawo's younger sister, and mother of Umi

Gikita   (ghee-kee-tah)   Akawo's brother

Gimari   (ghee-mah-ree)   Dayuma's younger sister ("Delilah" of Palm Beach)

Gingata   (gheeng-ah-tah)   Mintaka's young son

Gomoki   (goh-moh-kee)   Dayuma's relative and playmate. Killing of her father was first Auca spearing witnessed by Dayuma

Ima   (ee-mah)   an Auca hero

Ima   (ee-mah)   Dawa's father

Ipa   (ee-pah)   sister of Dyuwi; daughter of Wamoñi; married by force to Naenkiwi

Ipanai   (ee-pah-nah-ee)   mother of Akawo

Itaeka   (ee-tac-ca)   brother of Moipa

Jacinta   (ha-seen-tah)   Quichua woman; relative of Miguel; mother of Maruja

Karae   (cah-ra)   Dayuma's grandfather

Kimo   (kee-moh)   brother of Dabu and Maengamo; relative of Tyaento

Kinta   (keen-tah)   Ipa's young brother

Kipa   (kee-pah)   Gaba's brother

Kiwa   (kee-wah)   Dayuma's uncle

Komi   (coh-mee)   son of Gikita

Kominkagi   (coh-meen-cah-gee)   son of Maengamo

Koni   (coh-nee)   Nimonga's father

Maengamo   (man-gah-moh)   Gikita's wife

Maruja   (mah-roo-ha)   Jacinta's small daughter

Miguel   (mee-gel)   Dayuma's husband

Miipu   (me-ee-poo)   Ipanai's husband

Mima   (mee-mah)   Kara's cousin; mother of Gakamo

Mima   (mee-mah)   wife of Awañita

Mingi   (meen-gee)   enemy of Moipa

Miñi   (meen-yee)   young downriver mother; married to Dabu

Miñimo   (meen-yee-moh)   sister of Naenkiwi; first married to Wamoñi, then to Minkayi, Dayuma's half-brother, and to Warikamo

Minkayi   (meen-cah-yee)   Umi's little brother; Dayuma's half-brother

Mintaka   (meen-tah-cah)   Dayuma's aunt; sister of Akawo and Gami

Moipa   (mwee-pah)   notorious enemy of the Auca jungle; brother of Itaeka

Monga   (mohn-gah)   Awañita's son-in-law

Naenkiwi   (nan-kee-wee)   Moipa's young successor; husband of Dayuma's sister Gimari; "George" of Palm Beach pictures

Ñaeno   (*nyan*-no)   arrived with Dayuma's mother Akawo at first meeting with Dayuma after twelve years

Nambai   (nahm-*bah*-ee)   father of Moipa

Ñamae   (*nyah*-ma)   son of Maengamo

Nampa   (*nahm*-pah)   Dayuma's younger brother

Natani   (nah-*tah*-nee)   Kiwa's wife

Nimonga   (nee-*mohn*-gah)   older brother of Wiñaemi

Nimu   (*nee*-moo)   Dayuma's little sister; the name (meaning "Star") also given to Rachel by Dayuma

Nombo   (*nohm*-boh)   Dyiko's daughter; sister of Omaenkiri and Naenkiwi; wife of Gaba

Oba   (*oh*-bah)   Dayuma's younger sister

Obi   (*oh*-bee)   Gomoki's sister

Olimpia   (oh-*leem*-pee-ah)   Miguel's aunt

Omaena   (oh-*man*-nah)   cousin of Wiwa and Wiika

Omaenkiri   (oh-man-*kee*-ree)   Dyiko's daughter; one of Gikita's wives; sister of Nombo and Naenkiwi

Omaenga   (oh-*mahn*-gah)   Auca shot by foreigners

Omiñia   (oh-meen-*yee*-ah)   one of the Auca women at Hacienda Ila

Ompora   (ohm-*poh*-rah)   wife of Minkayi

Onae   (*oh*-na)   small daughter of Nombo and Gaba

Onaenga   oh-*nan*-gah)   Dayuma's younger sister, killed in storm

Pa   (pah)   father of Naenkiwi

Tamaenta   (tah-*man*-ta)   Ipa's baby

Tamaya   (tah-*mah*-yah)   Itaeka's wife; Dyiko's younger sister

Tañi   (*tahn*-yee)   father of Dyuwi

Tipayae   (tee-*pah*-ya)   an Auca hero

Toña   (*tohn*-yah)   Miñi's small son

Tuwa   (*too*-wah)   husband of Moipa's sister

Tyaemae I   (*tya*-ma)   Maengamo's mother

Tyaemae II   (*tya*-ma)   Maengamo's daughter

Tyaento   (*tyan*-toh)   Dayuma's father

Tyaenyae   (*tyan*-ya)   Wiñaemi's mother

Umi   (*oo*-mee)   cousin of Dayuma, daughter of Gami, and one of the Auca women at Hacienda Ila

Wagingamo   (wah-geen-*gah*-moh)   Tyaento's grandmother

Wamoñi   (wah-*mohn*-yee)   husband of Miñimo

Wani   (*wah*-nee)   father of Dayuma's cousin Umi

Warikamo   (wah-ree-*cah*-moh)   husband of Miñimo

Wato   (*wah*-toh)   small daughter of Nombo and Gaba

Wawae   (*wah*-wa)   Dayuma's older brother

Wiba (wee-bah) daughter of Awañita
Wiika (wee-cah) sister of Gami and Akawo
Wiña (ween-ya) Umi's sister; wife of Nimonga
Wiñaemi (ween-ya-mee) one of Auca women at Hacienda Ila
Wiwa (we-wah) sister of Gami and Akawo
Yaeti (ya-tee) father of Maengamo

Dayuma's Family Tree

Living today on the Tiwaeno River in Ecuador with other survivors of intratribal spearing, Dayuma is a member of a close-knit
Auca family group. Chart 1 indicates Dayuma's relationship to
other members of her family, living or dead, pertinent to her
eventful story. Chart 2 shows the relationship of Dayuma's uncle
Gikita to her aunts Maengamo and Mintaka, and other relatives
Kimo, Dabu, and Dyuwi. In Chart 3 the relationship of Dayuma's
brother-in-law Naenkiwi ("George") to certain downriver Aucas
is traced. Chart 4 shows the family connection of Moipa, murderer of Dayuma's father Tyaento, through her aunt Gami. Where
the names are identical, I and II distinguish the grandparent from
the grandchild. Shaded symbols represent relatives who appear on
more than one chart.

At marriage a man goes to his wife's hut for the first year or
two, after which he builds a hut of his own. At that time, the
household will consist of the man, his wives, and all of their
children by this or former marriages. Any mothers or mothers-in-
law who are widows, and sisters will often be included, either in
the same big hut or in one nearby. The man provides for the entire group.

Often two men who have married sisters will live, along with
their families, in one hut or in two contiguous ones, for economic
co-operation and mutual protection.

See pages 279–82 for a list of names.

DAYUMA'S

Chart 1

Key:
- △ Male
- ○ Female
- ‖═ Marriage
- ⌐‖⌐ Offspring

Gingata I

Ipanai

Wawae I

Mintaka
Dabu — Gingata II
Wiika

Wiwa

Maengamo — Komi, Ñamae, Tyaemae II, Dika
Gikita . . . . See Chart 2 →

Wamoñi

Gami

Ana
Oba — Dyuwi — Adyibae II
Gimari ("Delilah") — Bai
Naenkiwi ("George") . . . . See Chart 3 →
Onaenga
Nimu

Dabu
Akawo

Dayuma I
Karae
Omiñia
Tyaenyae
Koni

Tyaento I
Gami . . . . See Chart 4 →
Wiñaemi
Nimonga
Wiña

Dayuma II — Tyaento II ("Sammy")
Wawae II
Nampa

Minkayi II — Miñimo
Ompora

284

AMILY TREE

hart 2

hart 3

hart 4

Auca Indian Domain
in the Amazonian
Forests of Ecuador

A Downriver–Auca Area
B Area claimed by both groups
C Upriver–Auca Area

Napo River

Curaray River

Nushiño River

Villano River

Shell Mera

Pastaza River

Colombia

Ecuador

Peru

Pacific Ocean

Upriver Auca Area

- - - - - Dayuma's flight from Moipa's spears

N

Napo River

to Hacienda Ila

Arajuno River

Nushiño River

Grandmother Dayuma killed, grandfather Karae wounded by outsiders' guns ✗

Dayuma finds her mother, who is unwilling to flee with her ✗

Dayuma sees her mother's footprints ✗

Moipa spears Dayuma's father ✗

Dayuma's birthplace

Tzapino River

Moipa spears foreigners (Palm Beach) ✗

Dayuma turns back to seek her mother ✗

Dayuma accompanies Quichuas

Curaray River

Negro killed by Moipa ✗

Lahuano River

Challúa River

Villano River

Moipa spears Dayuma's family ✗

Nushiño R.

Moipa spears gold-hunters ✗

Tiwaeno River

Tiwaeno

Gikari's birthplace ✗

Gikari's place

Old Village

Oglán R.

Curaray R.

Dayuma meets Sevilla

Village where Maengamo and Mintaka were received by Quichua Indians

Arajuno ✗ Moipa spears Shell Oil-Co. workers

Chuya-Villano River

Villano

287

Nimonga & Wiña;
Minkayi & Ompora,
and children

Monga &
Boika, and
daughter

Dabu & family

Nombo & Dyiko
and children

Ipa & son;
Naeno, Wato,
Gakamo;
Mintaka & son

Gikita &
Maengamo
and children

Tiwaeno River

Dyuwi, Oba,
& daughter;
Akawo;
Gimari & son

Dayuma, Sammy;
Kimo & Dawa;
Rachel

Tiwaeno Village

After an absence of many years, Dayuma beams as she rejoins her family group. Aunt Omaenkiri sits in hammock with her children.